D1563940

*THE ANATOMY OF LOVE*

# THE ANATOMY OF LOVE

## The *Tristan* of Gottfried von Strassburg

## W. T. H. Jackson

Columbia University Press · New York and London 1971

*FOR ERIKA*

wir zwei sin iemer beide
ein dine ane underscheide

# PREFACE

This study of Gottfried von Strassburg's poem differs in many respects from its predecessors. I have paid little attention to many topics which have been regarded as staples of Tristan scholarship. Some, like religion, mysticism, sources, and the origins of the Tristan legend, have already been dealt with in far more detail and with more learning than I could ever hope to attain. Furthermore, they only have marginal significance for what I have tried to do. One important matter has been ignored for quite the opposite reason. I have not discussed Gottfried's use of the rhyming four-beat couplet because there is simply not enough detailed study of the subject available and to attempt such a study here would hopelessly distort my own work.

I have tried to show, by a careful reading of the text, that Gottfried's *Tristan* is a unique attempt to portray the overwhelming power of love and the essential incompatibility between it and the society in which Gottfried's contemporaries lived. The poet struggled with the problem of the correct vehicle to use to express his thoughts on the subject and decided to use the romance in spite of his opinion that its conventions committed it to a view of love and a solution of the conflict between love and society which were far different from his own. Thus the work is at once a positive statement of Gottfried's views and a study in the stylistic methods used to convey them and a negative reaction to the "game-rules" of the romance as developed by Chrétien de Troyes and brought into German by Heinrich von Veldeke and Hartmann von Aue.

In order to set the poem in context, it has been necessary to provide a brief and, as I am only too well aware, oversimplified account of the problem of sexual love as it appeared to educated men in the High Middle Ages. To this I have added a short discussion of the literary treatment of love found in the romances before Gottfried, particularly in the works of Chrétien de Troyes and in the lyric poetry of the troubadours.

The bibliographical material for the study of the poem is now easily available and up to date and there is thus no necessity for a detailed bibliography for this book. The basic information is provided in the "Bibliographical Note." Notes have been kept to a minimum. They are used only when a specific reference is required and are hence more frequent in the introductory chapters than in those on Gottfried's poem itself. The index is intended to be a guide to themes and treatment rather than to the occurrence of proper names. No attempt has been made to list the references to the two principal figures, since their names appear on almost every page.

I have used the names "Tristan" and "Isolde" throughout, even though Gottfried himself uses "Isot" as the normal nominative form. There is little point in attempting to follow all the variations of personal names which appear in the versions of the poem in different languages and periods. Only where a title is quoted have I retained the form which the author seems to have favored. Thus the principal characters will be designated as Tristan, Isolde, Mark, Brangaene, Curvenal, Gandin, Gilan, Kaedin, Marjodo, Melot, Morolt, Rual (li Foitenant), Urgan, Riwalin, Blanscheflur, Morgan. Where the name "Isolde" appears alone, it refers to Isolde the Fair. Her mother is called "Isolde the queen" or "the older Isolde." Her rival is "Isolde White Hands."

I have provided translations of the numerous passages quoted in Middle High German. There is, however, no way in which a translation can enable the reader to follow Gottfried's stylistic methods. These renderings, which attempt to keep close to the original, can only help him to see how the German text exemplifies them. The translations are my own, but I would like to pay tribute to the help I have received from the excellent prose version of the poem in English by A. T. Hatto in the Penguin series. I have used it constantly when studying such matters as narrative structure and development.

I am deeply grateful to my colleague, Professor Joan Ferrante, for her reading of a large part of the typescript and her excellent suggestions and to my student Setsuko Ohara, who edited the whole expertly, beautifully, and spontaneously. It is also a pleasure to pay tribute to the smooth efficiency of William F. Bernhardt, Senior Editor of the Columbia University Press, who returned a polished version of the manuscript to me in an unbelievably short space of time.

Once again it is an honor to record my debt to that most humane of foundations, the John Simon Guggenheim Memorial Foundation, which provided me with the free time to write.

*Columbia University*
*January, 1971*                                          W. T. H. JACKSON

# CONTENTS

   I. The Context     1

  II. The Poet and His Predecessors     31

 III. The Purpose of the Poem     48

 IV. Aspects of Love     64

   V. The Milieu     142

 VI. The Structure of the Poem     194

VII. The Texture of the Language     247

      Conclusion     270

      Notes     271

      Bibliographical Note     275

      Index     277

*THE ANATOMY OF LOVE*

# I

## THE CONTEXT

GOTTFRIED'S *Tristan* is a poem about love. Although it is a "chivalric" romance and calls upon many of the formal aspects, the conventions, and even some of the absurdities of the genre, it is not a "courtly" poem. Indeed, Gottfried leaves no doubt in the mind of his audience that he regards the courtly poem as an inadequate and shallow form. He proposes a thorough study of the love phenomenon, of the relation between the sexes in all its aspects—physical, intellectual, social, and artistic—and in his study he shows a ruthlessness and penetration which are not always obvious in the polished lines and bright colors of the story he tells. It is easy to be sentimental about the story of Tristan and Isolde and to weep over the fate of two unhappy lovers. Gottfried recognized the danger, and harsh words often remind us that the lovers are persons of free will, with whom we may sympathize but who are not the mere playthings of fate, whatever philters they may have drunk and whatever bonds they feel.

In its analysis of love, Gottfried's poem is closest to the *Roman de la Rose*—if we consider both parts of the *Roman*. For the first part is largely a presentation of the love phenomenon in the terms of allegorized courtly love and is incomprehensible except in the framework provided by earlier romances. The second part is a much more intellectual and philosophical analysis, and the two parts together provide a study of love from the points of view of two parallel but very different streams of medieval thought and feeling.

The attitudes toward love displayed in the vernacular romances and lyrics of the twelfth and thirteenth centuries cannot be regarded as typical of all thought of the period. Nor can they be regarded as isolated from it. The division of literature into "courtly" and "popular" is far too crude even as a generalization, and the term "courtly love"—which is an invention of Gaston Paris and not a medieval term—has very little meaning in serious literary criticism. Nevertheless chivalric romances do possess features in common and show some similarities in the treatment of love, by far the most important of which is the tendency to show the lady as being of superior qualities whose love inspires rather than degrades her lover. Such inspiration can take many forms and by no means all of them are idealized or even honorable, but they differ from the widespread medieval view that sexual love was essentially a degrading experience in most of its manifestations. A brief account of these common attitudes will be useful, but it should be emphasized that such an account must be based almost entirely on works written by men—and very occasionally by women—who belonged to a specific school of thought. An objective "evaluation of current attitudes to sex" is virtually unattainable in the Middle Ages, since every writer felt that the matter was so closely bound up with moral considerations that he could not merely describe what was happening. Even had he purported to do so, he could have done no more than give an account of his own, necessarily very limited, experience. There is no reason to think that ordinary people in their daily lives behaved very differently from ordinary people in any other age. Certainly the accounts of the lives of a group of men such as the Crusaders as given in the relatively detailed and near contemporary histories show that some were licentious, some ascetic, some one when they claimed to be the other, that a majority took advantage of sexual opportunities when they appeared, and that a minority were utterly happy in their marriages and never looked at another person of the opposite sex.[1]

The important difference in attitude toward sexual love between the Middle Ages and many, but by no means all, other periods is the strong sense of guilt felt by many persons in any intercourse between the sexes, not only in extramarital intercourse. Attraction between a man and a woman could be poisoned from the very start if either or both of the lovers were deeply sensitive to the effect on their immortal soul of any deep or passionate longing, as the tragedy of Héloise and Abélard shows, and the less casual such attraction was, the deeper was the sense of guilt it was liable to inspire in persons capable of feeling something more than physical attraction. Whether a sense of guilt in sexual matters is something embedded in the psyche of the human race is a matter for psychologists, not literary critics. Its obvious and visible cause in the Middle Ages was the ascetic tendency which is to be found in Christianity from its earliest origins. The Virgin Birth of Christ, which removed him from the stain of original sin, shows of itself the strong antisexual tendency of Christianity and set for others an ideal impossible of attainment. Only Christ himself could be born without sexual intercourse, and Christians were faced with a dilemma impossible of solution. They were commanded on the one hand to increase and multiply, to spread their seed over the earth, and yet they were told that the act which alone could produce this increase was sinful and indicative more than any other of man's fall from innocence and grace. Individuals took refuge in the form which seemed to them most appropriate. The cult of virginity received its strongest support from St. Jerome,[2] but he was followed by numerous writers—and by many who did not write. Yet it was clear that this choice, while avoiding sin for the individual, would fail to carry out the commandment to populate the earth. If everyone followed the example of Jerome and his societies of virgins, there would be no Christian population. The only solution was to regard lifetime celibacy as an ideal attainable only by an élite group of the population, those to whom it was given to crush the physical aspects of sex. A resolution of this kind might take the form of a mere contract, an abnegation in theory of all sexual life, one taken by all monks and nuns and which, like so many contracts, was often broken and caused the imposition of prescribed penalties. Sometimes, however, the renunciation of physical sex produced a sublimated mystical attitude which is illustrated best in the utterances of Mechtild von Magdeburg and the brilliant, if more restrained interpretation of the Song of Songs by St. Bernard.

Thus the sexual attraction which was forbidden in its fleshly aspects was made respectable and indeed desirable by its conversion into a yearning not for the flesh of one male or female but for the source of all love, the spirit of the One. Such sublimation was not a feature peculiar to Christianity. The individual human soul—indeed the being of any created object—was regarded by Plotinus and the Neoplatonists as being in a perpetual state of yearning for reunion with the one, the divine intelligence. Plato in the *Symposium* regarded such a spiritual desire as a higher form of love, and it was a central feature of many of the mystery cults. Plato makes it clear that he regards as the highest form of love a kind of mystical-intellectual attraction between two males, and it is precisely the elimination of the sexual and particularly the generative aspects of love which make this form of love superior to any between male and female. It is hard to tell whether Plato himself regarded this relationship as a reflection of the relationship between the soul of man and a higher force, but certainly such a position would be consistent with the doctrines of Neoplatonism.

Yet we should be very wary of making an assumption for medieval literature that would lead us to believe in the possibility of a direct trans-ference of the mystical love of the human soul for God to a similar love for one human soul by another. Mystical love is by definition and its very nature a yearning for return to a larger love, an envelopment in a larger entity, the extinction of the individual in a larger light. Transports like these were often phrased in erotic terms, to the discomfort of some readers, but I know of no instance where a writer explicitly describes his love for a human being in mystical terms. The problem is a very difficult one, since there are many works, particularly poems, in which it is not clear whether the author is referring to human or divine love, but such works belong for the most part to periods after the early thirteenth century and are hardly relevant to a discussion of Gottfried's work.

Far more important is the indirect effect of the mystical love concept on secular works, for it raised the possibility that there could exist be-tween man and woman a love purged of any sensual elements which would still be deeply felt and satisfying. It is impossible to define love of this sort, since those who felt it and wrote of it could not themselves have defined it accurately and its form certainly differed with every pair and group who practiced it, if "practiced" may be used of such a vague con-cept. The groups of noble ladies who surrounded St. Jerome would certainly have been horrified if they had been told that they were in love with him, yet what other expression can be used of such unremitting attention? Hennig Brinkmann long ago called attention to what we may call the phenomenon of epistolary love between nuns, often of noble family, and priests and others in minor orders.[3]

The idea behind such writings as these, whether conscious or not, was that the sinfulness, that is, the sensuality, could be removed from love by couching it in the terms of religion, of mysticism and charity.

This is a slippery path, for it was perfectly possible for love to be expressed in these and similar terms without any loss of sensual feeling. The terms can become a disguise rather than a true expression and they could and did lead to the evolution of a special vocabulary of love, much more in the vernaculars than in Latin, which was capable of great subtlety of meaning and which gave wide latitude to possible erotic interpretation.

It would be well at this point to mention an important point of terminology. There are several classical Latin words for love, of which the most general is *amor*, a very common word which can cover almost all shades of meaning. Vergil's *Aeneid* provides examples which range from Dido's love for Aeneas to the desire of the souls on the wrong side of the Styx to cross to the other shore. The word *cupido* is more restricted in meaning and "desire" is basic in its interpretation. It can refer to greed as well as sexual desire, which is expressed more directly by *concupiscentia*. *Venus* was, of course, a word used specifically of love between the sexes but rather by poets than as a technical term. Early Christian writers were handicapped by the fact that Latin lacked expressions for nonphysical love except the very general word *amor*. They therefore introduced the Greek word ἀγάπη but this was replaced by *caritas*, a Latin word indeed but one rarely used in Ciceronian Latin. Its meaning was confined to very specific aspects of *amor* and in particular to that love of one's fellow men which is called for by St. Paul. It is also used of love directed toward God, and Hugh of St. Victor makes it clear that he regards love as a force capable of different moral aspects according to the object toward which it is directed.[4] Thus *amor*, the love force, becomes *caritas* when it is directed upwards toward God but *concupiscentia* when it is directed downwards toward the flesh. It is easy to see the distinction when it is expressed in these terms, for love of God is easily distinguishable from desire of the flesh, but such a distinction is not so easily made in respect of human beings. Was it possible to exercise *caritas* to an individual person? This was clearly so in the case of the parable of the Good Samaritan, for here there was no sexual problem. Could a man feel such a "higher devotion," *amor sine concupiscentia*, for a woman? This is the problem which exercised the talents of many authors in the second half of the twelfth century and the centuries which followed. We have seen that one solution was "epistolary love" but this can hardly be regarded as a conscious attempt at a solution of the problem. In his well-known treatise *De Amore*, Andreas Capellanus indicates that the problem had been considered theoretically, for he notes the existence of *amor purus*. This, apparently, was love for a woman which stopped short of intercourse. It is hard to see how it could be described as *purus*, since physical caresses were by no means excluded. Indeed, the impression one gains from Andreas' account is that *amor purus* obeyed the letter of the law in refraining from intercourse while offering the parties a considerable amount of enjoyment. It is scarcely surprising that one of the participants in Andreas' dialogues, a woman, describes it as ridiculous, and it is hard to escape the conclusion that Andreas was himself writing tongue in cheek.[5]

What is much more important than Andreas' own remarks on the subject is the evidence that his work supplies that the possibility of non-sensual heterosexual love was being seriously considered, that it was possible for a man to love a woman as a woman, and not merely as another Christian soul, without committing sin. The line was finely drawn, for it is clear that the distinction between sin and innocence was legalistic. Sensuality is abundantly in evidence but the "sin" of intercourse is excluded. Such a concept of love could be interpreted differently. Sensuality itself could be excluded, and love could consist entirely in contemplation, not because of any feeling that sin was involved in intercourse but because the lady was felt to be unattainable for different reasons. We have thus arrived at the general position of the writers of the troubadour lyric.

These various attitudes to love shade into each other, and it is pointless to look for any specific source for the ideas found in one type of poetry and still more pointless to set up a system of courtly love compounded of elements from many sources and attempt to trace its origins in medieval terms. By the end of the twelfth century there were as many attitudes as there were authors. Nevertheless there are certain literary and social attitudes which should be understood.

The asceticism of early Christianity led to the praise of virginity and the cultivation of celibacy, the rejection of physical pleasure and sexual love as goods to be sought by man who wished to save his soul. The ideas were propounded almost entirely by males and it is therefore scarcely surprising that the female should be regarded as naturally disposed to sin and a potential danger to men. After all, the first woman was the direct cause of the Fall and her yielding to the blandishments of the snake had led directly to knowledge of sex and to the sin of sexual pleasure. Before her act Adam and Eve had been unconscious of their sexual differences in any sinful sense. The question of how their children would have been conceived was one which the theologians found hard to answer, but one thing was clear—woman was the instrument of man's destruction and had continued to be so throughout the ages. History abounded with examples, and these were diligently collected by enthusiastic woman-haters to form a corpus of violently antifeminist literature.[6] Some of it consisted of mere tales, some of it was incorporated into *exempla* or sermon material. If it were confined to Latin writers or Christian apologists, it would concern us very little in the study of *Tristan*, but the Christian antifeminist literature is a manifestation of a much more fundamental attitude which affected in one way or another many forms of secular poetry.

Greek myths abound with stories of men sacrificed to destructive love: Hippolytus dies because of the mad passion of Phaedra, the daughters of Danaus murder their husbands, Medea spreads destruction wherever she goes, and Hercules dies because of his wife's attempt to keep his love by sending him a shirt dipped in the blood of Nessus. The female gods rejected at the judgment of Paris pursue their revenge not only against Paris himself but against the whole Trojan race. There is no doubt that many of these stories are based upon or inspired by the sacrifice of the male consort of the various manifestations of the Mother goddess, the destruction of the transient male principle in fertility by the eternal female. Certainly Greek literature was deeply affected by this feeling of the destructive power of love. It is clearly apparent in the *Oresteia* of Aeschylus and in many of the plays of Sophocles and Euripides. Briseis, we should remember, is the cause of the quarrel between Agamemnon and Achilles, and even though Homer appears to regard her as a piece of property rather than a person, later writers emphasized the personal relationship as a cause for Achilles' reluctance to let her go, just as they found in Achilles' love for Polyxena, daughter of Priam, the reason for his death.[7]

Passionate love meant destructive love if it were not contained by the bonds of marriage—a relatively rare occurrence in literature—or directed toward an object such as a courtesan or slave girl, whose powers for evil were limited. The lyrics of Catullus to Lesbia, for all their fire and deep passion, emphasize death and destruction far more than light and laughter,

as even a superficial study of their imagery will show. By far the most
famous and most influential example of the destructive power of love is,
of course, Dido in Vergil's *Aeneid.* There can be little doubt that her story
appears in the work simply to show this destructive power. It should be
remembered that Vergil was writing at a time when the memory of the
corruption and downfall of a great Roman, Antony, at the hands of Cleopatra was still fresh. An Eastern woman, a sensualist (as the Romans saw
it), a person of exotic amatory talents had not only destroyed Antony but
had almost brought down the Roman dominion with him. Only the presence
of Augustus, totally unaffected by passion, had saved the state and forced
Cleopatra to take refuge in death. Whether these were the true facts is
irrelevant—they formed the picture which the Romans desired. Vergil
wishes to show that this same problem faced their first ancestor, that he
too had been seriously tempted by an Eastern queen whose unrestrainedly
passionate nature had led him to believe that true happiness could be
found with her and through her attitude to life. Only the direct intervention of Jove and Aeneas' own readiness to see his error saved him and
the state—and also sowed the seed for the rivalry with Carthage which
came nearer to destroying Rome than any event in her history. Dido too
finds refuge in self-destruction. Vergil's poetic genius makes Dido into a
figure for whom we can feel only the deepest sorrow. She seems to us an
individual sacrificed to statecraft, a pitiable female tossed aside by a
ruthless and ambitious politician. Aeneas' excuses do not ring true. It
seems unlikely, however, that most Romans would have shared our feelings.
Aeneas was wrong to allow physical attraction to blur his judgment—and
we should not overlook Vergil's skill in emphasizing the essentially sensual
nature of Dido's hold over Aeneas. Many medieval readers of Vergil
would be entirely in sympathy with this attitude, as we can tell from the
inclusion of Dido in the lists of the antifeminists. Even Dante is far from
sympathetic. Vergil has very little to say about the personal aspects of the
later, purely political union between Aeneas and Lavinia and it was left
to the author of the French *Roman d'Enéas* and his German adapter
Heinrich von Veldeke to write their love story. We shall have occasion to
discuss it later.

Vergil wrote the most famous story of the conflict between passionate
love and the society in which such love must exist. He was exemplifying
for all time one of the fundamental conflicts of life—deeply felt physical

attraction, often accompanied by idealism and a search for a better existence, clashing with social conventions, the advice of elders, and the rules laid down to maintain a community. Medieval society, highly stratified and class-conscious as it was, felt this conflict as keenly as the Romans, indeed even more keenly, for to the Roman belief that love should not wreck society there was added the strong distrust of sexual love in any form which has already been discussed. Few medieval writers take up explicitly the general problem of the conflict between love and society, and only Gottfried makes it one of the central features of a great work of art. Other artists sought their own ways to present and resolve it and of these the most important is the well-known dilemma of the hero who has to balance love and other demands of his milieu, the courtly dilemma. Earlier Greek romances, of which a few survive, apparently sentimentalized the problem. The lovers were usually of perfectly acceptable social station and attracted to one another but kept apart either by their own pride, by their parents, or by physical barriers. Such romances usually showed their lovers passing through a series of adventures, of hairbreadth escapes from total disaster, of capture by pirates, of rendezvous missed by ill-luck. The pattern is well known, since it can be found in Shakespeare's comedies and a host of other works. There are many medieval representatives of the type, of which *Floire et Blanscheflur*, extant in several languages, is an excellent example. In such works the love problem is presented on the simplest possible terms, a conflict of personalities or a struggle with events. There is no evidence that the authors were aware of, or at least that they wished to discuss, Gottfried's question: Is love in its deepest form compatible with Christian society, and if it is, what concessions will each have to make? Such speculation goes far beyond the Christian question of the sinfulness of sexual intercourse, for Gottfried's conception of love is that lovers should be utterly dedicated to it in a way which includes physical love but makes demands going far beyond it and controlling all their actions.

All Christian writers, as we have said, were fully aware of the necessity of working out an accommodation by means of which sexual life could be permitted. Virginity and celibacy might be ideals, but for most—fortunately for the continuation of mankind—they were unattainable ideals. Marriage was the best solution for the great majority of people, but all Christian apologists make it clear that marriage is not a legitimized way of sexual indulgence. Marriage was for the procreation of children, and all sexual activity within marriage should be directed to this end. Any attempt to thwart such procreation was a sin. This was the official view but it was perfectly well recognized that it was largely a fiction, and writers from St. Paul on recognize the importance of marriage in directing sexual energy into legitimate channels. The "marriage debt," the need for a woman to yield to her husband, is widely recognized and a woman does not sin in rendering it.

Yet we should not overlook the importance (for medieval views of love and marriage) of this legalistic concept. It encouraged the view that marriage was essentially a contract for the production and rearing of children, a view that appealed strongly to a society which admired legal attitudes and thought of children as copies and extensions of their parents. Love had little place in such an arrangement, and the sanctity of marriage rested not so much on a desire not to injure one of the parties as on a contract which must be kept. Adulterous queens were executed for treason. If love grew in such a marriage, that was a fortunate accident. It was more likely to spring up outside it, either before or after marriage, and was thus by its very nature antisocial in the narrow sense. Nor was it as evil, compared with marriage, as might appear at first sight. For was not sexual indulgence within marriage also evil? To "lust after a woman" in thought or deed had been condemned by Christ himself. It was the willing which mattered rather than the context in which it occurred. Andreas Capellanus is thus perfectly correct when he says that love and marriage are incompatible, although I doubt whether he meant it quite in the way described here. If people loved outside the bonds of matrimony they might commit the sin of fornication—but it was possible to commit the same sin with the marriage partner. All this is not to suggest that there was no such thing as adultery in the Middle Ages, except in a social sense. But there was a great deal of confused thinking and there were many opportunities for specious and casuistic argument. In view of the official attitude that marriage was an arrangement for the perpetuation of the race, it is easy to see that love between the sexes which did not involve procreation or the act of procreation would be better practiced outside the marriage bond than within it. Here we have the starting point of "troubadour love." There were many other factors involved, but the beginning was here.

The problem of generation and its place in the divine order had exercised several of the best minds at the school of Chartres. These authors, Bernardus Silvestris and Alanus de Insulis in particular, thought of the perpetuation of the human race as an essential part of the divine purpose.[8] The act of generation is thus also divinely ordained and is under the supervision of the goddess Natura, who is envisioned as the agent of God. It does not appear that these poets consider that there can be any question of sin in such an act. Sin consists rather in its perversion, as Alanus makes very clear in his *De Planctu Naturae*. So long as sexual relations are intended for procreation, they are wholesome and wholly consonant with God's plan. But homosexuality and wrongly directed heterosexuality not only defile the individual but constitute blasphemy in the sight of God.

It is this point of view which is taken up and adapted by Jean de Meun, the author of the second part of the *Roman de la Rose*. He is much less concerned with the cosmological problem of the perpetuation of man within the universe than are his two predecessors. For him the question has become one of social realities. The love depicted by Guillaume de Lorris in the incomplete first part of the *Roman de la Rose* was essentially sterile. The stress on purity, unattainability, allegory, posture, form, and tradition showed all too clearly, so far as Jean de Meun was concerned, that his predecessor was thinking in terms of distant love, of the love of the troubadours, of love outside marriage and with no procreative purpose. His task, as he saw it, was to take this allegory, which was based on the courtly tradition, and use it in the way of Bernardus and Alanus to show the power of Venus the creator, the goddess of love in the service of Nature, the desire which, when rightly used, ensures the continuity of the human race. The end of the allegory must inevitably be the plucking of the rose but under the auspices and guidance of Venus genetrix, not of Narcissus.

It is hard to say whether Jean de Meun understood fully what Guillaume de Lorris wished to convey. Certainly he had no sympathy with it. Love between the sexes is a part of Nature's purpose, and Jean de Meun goes to great lengths to show love functioning as an essential part of the cosmos, but it is only the purpose of procreation which is important, a purpose which man shares with all animals. If we are to talk of love in any real sense, we must divorce it from sex. It must be founded on the mutual recognition of virtue, it must be a love of all human beings, love of God. These alone are higher forms of love and, according to Jean, no amount of fine talk and pretty words can make sexual love into anything but a primitive, if necessary desire which is more than likely to cause trouble, evil, and sin. Such an attitude inevitably saw happy marriage as the only solution to the need for procreation combined with affection. Chaucer's work, largely influenced by Jean de Meun, studies this problem of love and marriage from many different angles.

Yet it must be admitted that at the beginning of the thirteenth century there was little attempt to fuse the intellectual tradition as it referred to generation and the concept of love outside marriage which was concerned only with the feelings of the lovers themselves. Children as the fruit of love in marriage are not a part of the courtly tradition—with the notable exception of Wolfram's *Parzival*. If children appear, it is to provide a story motif, as in the *Amis-Amiloun* romances, or to provide a second part to a story, as in Chrétien's *Cligès*. The marriages were not contracted for the purpose of generation, and the appearance of the children has no connection with the love motif. The romances terminated either with the fulfillment of love or with destruction because of it.

This absence of any reference to children in courtly romance and troubadour lyric should not surprise anyone who has realized the gulf between contractual marriage and love, but some critics have seen in the sterility of such love the influence of un-Christian ideas, whether Moslem or Catharist. The question of formal resemblances between Arabic and Provençal lyric is not relevant here. It should rather be pointed out that very few of the world's love poems do have reference to the production of children. It is the beloved, not the results of the possible union, which provides the inspiration and there would be something ludicrous about sophisticated love poetry which raised the question of family planning. The charge of sterility arises presumably from the frequent statements that the troubadour regards the lady as too good for him, superior in virtue and beauty, utterly unattainable. But no troubadour poetry that I know specifically renounces desire. If the troubadour could renounce desire, his problem would no longer exist. His yearning may be sterile in its results but it is not willed to be sterile. Any attempt to connect such an attitude with the Catharist heresy is unjustified. The Catharists rejected marriage because its purpose was generation, and generation would continue the flesh. Since flesh was the creation of the force of evil and trapped the scintillae of the spirit, the dissolution of all flesh was desirable. It is natural that their orthodox opponents accused them of unnatural vices—somewhat illogically, since they also advocated celibacy as the highest good. There is no evidence, however, that any troubadour belonged to a Catharist group, and even if he had, he would have had to reach the highest grade of "perfectus" in order to practice complete celibacy. Most Catharists lived normal married lives and produced children. The efforts of modern critics to show that "sterile love" in the lyrics is of Catharist inspiration and that some poems are allegories of the Catharist church are as fanciful as they are erroneous.[9]

The writer of the twelfth century thus found himself faced with a number of conflicting views. Marriage should have no emotional connection with sexual love, yet love outside it was a sin. Marriage was for the purpose of procreating children, yet the act of procreation was sinful, unless the participants had the procreation of children in mind. Celibacy was a higher state than marriage, yet the race must be continued. Woman led man into evil, yet Christ's mother was a woman. It was clear that no one solution could be found to such problems. Compromises had to be made and accommodations found. For all of these views were opposed to the essence of all love poetry—the sublimation of sexual feeling into adoration, the raising of the status of the lady to that of a being perfect in every physical and moral characteristic. There is no need to seek for the "origins" of such an attitude, for there would be no love poetry without it. The problem is rather to observe how it was adapted to the social and intellectual conditions of contemporary society.

The most significant attempts to solve the problem of love were those made within the framework of so-called courtly literature. They were made by persons with close connections to certain centers of artistic effort and discussion which can be identified with the courts of great nobles. It should be emphasized that we really know very little about these courts, and such knowledge as we have is derived from sources which are far from objective in their evaluations. It is probably true that the power of many of these courts as literary centers began with their patronage of Latin writers whose interests were literary rather than theological. The court of Henry II in England is an excellent example, since the presence there of such writers can be proved. Those courts, however, which were centers of literary production in the vernaculars cannot be shown to have such antecedents.[10] Obvious examples are the courts of the counts of Toulouse and of the lord of Marseilles, of Champagne, and of Henry the Lion in Germany. It is probable that such Latin intellectual life preceded that in the vernaculars and that it was largely in the hands of court chaplains, the *capellani*, whose duties included the teaching of the children at court, both those of the reigning family and those of their associates. A man of character and intellectual distinction could have a great deal of influence in a position like this. Most of his pupils, male and female, would probably be glad to escape from his tutelage, the former to practice jousts, tournaments, and the serious arts of war and the latter to their embroidery and household cares. Yet a residue remained, not only the males who were destined for the church but those who were interested in literature, even though their main business was government, and the ladies who had ample time for literature if they wished to pursue it.

Life in the twelfth century, while still crude and uncomfortable, was infinitely more settled than it had been at any time since the Roman peace. In Western Europe at least there were no mass movements of peoples, town life was reviving, a money economy was returning, and the powerful could live in relative ease. The courts of great nobles, dependent on wealth derived from landed property, were the only possible centers of intellectual life, and it must be remembered that while war, sometimes destructive war, was a normal hazard, there was nothing to compare with the raids of the Norseman. Under such circumstances culture became fashionable at some courts among some people. Its extent should not be exaggerated. We really know very little about the size of the audiences for "courtly" literature but it was probably quite small and it probably had a strong female element.

References to female patrons of literature are relatively numerous,[11] and many of the names appear in the *vidas* or biographies of the troubadours as the "actual" person who was the beloved to whom a lyric was addressed. Such identifications are very rare in German literature of the period. The evidence, while by no means conclusive, is strong enough to suggest that these women may have been the centers of a "salon" at some of the courts and that they may have been responsible for the strong feminine orientation in "courtly" literature. For there can be no doubt that the feature which distinguishes "courtly" literature from the vernacular narrative poetry which preceded and to a limited extent paralleled it is that courtly literature accords to women a high status and central position in the work, while vernacular narrative poetry, if it mentions women at all, does so only in a social and political context.[12] These women are shown as wives, as mothers, as daughters, as faithful companions, even as fellow warriors, but never as lovers.

The difference between the two types goes much deeper than the role of women. The older narrative poems—and in this category the *Nibelungenlied* is included—are "public-minded." They are essentially political in orientation. Their heroes fight wars, and the events portrayed make and break whole peoples. Thus heroes are always rulers, whose actions are of the utmost significance to hosts of unnamed individuals. The virtues of these heroes are public too, the virtues of rulers, and among such virtues the art of loving could not possibly be included, for in such a world the relation between man and woman was determined entirely by their position and duties, not by their individual preferences and personal feelings. How ruthless the logic of these "public-minded" works was can be seen by the—to me—complete failure of the author of the *Nibelungenlied* to integrate into his work the love idyll of Kriemhilde and Siegfried, a relation which he was obviously attempting to base on the conventions of the *Minnesang* and which is equally obviously incompatible with the conditions of his poem.

Courtly romance, on the other hand, is "private-minded." Its heroes fight not wars but tournaments, and even though the contemporary joust—better described as a "bohurt," a kind of free-for-all fight on horseback—was a scrambling affair which bore little resemblance to the highly formalized ceremonial of the later Middle Ages, it was still an amusement, a part of a fighting man's leisure time, not a serious incursion into the relation between governments. These same heroes may be entitled kings, dukes, and counts but they are not thought of as rulers. In the courtly romance everyone, whatever his rank of nobility, is a knight. There is a deliberate leveling process, which eliminates all question of ruling and administering, and substitutes for it a total concern for the individual as a nonpolitical being. Knights were, of course, originally simply mounted fighting men, mounted because they were thus more efficient on the battlefield. Such a definition has little relevance for the courtly romance. Here the word "knight" is used in a purely literary sense, to represent a man from whom certain standards of culture and behavior can be expected. In the later Middle Ages the standards of literature were assumed to have been the standards of contemporary society, and nobles of the fourteenth century modeled their behavior—at least when it was politic to do so—on that of the knights of the romances. The stories which are attached to Edward, the Black Prince, and the Chevalier Bayard provide excellent examples. The literary knights of the twelfth century were undoubtedly well ahead of their contemporaries in manners and polish. They were intended as an example, not as a representation, and furthermore the ideals they stood for were not entirely those which the male inhabitants of contemporary courts would have desired.

Bravery, loyalty, and generosity (to those of the right social standing) have always been the ideals and usually the characteristics of a warrior class, and the semiprofessional fighting men of the twelfth century were no exception. In this respect there is no difference between the ideals of the romances and those of the national epics. Knights in romances, however, spend little of their time in fighting and none of it in war. Their fights are tests of courage or perhaps more accurately demonstrations of skill under very specific circumstances. (It is no accident that many of them have to stand the test of fighting Gawain.) The qualities which distinguish the knight of the romance from the warrior of the epics are those connected with his nonfighting activities, his life at court, in other words, his leisure. This is the part of a warrior's existence which has hardly a place in *Beowulf* and the *chansons de geste* and very little—and then for quite different ends —in the *Nibelungenlied* and the *Cid*. The characteristics are those of appearance and behavior in civil surroundings. Some are superficial— fine dress, courteous behavior, cleanliness, fair speech, a good seat in the saddle—while some demand more understanding and artistic ability— knowledge of singing, of poetry, of instrumental music. It was rather the ability to appreciate artistic achievement than skill in composition or performance that was required. There are few romances in which the hero is an artist—we shall have a good deal to say on this subject later—but in all of them an appreciation of music, of a well-told tale, is required. Yet in most romances the emphasis is on good manners and courteous behavior, on the correct deference to ladies of rank, on the kind of flattery which is intended to please rather than deceive. The female effort to impart polish to social life is clearly in evidence, and it is in this context that we must consider the love passages in courtly literature.

First we should notice the influence of lyric poetry on love concepts and dismiss once and for all the idea of a unified concept of "courtly love." There is no evidence that the writers of the twelfth century envisaged such a concept, and to attempt to force the many different types of love found in medieval courtly literature into one mold is a Procrustean task indeed. The concept of love found in the lyric of the troubadours is usually stated to have begun with the works of William IX of Aquitaine, but any careful study of those works reveals that it is rather a desire for continuity and a tradition that has allowed critics to find in his work the elements which are so characteristic of the later troubadours. A more reasonable beginning would be with Jaufre Rudel whose *amor de lonh* may be regarded as a firm principle of the lyric love-concept. For it is not physical separation which is the main consideration here so much as that of the unattainability of love. Love is reached through the eyes, through the vision of the beloved, and the heart is thus irretrievably lost. It is questionable whether, at this period of the twelfth century, there was any conscious intellectual basis for the eternal image of ideal love which the sight of the beloved fashioned in the lover, any philosophic idea of the *imago* of the lady compared with the concept of ideal beauty. The poems seem to indicate rather a love rendered hopeless by distance in rank and position, a feeling of inferiority on the part of the male. If Jaufre really was "Prince de Blaya," as his *vida* says, a problem of rank could hardly exist and we must ask ourselves whether such differences were not perhaps a pose.

Many of the troubadours were professionals, men of the lowest ranks of the nobility or of humble birth. For these men to aspire to the love of a great lady was clearly impossible, and if they really loved such a lady, their cries of despair were well founded. Devotion to her would indeed be a hopeless love, which must inevitably lead to despair. Fulfillment, any love in the physical sense, was theoretically impossible. Of marriage there could be no thought. The lady could, of course, stoop to an illicit affair. No doubt many did, but such an affair could not be the solution to the problem for a sensitive man, for the very fact of indulging in it would lower the lady's status in the poet's eye and render her unworthy of his love. Whatever view we take of the origins of the love concepts to be found in the lyrics of the troubadours, we cannot afford to neglect the problem of difference in rank. The professional poets probably began to conceive of love as a form of liege service, and their noble imitators took it up because it afforded an ideal means of writing love poetry without overt eroticism.

Lyric poetry can be thought of as a form of service to a mistress and was indeed so thought of. All the great troubadours and many of their German successors either imply or state explicitly that their works are designed to present their lady to an artistic audience and to raise her reputation. Their threat in moments of utter despair is that they will refuse to continue their celebration of her in song. A poet serves his lady as a warrior serves his lord; he raises her reputation by his songs as a knight raises his lord's reputation by his prowess. Such a relationship could not, however, be one-sided. The acceptance of such service called for reward, for some act on the part of the liege lord or the lady which acknowledged the service rendered and enhanced the reputation of the poet as that of the lady had been enhanced. But how was such a reward to be given and what was it to be? The only true reward must be that the lady granted her love. Yet she could not in honor do so, for if she did, that very excellence which the poet celebrated would be lost. This is not a rejection of the physical act of love as sinful but the rejection of loss of honor brought about by the lady's stooping down to a man beneath her. It cannot be too strongly emphasized that the troubadours do not reject physical love; they simply regard it as impossible of attainment in the context they envisage and therefore they are perpetually seeking a substitute and failing to find it. Their poetry is an unsuccessful attempt to find a state of equilibrium between the power of attraction of the lady's virtue and beauty and the sense of rejection which comes not only from her cruelty but even more from the poet's own sense of his unworthiness. The point of equilibrium is never discovered and love must thus remain a matter of unending tension.

The poets take refuge, poetically, in a series of images of beauty through which alone they can gain some recompense for the fact that the highest beauty is beyond their reach. Their love is tragic in the sense that it must forever be unfulfilled. But there is in it an element of Keats's *Grecian Urn*. For what is unachieved cannot be destroyed and the poet's love has a timeless quality unaffected by the lady's age or the poet's lack of success.

There is no reason for thinking that this concept of love was the only one to be found in lyric poetry. The *alba* or dawn song and even more the *pastourelle* show none of the inhibitions of the *canzon*, for these two genres take no cognizance of differences in rank and are not concerned with the unattainability of love—or with the problems of service and reward. In some senses they are more realistic, for they reflect existing conditions more accurately than the *canzon*, but all have their own milieu, their own sets of conditions, which need not correspond to anything in real life.

The love situation in the Provençal *canzon* undoubtedly influenced the narrative genre cultivated in the north of France, but there can be no question of a mere transfer of the ideals of the one to the other. We can trace the development of the romance more easily than that of the lyric, and there is no evidence at any point of the kind of substitute sublimation of the service-reward concept which we find in the lyric, nor of the idea of song or poetry being in itself a service worthy of reward.

The first romance in which the question of love is of great significance is the *Roman d'Enéas*, and the manner in which the love problem is handled is worthy of closer examination. The love passages between Aeneas and Dido follow those in Vergil's *Aeneid* closely. The author shows us a Dido completely at the mercy of her passion and Aeneas in grave danger of succumbing to more than mere sensual attraction. The changes made by the author of the French romance are such as to eliminate the sympathy which the reader might feel with Dido and in particular her own doubts.

The love affair between Aeneas and Lavinia is the author's own invention, for Vergil has nothing to say of love between the two. The essence of the arrangement was that it should be purely political, and so it begins in the French poem. Lavinia is already betrothed to Turnus, and the engagement is strongly supported by her mother. When the message arrives that Latinus has promised Lavinia to Aeneas—whom she has naturally never seen—Lavinia is intrigued by the thought of a new man in her life, but her mother proceeds to blacken the character of Aeneas in no uncertain way, chiefly by saying outright that he is a homosexual. Lavinia is represented at first as a complete innocent, but her knowledge grows remarkably in the course of a few days, and she is seen debating with herself whether such charges can be true and what effect they would have on their relationship. A love monologue, indeed, but hardly one of sublimated yearning.

The turning point in the affair comes at the first sight of the beloved.

Lavinia is in a castle which is being besieged by the Trojans and she catches her first glimpse of Aeneas when he is making a tour of inspection. What follows on both sides is a series of sensuous visual impressions. The idea of the eyes as an instrument of love, of the shattering effect of the visual image of the beloved on the other partner, is fully exploited. Yet all of the inner monologues recorded by the author, the daydreams and yearnings, are couched in highly erotic imagery. Lavinia and Aeneas both feel the misery of their situation. They are separated by physical distance and political problems but neither is in any doubt about the kind of love they need and are determined to have. This is not the *amor de lonh* of Jaufre Rudel but physical love which must overcome physical handicaps. Each thinks up good reasons why the other may reject such a union, but these are the natural hesitancies of lovers who regard their beloved as superior not only to themselves but to all mankind.

The love affair of Aeneas and Lavinia has a happy ending. Love and politics join in bringing them together and the author has set a pattern for future romances. He has defied Vergil's separation of sensual love and social union and argued that the two can be compatible. In doing so he has by no means eliminated the physical aspects of love but has expressed these aspects by a new type of erotic imagery and in particular by allowing the lovers to describe their own feelings, feelings often not fully understood by themselves, in a series of monologues or occasionally dialogues with a third person. The technique was by no means new. Ovid had used it freely in his *Heroides*, which was widely read in the Middle Ages. The novelty lay rather in substituting for direct desire a more sublimated, a more distant, a more indirect approach which laid stress on looks, gestures, trifling acts which might signify affection. We are presented with a kind of mental courtship. The lovers in the *Enéas* cannot physically approach one another because of the military situation, but the technique was to be extended to situations where there was no barrier but the lovers' own feelings that they were unworthy and that any advance could be met only by a rebuff or, worse, by laughter. The lovers must therefore take refuge in imagery.

It is important to notice the literary context in which this innovation in the treatment of the love appears. The story was fixed and for most, if not all, medieval readers it was historical fact. The desperate anxiety of the ruling families of Western Europe to trace their descent from Trojans and thus equate themselves with the rulers of Rome is proof enough of their belief. Yet the story of Aeneas was remote. It contained some elements, particularly the intervention in human affairs of the pagan gods, which no Christian could accept, nor could it be connected with the recent history of a Western European people, as could the *matière de France* with France, the *Cid* with Spain, and, when it was first set down, *Beowulf* with England. The story of Aeneas was thus less political, less public-minded. Its wars were remote and in the medieval versions they were restyled to appear as tournaments rather than battles. (Vergil's battles are also fully stylized but this was less obvious to a medieval audience than to us.) It would be wrong to say that the work is concerned with the leisure time of a knight, but it is true that in the second part of the work the author has deliberately reshaped his text so that the political considerations—the establishment of Aeneas as the hero of Latium and the ultimate founder of Rome—are subordinated to the love affair with Lavinia. Balance is achieved by the defeat and death of Turnus, which at once establishes Aeneas as a military hero and eliminates his rival. The author follows Vergil in providing Aeneas with an excuse for killing the defeated Turnus, for he sees on his enemy's finger the ring he had taken from Pallas whom he had cruelly slain. There is thus no need for Aeneas to be chivalrous. No one can doubt that Aeneas the lover is more important than the political figure.

The romance had thus been turned in a significant direction. Whatever the story used may have been originally, the interest must be shifted to the prowess of an individual hero and his relation to a woman. In the *Roman de Troie* of Benoît de Ste Maure the process may be observed clearly. The Latin accounts of the Trojan war ascribed to Dares Phrygius and Dictys Cretensis, the former of which was apparently Benoît's principal source, show the love of Achilles for Polyxena as the principal event of the war and the failure of the Greeks to yield to Achilles' demand for a peace so that he could marry her as the cause of his wrath—and also of his own death. Thus political and historical events are closely bound up with the love of a hero. Benoît follows his source in this but he adds another story of perhaps greater significance. Troilus is mentioned as a minor warrior by Homer and he appears in Dares' account, but Benoît himself seems to be responsible for the story of his tragic love for Briseida, which proved so fertile for Boccaccio, Chaucer, and Shakespeare. In

Benoît's story love is shattered on the demands of politics. His lady is compelled to join her father by the terms of an agreement between Greeks and Trojans, and when she is separated from Troilus her love is not strong enough to resist the wiles of the handsome Diomedes. Thus love is sacrificed on the altar of political expediency, but the interest of the reader is concentrated on the lovers, not on politics. We do not feel that Troilus was allowing his attraction for Briseida to interfere with his duty to Troy but that an inflexible political system was ruining the lives of two innocent people. The difference is important. It is the individual who matters, not the political and social entity of which he is a member. Troilus' tragedy is due in part to the fickleness of women but even more to the harshness of war. The Trojan war, in fact, becomes little more than a background against which the tragedies of Achilles and Polyxena, Troilus and Cressida are worked out.

It was almost certainly the desire for a flexible historical milieu which led to the popularity of the *matière de Bretagne*. It is difficult to determine from the extant evidence how far the story of Arthur was regarded as history. Certainly the Celtic peoples regarded him as an important figure and furthermore one who was likely to return. But it is not with the writings of the Celtic peoples that we are primarily concerned. Geoffrey of Monmouth, with a brilliance to which scant justice has been given by some critics, attempted to make this vague figure a part of the history of Britain.[13] He realized that the figure of Arthur was sufficiently exotic to be fashioned into the form he wanted—that of the ruler of a court whose culture and polish far surpassed not only that of his contemporaries but that of the much vaunted Romans and thus, by implication, that of their professed successors, the Franks of Charlemagne. Geoffrey's declaration that the court of Arthur "was at that time raised to such a degree of dignity that it was superior to all other kingdoms in fullness of riches, in luxury of ornament, and in the courtliness and wit of its inhabitants" undoubtedly went far toward establishing its reputation for culture and manners, but the use of that court as a background for chivalrous deeds was already firmly entrenched in France. For French audiences the court of Arthur was a never-never land, far removed from their own history and therefore not susceptible to the kind of historical interpretation which was necessary in discussing the deeds of Charlemagne. For most French authors, Arthur's court was no more than a background, a place where certain ideal values ruled. There are no wars, no taxes, no life-and-death struggles. For twelfth-century France, Arthur's court provided an opportunity to illustrate those literary values for literary knights which we have already discussed. The figure of King Arthur is utterly unimportant. It is the milieu of his court which is significant and quite obviously this could be adjusted to elevate the qualities which the author admired without any reference to historical accuracy. We should beware of thinking that "Arthur's court" is the same wherever it appears. The British tradition was much more bound to history than the French and German, and Arthur as an individual plays a much more important role.

The earliest extant Arthurian romances are those of Chrétien de Troyes and there has been no lack of critics who believe that he "originated" the genre.[14] The discussion is rather pointless, since Arthurian romance as a specific literary genre does not exist. What we have are romances in which Arthur's court is the representative of certain values. It would hardly have been possible for Chrétien to write his romances in the way that he did if his contemporaries had not already a clear conception of this function of the court. None of his works is comprehensible without such knowledge and in none of them does he explain the qualities which make Arthur's court important. There is an even more important indication of this assumption of knowledge in the audience. All Chrétien's romances treat the Arthurian values ironically. In none of his works are the Arthurian ideals the ultimate toward which the hero strives but rather a base from which he can move to higher things. A detailed study of Chrétien's attitudes would be out of place here, but his work was so influential that a brief indication must be given of his attitudes to love.

It seems not unlikely that Chrétien had some sort of a program in mind in selecting his stories and in his treatment of them. Certainly each romance takes up the question of love in society from a different point of view and not, as has so often been assumed, as a mere example of courtly love. In *Erec* the first meeting between the hero and the heroine shows none of the "mysticism of eye and heart" which we have noted in the lyric.[15] She greets him fittingly—and takes his horse to the stable! There is, after all, no one else to do it. When Erec selects her as the lady for whom he will win the sparrow hawk, he does so purely because he needs someone and because, in spite of her mean dress, Enid is beautiful. The arrangement is made with her father, and Erec promises to marry her

in exchange for her services. Enid has no part in the negotiations. No one
mentions love. The whole transaction is calculated to a degree rarely
found in romance. It also conforms very closely with actual medieval
practice.

Chrétien goes to considerable lengths to show that Enid is not like
the female members of Arthur's court. She is shown not only at her
first introduction but throughout the poem as far less sophisticated and
far more attractive than Guinevere and her ladies. She lacks their wiles
and their determination to profit from the game of love. Her affection
for her husband is sincere. Erec enjoys the physical beauty of his wife,
but it requires all the agonies of the later part of the poem to make him
appreciate her other qualities. Much has been made of the necessity for
*mesure*, for a balance between love and prowess, but surely the real lesson
of the poem is that true love can develop within marriage, that concupis-
cence—of which Erec is undoubtedly guilty—is not a basis for success in
marriage but rather full understanding. In this poem Chrétien is far from
advocating the love of the Arthurian court, as represented by Guinevere
and her ladies, and he reinforces his point by the introduction of the "Joie
de la Cort" episode in which we are shown what happens when Enid's
conduct is reversed. For the whole point of the episode is to demonstrate
the evil effects of the dominance of women when that dominance is based not
on love but on desire for power. In *Erec* Chrétien has written a poem
about love in marriage and has shown how it can be made successful.
Thus he has attempted a solution of the problem which exercised all his
contemporaries. His solution is based on mutual trust. It may be added
that Chrétien shows no signs of regarding sex within marriage as sinful.
His problem is social rather than religious.

In *Cligès* the poet is concerned with a totally different question,
or rather with a pair of questions, impediments to marriage. Between
Alexander and Sordamurs the only impediment is the artificial one set
up by the exponents of the love game. The two are perfectly well matched,
their social standing offers no obstacle, but they have been educated to
think that love is a mystical thing with its own ceremonial. Each believes
that the other is unobtainable, the man because the lady is of a beauty
and virtue far beyond his grasp, the lady because it seems that he will
never make a declaration and she is too shy to encourage him. Chrétien
makes sport of the whole cult of love, with its hairs sewn into shirts

and its adoration of the things which the beloved has touched. The second part is more serious, for here we are faced with the problem of extramarital love. Cligès has every right to be angry with his uncle, for he has broken his oath. The sympathy of the audience is with Cligès, but can it remain with him after the cynical expedients to which he resorts to win his uncle's wife? Surely adultery remains adultery in the sight of God even if the lady has been given up for dead and lives in a (richly furnished) sepulchre. Chrétien cannot have meant us to take seriously his proposed solution of the uncle-aunt-nephew triangle. Fenice differs from Isolde only in being more dishonest. She deceives her husband before her apparent death and deceives him again—and herself, apparently —when she goes to Cligès. It is perhaps significant that the guilty pair finally do what they should have done in the first place—flee to Arthur's court, which is the only place where such conduct is tolerated.

It seems to me that in *Cligès* Chrétien is attacking the whole cult of love outside marriage.[16] He is merely ironical at the expense of the trappings of the love game in the first part, for a decent marriage is ultimately made in spite of them, but he is savagely critical of the cult which regards love as more important than marriage and which believes that, if the two are in conflict, it is the marriage which should be sacrificed. There is no evidence that there was any motive behind the "love" of Cligès and Fenice but physical attraction. Not quite the same can be said of the attraction of Guinevere for Lancelot. He is under the spell of her beauty, it is true, and he desires above all to possess her physically, but there is in all his conduct a degree of sublimity which transcends the ridicule to which he is subjected. There is no doubt that he is the greatest of knights. He can win anything at any time. Yet he is prepared to sacrifice all this for a look or a smile from the Queen. The spirit of sacrifice is strong in him, and even were he not to be granted any reward he would still love the Queen desperately. The question which Chrétien raises and leaves unsolved is whether the Queen—or any woman of the court over which she presides—is worth such adoration. Chrétien's portrait of her is unflattering in the extreme. All her actions are designed to show her power over the wretched Lancelot, and the sight of a truly great man's being reduced to a lady's puppet is highly unpleasant. Here was the power of the lady carried to its extreme, the "Joie de la Cort" attitude taking over the whole Arthurian court. Clearly Chrétien did not believe that such conduct could endure, for it would destroy the court which fostered it. If Arthur stood idly by to let such things happen, he was much to blame.

I find it hard to escape the conclusion that Chrétien, in *Cligès* and *Chevalier de la charette*, is rejecting the whole concept of a solution to the love problem outside marriage. The hypothetical Arthurian court might be a place in which fancy could solve the problem by making love into a sport and thus encouraging men and women to indulge themselves to different degrees under the cloak of a highly formalized love game. The evidence is insufficient to allow us to determine whether the salon of Marie de Champagne operated on the same principle, although Andreas Capellanus gives us grounds for such a belief. The Arthurian court might be a model of manners and civilized behavior which encouraged conduct far superior to that of most of Chrétien's contemporaries, but Chrétien did not believe that the romances built around it should develop the lyric thesis of extramarital love.

*Yvain* has usually been regarded as a kind of mirror-image of *Erec*, and it has been stressed that both works show their heroes attaining *mesure*, Erec by realizing that his passion for his wife must not prevent him from using his knightly prowess to aid the unfortunate, Yvain by being forced to reexamine his conception of knightly adventure and to realize that such prowess has no validity unless it is used in combination with love, for Laudine and all women. The two poems do indeed present the problem of balance, of competing qualities, but it would be ludicrous to regard Erec's relationship to Enid as in any way equivalent to that between Yvain and Laudine. Although the marriage of the former pair begins as a contract, it soon leads to deep affection on both sides. The problem faced by both is the meaning of true marital love and they attain that knowledge. We have no such certainty about Yvain and Laudine. Quite the contrary. Chrétien describes the beginnings of Yvain's passion for Laudine with all the terminology of the "mysticism of eyes and heart." He sees her and is smitten. There is no question of communication, because Lunete's ring has already made him invisible. We have been prepared for Yvain's behavior very carefully—by his excessive concern for his cousin's honor in an incident which took place fourteen years before, by his impression of the fountain and its contrast with the down-to-earth attitude of the giant herdsman. He is ready for all the trappings of "courtly love" and believes in full in the concept "amor vincit omnia," even when one of the things to be overcome is the lady's natural repugnance toward the man who has just killed her husband. Yvain obtains his wish. He marries the lady after going through the motions of handing himself over completely to her power. Yet she does not say that she loves him. She accepts him as a guardian of the fountain, an office which he soon abandons, and it is in this capacity that he is readmitted to her favor at the end of the poem. After all his brave deeds in defense of distressed womankind, the best he can obtain from Laudine, his lawful wife, is a promise to take him back because she has sworn an oath to Lunete. There is no evidence that the "political" marriage of Yvain and Laudine resulted in wedded love. Hartmann von Aue, in his German adaptation, realized this full well and added a scene in which Laudine begs for forgiveness and a true reconciliation takes place. Hartmann believed in the courtly mystique, as Chrétien did not, and he therefore failed to appreciate his predecessor's irony.

Chrétien's romances are the most consistent attempt in medieval French literature to grapple with the problem of love and society. The best solution is that propounded in the *Erec*, where lovers joined in a social contract find love and mutual understanding. Physical passion plays an important role in their love but it is combined with a realization of the importance of their role in society. Both are far superior to their counterparts at Arthur's court, whose ideas of love they prove to be hollow. Yvain tries to put these Arthurian ideals into practice and fails. He finds that they cannot be seriously applied to the situations in which he finds himself and that he must rise above them if he is to find happiness with Laudine. The issue is deliberately left in doubt. Both *Cligès* and *Chevalier de la charette* illustrate the total collapse of the courtly concept of extramarital love, the former by its proof of the essentially immoral nature of the two participants and the shallowness of their love, the second by the degradation of a noble nature in its pursuit of the unattainable, the love of the highest woman in the land in spite of her marriage.

Yet Chrétien's romances, with the possible exception of the *Chevalier de la charette*, remain comedies in the medieval sense of the term. All of the participants achieve their goals, they are accepted as part of the society with which they wish to be integrated. The harmony which exists at the beginning is restored at the end, even though the hero and heroine in two of the romances, *Erec* and *Yvain*, have actually transcended this social harmony and attained a higher form for themselves. The romance as a genre is essentially the comedy of love, for it proves—or purports to prove—that love can be reconciled with the demands of society and that a society can be so shaped that it recognizes the demands of love and adjusts to them. The Arthurian world is ideal for this purpose, as we have seen.

There can be little doubt that the Arthurian world, as it is depicted by Chrétien, is female-oriented. It is characteristic of this world that the actions which begin *Erec* and *Yvain* are both closely connected with Guinevere, not Arthur, who is a passive bystander. The concept of service to the lady is closely linked to this female orientation, as are many of the characteristics of the romance itself—its interest in dress, festivals, appearance. Thus the social orientation is largely feminine. But is this true of the development of the plot and characterization? The hero in all cases is largely employed on adventures which involve aid to females, but all such adventures are considered from the masculine point of view. The lady may be the instigator, the person for whom the actions are performed, but she is not the person in whom the writer of romance is interested. Any reader of the romances of Chrétien de Troyes would be rather hard put to it to describe the character of his heroines in any but the most general terms. Laudine hardly exists except as she is seen through the eyes of Yvain, Guinevere is depicted as an embodiment of the demanding female, the female characters in *Cligès* are little more than puppets pulled by the strings of courtly cliché. Only Enid may be said to exist as a person in her own right. The romance is interested in the effect of love on the male. When the stories open, all of the heroes except Perceval are fully developed within the limits of the society to which they belong, except that they have no permanent attachment to any lady. Erec and Yvain are bachelor knights but they are full and honored members of Arthur's entourage. Both Alexander and Cligès are fully trained in everything but love and even there they are perhaps overconscious of the rules. Lancelot appears to be an exception. His love for Guinevere is already in full flower, even though we are not aware of the fact at the very beginning of Chrétien's poem, but he is nevertheless a fully trained knight who needs only to gain acceptance by his lady. There are no "enfances" in these poems, no periods of training, no attempt at showing how society affected the man in any regard except that of his relation to one lady. In every case the training he has already received proves inadequate and he has to work out for himself the problem of reconciling the inadequacy of his preconceptions with the reality of love in marriage.

It is thus that we must understand the formal structure which is obvious in Chrétien's complete romances, particularly the *Erec* and *Yvain*: harmony, disruption, restoration, chaos, struggle, harmony. The original harmony is a false, inadequate state for the hero (but not for the court, where it is normal), although he does not realize it. Its disruption is brought about by an incident alien to courtly behavior, and its apparent restoration by adventures which superficially are entirely within the Arthurian range but for the hero have much more profound implications. There is constant tension between the values of the Arthurian world, represented in *Erec* by Guinevere and her ladies, in *Yvain* by Gawain, and the true values which the hero himself does not yet understand. The chaos is brought about by the inadequacy of the Arthurian measuring rod, the demonstration, in different ways, that "adventure," in the shallow sense in which it is normally used, is an empty pursuit and that service to a lady must be meaningful in general human terms. The harmony which is restored at the end of the work is thus quite different from that at the beginning. It is a harmony between two human beings which is independent of the virtues of the Arthurian court, even though the principal characters continue to live in it or in close association with it. The whole point of Chrétien's work is thus to show how a man, as an individual, must evolve a relationship with his lady which will enable him to fulfill himself as a member of society—not merely of the Arthurian court—and also to live a life of sexual harmony with his partner, with each contributing to that harmony. In evolving this new pattern the hero becomes a much greater man, but it should be noted that only in the *Erec* is the hero's career crowned with complete success. Love in marriage is a difficult pursuit.

How dependent was Chrétien on Christian religious standards? Attempts have been made to show that *Perceval* is a religious allegory and that the Christian concept of charity plays an important part in the growth of Yvain.[17] The former is hardly relevant to our discussion and the latter is very hard to prove. Obviously Chrétien thought in a Christian context, but it is hard to make connections between the behavior of his characters and specific points of Christian doctrine. He was writing essentially secular works whose object was to demonstrate the development of individuals within a precisely described social milieu. Their lives are determined not by considerations about the ultimate fate of their immortal souls but by a desire to reconcile sexual happiness with the correct employment of those talents, social and chivalric, with which they have been endowed. They must develop a sense of responsibility in the use of physical strength and a sense of proportion in their love for a single, chosen woman.

The technique of the courtly romance reaches its zenith in the works of Chrétien de Troyes. He uses to the full the "game-rules" of the genre, the conventions within which his heroes function. These game-rules have no necessary connection with life at court, present or past, contemporary or historical. They are designed to allow the development of a person in specific directions. Chrétien's knights are members of this society and of no other. They are not actual medieval aristocrats or knights of any order but characters whose conduct is circumscribed by rules which limit their behavior to specific areas and to specific patterns. The romance exploits the variations possible within these rules.

Chrétien is concerned to illustrate the morality within the system but recognizes and exploits to the full the potential absurdities. Complete devotion to a lady is feasible and commendable if the lady is Enid but if she is Guinevere the act of adoration becomes an act of absurdity. Chrétien was able to exploit these weaknesses with irony and humor but he did not overcome the fundamental defect of the game-rules—that the lady who is so worshipped is a shadowy, tenuous figure of no interest to the reader. In a female-oriented society the females are merely the objects of male attention, accepting or rejecting the love of the males but virtually never revealing their own true feelings. Yet surely the knight's attitude can be made credible only if the lady is herself a person, a participator in love rather than a mere recipient. It is this element of mutuality, of sharing, of equality, which Gottfried introduces and which raises his work above the level of the "courtly romance."

# II

# THE POET AND HIS PREDECESSORS

WE SHOULD SAY at once that nothing is known of Gottfried von Strassburg. Even the identification with Strassburg rests on remarks made by the continuators of his poem—there is no evidence in the *Tristan*. In the anthology of lyric poems contained in the manuscript called the *Grosse Heidelberger Liederhandschrift*, several poems are ascribed to a "Meister Gottfried von Strassburg," but there is no *certainty* that this is our poet, although the identification seems natural. What connection Gottfried has with Strassburg is unknown. He may have been born and have lived his whole life there or merely have worked there during the years in which his reputation grew. It is significant that all of the early manuscripts of the *Tristan* can be assigned on paleographical grounds to the Alsace region and there is some evidence to connect them with Strassburg and even with one scriptorium in the city.[18]

More important than this speculation is the question of the significance of the designation "Meister"—if indeed the title is anything more than a guess by the compiler of the lyric anthology. To equate the title "Meister" with the bourgeoisie is an error. The inhabitants of Strassburg were not a well-organized group of tradesmen and artisans at the end of the twelfth century. It is much more likely that "Meister" is to be understood in its other sense of *dominus*, a man educated for the church but not necessarily in orders. There is no doubt that Gottfried had received such an education. He uses classical references with far more frequency and, in spite of an occasional lapse, far more accurately than most medieval writers and, what is more important, he uses them naturally, as an integral part of his work, not as mere illustrations or *exempla*. He is clearly acquainted

with the rules of formal rhetoric and can handle them so easily that
he is able to manipulate them for his own stylistic purposes. Although he
makes no overt references to the formal training in music which formed
part of the quadrivium, his numerous references to the latest fashions in
song and to the new modal school show his close acquaintance with and
deep interest in both the theory and the practice of music.[19]

We may assume that Gottfried was well trained in the trivium and
quadrivium, but it is much harder to determine the extent of his knowledge
of philosophy and theology. There has been a great deal of scholarly
speculation on the subject, but much of it attempts to prove a depth of
theological knowledge and interest which cannot be demonstrated.[20]
Gottfried was writing a poem, not a work of philosophy or theology, and
the presence of ideas in his work which correspond, in general terms, to
those found in specific religious writings does not necessarily prove
acquaintance with those writings, although such acquaintance cannot, of
course, be excluded. It shows rather that the ideas were "in the air" and
accessible to an educated man. Although the parallel is far from exact, the
situation is not unlike that in which information about Freudian psychol-
ogy, much of it secondhand and much of it inaccurate, is available even
to those with no firsthand knowledge of Freud's works.

Several critics have shown with considerable probability the influence
of mystical writers on Gottfried, and the importance of the sermons of
Bernard of Clairvaux has been proved as conclusively as anything could
be without actual citation by the author.[21] Gottfried Weber is probably
right when he says that all the great religious movements of the time—
"Augustinism, the works of Bernard of Clairvaux, the Victorines, Abélard,
the Catharists, the Amalricans, the School of Chartres"—are concentrated
in Gottfried's work.[22] He knew of them and they formed part of his
thinking. How *consciously* he used their ideas in shaping his own is a
different problem and an insoluble one. Gottfried's work was written in a
Christian context. We shall discuss later how important Christian ideas
were for Gottfried's own concept of love.

There is no doubt about the importance of one aspect of Christian
teaching, that of allegory. The early Christian apologists inherited from
classical and Hebrew scholars the system of interpreting works on several
different levels. The technique was of particular use to Christian writers
when they were faced with the problem of reconciling the Old Testament

with the New and of producing from their interpretations of both a unified theology. We should not expect to find in every case the meanings "ad litteram," "per allegoriam," "per moralitatem," "per anagogiam" which represent the complete series of allegorical steps. Even in theological works it is unusual to find all four. The importance of the technique for secular writing is that it enabled authors to present a story which need not be interpreted, but could be, on a higher level. In most poems there is only one level of allegorization. We should distinguish very carefully the personification allegory, such as the *Psychomachia* of Prudentius or the *Roman de la Rose*, in which the author has set general abstractions in a well-known literary-genre frame (Vergilian epic, courtly romance), and the poem which exists in its own right as a narrative or lyric work but which can be understood on a higher level. Certain parts of Gottfried's *Tristan* are specifically allegorized by the author, but there is every reason for thinking that he intended other parts and possibly the whole poem to be read allegorically. Certainly some parts, such as the literary excursus, must be read on two different levels if they are to be understood correctly.

In general it may be stated that Gottfried had a broad acquaintance with the religious thinking of his time, that he understood the techniques of religious thinking and their application in writing, and that he was particularly well versed in the writings of the chief mystics. He was prepared to use this knowledge in a bold and imaginative way.

THE TRISTAN STORY

Why did Gottfried choose the Tristan story as the vehicle for his only major work and for what he clearly intended as a study of the love problem in all its aspects? He says that he followed the version of Thomas of Britain and the statement is significant, not only because it is one of the few definite statements by a German author about his immediate source, but because the version of Thomas had steered the Tristan story in a direction very different from that of its earlier versions. It was the only version, except, perhaps, that of Béroul, in which love for Isolde was of more significance than the honor of Tristan himself.

Since no early versions of the Tristan story are extant and the dates of the extant versions are difficult to determine, we are forced to fall back on reconstructions. All the evidence seems to indicate that the early Celtic stories told of a love story very different from that which we normally associate with the names of Tristan and Isolde. The most significant element of the older story was the reluctance of the male lover and his inability to escape from the curse which was imposed on him. If, as seems probable, the earlier versions followed the pattern seen in the story of Diarmaid and Grainne, Tristan was not in love with Isolde in any real sense. She was attracted to him, presumably on purely physical grounds, and was determined to make him her lover. He resisted obstinately because it was inconsistent with his honor to take as mistress his uncle's wife or betrothed. He breaks down because of a challenge to his manhood (the splashing-water incident which occurs in the extant Tristan stories but always in connection with Isolde White Hands, not Isolde the Fair). The love affair ends in tragedy when Isolde's husband revenges himself on his wife's lover, as he was perfectly entitled to do, and Tristan in his turn strangles the woman whose desires had brought misery to all who came in contact with her.[23]

During the twelfth century or earlier, this story was considerably modified. Certain elements were introduced which changed the relationship between uncle, nephew, and wife and shifted the sympathies of the audience. The obligation of the uncle to the nephew was increased by the Morolt incident, which meant that the uncle owed his kingdom and his life to his nephew. Further, the bride was actually won by the exertions of the nephew. The uncle would not have had a bride if his nephew had not won her by risking his life at the Irish court. The lovers come together not because of the lust of Isolde for a handsome man but because they accidentally drink a love potion which makes it quite literally a matter of life and death for them both that they should stay together, either for a term of years or forever. Neither of the lovers has any choice in the matter and the tricks to which they must resort are justified by the danger to their lives.

Yet it cannot be said that there is anything noble about their love. It is on a purely sensual level, and no attempt is made, so far as we can see from the fragmentary state of the texts, to show that Tristan's love for Isolde, or her's for him, is on any higher level than that of Mark for his bride. As a result the story becomes very largely a contest of wits between Tristan and his uncle. How long can Tristan succeed in tricking Mark and what will happen to him when he is discovered? The monstrous nature of the penalties proposed—the handing over of Isolde to lepers or burning her at the stake—shows that the tension exists not between the lovers but between uncle and nephew. Who will win? The lovers are faithful because they have to be, but they and the audience realize the dishonorable nature of the relationship into which they have entered. The story in which they appear can therefore follow two main lines of development: a cynical deluding of Mark and a corresponding savagery on his part, so that the death of Tristan becomes an obsession with him—such is the main purport of the prose romances—or a study of the decay of a knight's honor. So far as can be judged from the fragments, the treatment of Eilhart von Oberg sought to show how a great knight was corrupted by a sensual passion over which he had no control.

Very few of the medieval Tristan stories are concerned with the study of love. For most of them the liaison between Tristan and Isolde is an adulterous passion with no extenuating moral circumstances. It is justified only by the love potion. The passion is frankly sensual, it unites the lovers in body but not in soul, and it is utterly destructive not only of the lovers but also of the society in which they function. That society was not orig-inally Arthurian. It did not condone adultery, whether in theory or practice. The story is told from the point of view of a knight whose primary duty is the service of his liege lord. His mad passion prevents him from carrying out that duty and he is destroyed. Love, in this society, cannot be reconciled with chivalric duty. It is the kind of love which almost de-stroyed Aeneas, fatal, undisciplined, irresistible.

We would do well to bear in mind that there is no chronological development in the character of the love story.[24] The usual but by no means universally accepted datings of the most important versions of the Tristan story are these:

| | |
|---|---|
| c. 1165 | Oldest extant lay of Tristan |
| c. 1170 (but may be anywhere from 1150 to 1190) | Thomas of Britain |
| c. 1170 | Eilhart von Oberg |
| c. 1190 | Béroul |
| c. 1210 | Gottfried von Strassburg |
| c. 1225–35 | First French prose version |
| 1226 | Brother Robert (Norse version of Thomas) |
| 1230–35 | Ulrich von Türheim—continuation of Gottfried's version |

| c. 1290 | Heinrich von Freiberg—different continuation of Gottfried |
| c. 1300 | *La Tavola Ritonda* (contains Italian version of Tristan story) |
| c. 1300 | *Sir Tristrem* (Middle English) |

All of the extant versions which antedate Gottfried's are fragmentary, not because, like Gottfried's, they were left incomplete but because of the transmission of the text. Eilhart's version exists in fragments of the whole work (611 lines) which can be supplemented by references to the German prose version first printed in 1484 and by thirteenth-century reworkings of the story. From these it is possible to determine Eilhart's approach to the story and to grasp what remained the "normal" attitude of German audiences to Tristan's love affair. It is quite clear that not only before Gottfried wrote but during his lifetime and for the next three centuries the love affair was regarded as sinful and destructive. Isolde drags Tristan down from the high level of honorable knighthood to that of a sly adulterer and betrayer of his uncle's trust. Death is the only possible conclusion to such a relationship. There is little sympathy for Mark, who is depicted as cruel and brutal but not man enough to avenge himself. It is ironical that both the authors who "completed" Gottfried's work were fully in sympathy with this attitude. The lovers are sinners and are surely doomed to Hell (as they are in the *Commedia*) and, as Weber points out, Tristan's marriage to Isolde White Hands is regarded as the one good deed he performs after his meeting with Isolde the Fair.[25]

Such evidence as we have seems to indicate that the French romances also regarded Tristan and Isolde as unhappy lovers but nevertheless sinful. The stress, however, is rather on their individual adventures than on any development of love, and the huge extant versions of the French prose *Tristan* are collections of accounts of trickery and furtive meetings rather than properly constructed works of art. Thus when Gottfried says that Thomas of Britain alone has told the story aright, he is perfectly correct in the only sense that mattered to Gottfried—Thomas was the one author up to that time who wished to study the love of Tristan and Isolde sympathetically. There is no question of whether he did or did not include a particular incident; such matters, even when Gottfried mentions them, are quite insignificant compared with the new approach to the whole story which Thomas undertook. He showed the lovers seeking a solution to a situation which was being studied by Chrétien and other poets: How can love be reconciled with a social order which recognizes sex only in marriage but regards marriage as a contract made without love? Thomas saw in the Tristan story an opportunity to explore this problem in the light of the views current in some circles—the courts of Eleanor of Aquitaine and others that we have mentioned—namely, the view that love could be more important than either the sanctity of marriage or the prohibition of sex outside it. Under such circumstances the marriage remained in being, but love could be carried on—provided it was kept secret. In such an arrangement the element of deceit was bound to be strong—this element was already present in the Tristan story—and the love was in the end bound to come to a tragic conclusion—as the Tristan story did. The problem faced by Thomas was to shift the emphasis from the decay of knighthood as a result of sensual indulgence to love which rose above the obstacles it faced and appeared to the audience as worthy of sympathy rather than condemnation. To do this it was necessary to present existing relationships in a new light.

There are certain fixed events in all the versions of the Tristan story but they are manipulated very differently by the various authors. The birth and upbringing of Tristan is a standard form—the boy deprived of one or both parents by death and in some case also of his birthright by a usurper, who is educated by a faithful retainer. Even when Tristan's father does not die shortly after his birth, he is not an important character except to provide motivation, by his death, for an act of revenge by Tristan. In some versions this act of revenge is extremely important.[26] In Eilhart's version the boy's training is the standard upbringing of a knight, with a stress on physical prowess, and in this respect there is clear evidence of a shift in emphasis by Thomas, for he—and still more Gottfried—stresses those features of good manners, learning, and training in the arts which were characteristic of the female-oriented knights of the romance. The theme continues when Tristan arrives at Mark's court—by accident, not by design, as in Eilhart. Thomas stresses that it is the boy's artistic skills and knowledge of hunting etiquette which provide an entrée for Tristan into Mark's court. Moreover, Tristan uses his skills to make himself a place at a court which, so far as he knows, is foreign. He can expect no favors but relies only on his merits, whereas Eilhart's hero intends to ingratiate himself with a ruler whom he knows to be his uncle and is merely waiting for a suitable opportunity to reveal his identity. The two situations are very different and it is a difference which persists, for the hero in the Gottfried-Thomas version is an adventuring wanderer throughout the poem in a way that Eilhart's Tristan, a permanent if erring inhabitant of Mark's court, is not.

The battle with Morolt is always a part of the Tristan romances. Nevertheless its function varies considerably from one version to another. It may be assumed that the incident always had two principal structural purposes—to bind Mark closely to Tristan because of the great service he performed in saving the kingdom at the cost of a dreadful wound and, perhaps more important, to connect the winning of Isolde with this incident, so that Tristan's love affair and his treason toward Mark are directly connected with a service without which Mark himself could not have survived. The character of Morolt varies considerably. He was undoubtedly a monster in earlier versions, and his demand for large numbers of children as tribute recalls, as Gertrude Schoepperle says, the eater of human flesh.[27] His superhuman strength is described in all versions, but the fierceness of his demeanor varies greatly. In Eilhart's version he is a savage fighter, although he recognizes Tristan's bravery. The use of the poisoned sword is an essential motif and one characteristic of an uncivilized fighter. The difference between the Eilhart version—and presumably other early versions—and that of Thomas lies in the fact that Morolt reveals to the wounded Tristan that he can be cured by his—Morolt's—sister, the mother of Isolde, and only by her, and offers him life at the expense of Mark. Thus Tristan's devotion is made all the more significant by Thomas and his subsequent visit to Ireland is a deliberate search for a cure rather than the pointless and presumably final voyage of a dying man.

The whole treatment of the incident is much more sophisticated in the Thomas-Gottfried version and much more closely integrated with the subsequent love conflict. Tristan's cure is effected in Eilhart only because the king of Ireland pities his condition. (The link with the education of Isolde, a most significant change, seems to have been the invention of Thomas.) Tristan is cured by herbs sent by Isolde but he leaves Ireland without ever seeing her. Thus when he sets out in search of the lady of the yellow hair whom alone Mark declares he will marry, he has no idea that she is Isolde or even that she lives in Ireland. Once again it is pure chance which throws Tristan ashore on the Irish coast, pure chance that informs him that the king will offer his daughter in marriage to the slayer of the dragon, and pure chance that it is Isolde who finds him in the brook and ends his quest for the lady with the blonde hair. The structure is thus improbable and unsophisticated in the Eilhart version. Far too much is left to chance, and Tristan's acts are determined by fate—or accident— rather than calculation, even though it may be Eilhart's intention to show the intervention of a deterministic fate. It is Thomas who introduces the element of calculation and Gottfried who carries this element to its logical conclusion. Tristan knows that he is going to Ireland, he obtains his cure in exchange for instruction of Isolde, he knows of the dragon-slayer's reward and goes back to Ireland with this knowledge. When he is discovered by Isolde and her mother, he is recognized as Tantris the minstrel and has to find an explanation of his return. It is not until he has been at the Irish court for some time that the notch in the blade is discovered, and Isolde has to be held back from taking vengeance for her uncle. In Thomas, as in Eilhart, it is fear of marriage with the seneschal which deters her but in Eilhart she soon gives up her anger, and it is she who asks her father to pardon Tristan for any deeds he might have done. Eilhart does, however, offer an explanation of why Tristan does not take Isolde as his own wife —as he was perfectly entitled to do. He is, says Tristan, too young. Thomas does not raise this point, although it is important. If Tristan had chosen to ignore his uncle, he could have married Isolde himself and presumably have succeeded to the kingdom of Ireland. Once again, Tristan is making a sacrifice for his uncle. Thomas stresses, as Eilhart does not, the opportunities that his hero had to cheat Mark, opportunities which he rejects out of loyalty to his uncle. Yet Eilhart clearly regards Tristan as closely attached to Mark and the core of his work is the uncle-nephew relationship which is disturbed by the relation to Isolde, unwilled and yet inescapable. Thomas also makes much of the loyalty issue, but the difference between the two treatments lies in the fact that Eilhart is interested only in the principle of loyalty and understanding between uncle and nephew, whereas Thomas and Gottfried are interested in the moral conflict within the minds of the participants.

The same disparity appears in the treatment of the love potion. In Eilhart's version the potion is all-important. It really controls the destinies of the lovers, and they cannot escape from it for four years without physical death. Eilhart emphasizes over and over again that the lovers realize the immorality of what they are doing but are powerless to work against the potion. The very fact that it has an effective limit of four years stresses this mechanical dependence. Tristan and Isolde cease to be rational creatures. They are mere puppets of love and are completely in its power. It would be hard to imagine a more effective way of disparaging the love phenomenon.

Gertrude Schoepperle pointed out long ago that Eilhart's treatment changes in the later parts of his poem.[28] In the part of the action which occurs before the return from the forest, all the emphasis is on the powerlessness of the lovers. Their will means nothing. They realize the wrongs they are committing but cannot help themselves. Their love is altogether evil, both in their opinion and that of the author, and the only excuse for their conduct lies in the power of the potion over them. After the four-year term expires, they can live without seeing each other, Tristan does consummate his marriage to Isolde White Hands, and both he and Isolde are much more responsible for their acts. Those acts are just as reprehensible and are now worthy of total condemnation. Tristan is unfaithful to his wife, as Isolde is unfaithful to her husband, and death is their reward.

Eilhart's version and indeed most versions of the Tristan story except those of Thomas and Gottfried delight in the multiplication of examples in which the lovers deceive or attempt to deceive Mark. Those which precede the exile in the woods—the slandering by the king's servants, the meeting under the tree in which Mark is concealed, the jumping of the flour-strewn floor, and the condemnation of the lovers—are all designed to show the progressive undeceiving of Mark and the hardening of his attitude. They are not particularly indicative of any great skill or cunning on Tristan's part, since he acts rashly under the influence of the potion. Mark's act in handing over Isolde to the lepers suitably punished her sexual promiscuity by giving her to men whom medieval opinion regarded as horribly lustful because of their disease.[29] Tristan effects a rescue by prodigious feats of physical skill and takes Isolde away to the forest. His return to court after much misery is brought about by Mark's discovery of the sword between them—and also by the fact that the four-year term of the potion has expired.

From now on Tristan embarks on adventures which often have little connection with Isolde. She is still his mistress, her image is still before his eyes, but he can be separated from her and live and he does in fact leave her voluntarily. The relation between them is much more like the alternating storm and sunshine of the Lancelot-Guinevere affair than the earlier obsession, and while Isolde can be an imperious mistress, Tristan can be an unfaithful lover. It is hard to find any approval of Tristan's conduct in Eilhart's work, except when he consummates his marriage to Isolde White Hands. The stress is in any case not on the question of approval or disapproval of the lovers' conduct but on an account of the extraordinary ruses which they used to circumvent the watchfulness of Mark. The series of such tricks in Eilhart's version is long—the blades at the bed, the lover in the thornbush, Tristan the leper, Tristan the fool, Tristan the pilgrim, Tristan the minstrel.

Thomas changes this approach completely. To him, as to Gottfried, it was inconceivable that the love of Tristan and Isolde could degenerate. It might and did become more refined when the lovers were forced to separate; it was exposed to much more severe trials and Tristan's loneliness led him to try to console himself for the loss of one Isolde by taking another. Yet it remained noble. Thomas, therefore, increases the number of deceptions attempted on Mark *before* the exile in the forest and eliminates most of those which come after. The first incident, the discovery of the queen and Tristan together by Marjodo, corresponds to the general accusations made by the barons in Eilhart's version and serves as a preliminary warning to Mark, who begins to test Isolde's loyalty by asking who is to be her guardian during a pilgrimage he proposes to take. Her selection of Tristan intensifies his suspicions and her subsequent efforts to allay them by declaring that she hates Tristan are not altogether successful. The incident of the meeting under the tree is the result of Mark's continuing suspicions and reflects brilliantly the state of his mind —his willingness to be convinced of Tristan's guilt and his reluctance to believe the evidence when it is before his eyes. The incident of the flour-strewn floor provides indisputable evidence, yet Mark does not take the direct action which Eilhart describes. Again he tries to let others make the decision for him, and the highly complex incident of the ordeal of the hot iron, completely unknown to Eilhart, is the result. It is a natural projection of the state of Mark's mind as Thomas sees it, just as Mark's decision to hand over Isolde to the lepers is natural to Eilhart's king. Mark has no desire to make a decision himself, for, after all, it is just possible that Tristan's conduct was innocent, and he therefore decides on the ordeal which will place the decision in the hands of a higher power. The fragments of Béroul's version also contain an ordeal scene, but attitudes are very different from those in Thomas' and Gottfried's version. Tristan is disguised as a leper, and there is more crude byplay than sentiment. Here as so often the scene is designed to show deception being practiced on Mark rather than to throw any light on the character and motives of the lovers. For Thomas and even more for Gottfried it is a confrontation between the morality of the lovers and the morality of the society in which they live. It is no accident that Tristan is disguised as a pilgrim, not a leper.

It is not clear in Thomas' version why Tristan does not return to court after Isolde's success in undergoing the ordeal. If she is innocent, he is also, but it was tactful to stay away. The incident of Petitcreiu, the dog whose bells give forth magic harmony, is found only in the Thomas-Gottfried version, and its introduction shows a very different intention from that of Eilhart. This is not a deception incident nor an attempt to visit Isolde. It is the first of the attempts to show the establishment of harmony at a distance, love without the physical presence of the beloved. Tristan wishes to give sensuous pleasure, even though he cannot share it. Isolde refuses such pleasures unless they can be shared. Structurally, the incident is closely related to Tristan's attraction to Isolde White Hands. Isolde's inability at this stage to be happy without the physical presence of Tristan leads to her request for his recall and to the subsequent banishment to the wilderness.

Eilhart's account of their life in the woods follows immediately after the leper incident and is a natural continuation of it. The lovers are fleeing from Mark's wrath. Thomas, as we have seen, moves more slowly to the scene in the grotto because he has to prepare the reader for the gradual change in the lovers' attitudes. Nor are the lovers driven out in the conventional sense. They are not caught in any act of adultery by Mark or his creatures, but their affection for each other, expressed in looks and general behavior, simply becomes so obvious that Mark cannot bear it. Thomas' change is significant. Eilhart is concerned only with actual sexual aberrations, with acts of adultery which Mark may detect or not but which in any case rouse him to bestial anger. It is with such acts, either actual or attempted, that almost the whole of his version is concerned after the marriage of Mark and Isolde. Thomas departs so far from this attitude that he shows the king dismissing the lovers from his presence not as punishment but simply to rid himself of a torture which has become intolerable. They depart together, hand in hand, and there can be no doubt in the mind of Mark or anyone else that they will be together in exile. Thomas and Gottfried show them parted from normal civilization. Their separation from the life of the court is not so much an exile as a transition to another sphere. There is no stress on the poor quality of their food or their misery from the squalid conditions in which they are forced to exist. Quite the contrary. Their life is idealized and both attain a degree of happiness which is not only higher than at any other time in their lives but higher than that achieved by any other character. Thomas, like Chrétien, shows that idealized extramarital love is, in the end, not possible at the court of Arthur or any other monarch but only where no society exists except that which the lovers themselves set up. The subject will be discussed in detail later.

In all the versions of which we have any knowledge, the lovers return to court because their hiding place is revealed to Mark and he sees them sleeping with a sword between them and is, rather illogically, convinced that they are innocent after all. They are allowed to return to court, but in Eilhart's version Tristan is banished immediately after he has delivered Isolde to the king, in spite of his pleas to remain. From now on his energies are mainly devoted to seeking means of illicit meetings with Isolde—except when they are estranged as the result of the false accusation by Breri that Tristan had refused to turn when asked to do so in Isolde's name. It is this estrangement that leads to the consummation of Tristan's marriage with Isolde White Hands but by no means to the cessation of the attempts to deceive Mark.

Thomas' lovers return to court under very different circumstances. Mark summons them back to court and they obey. Refusal is impossible, for it would mean that they had once and for all cut themselves off from society—lost their honor, as Gottfried would say. They must therefore sacrifice the private society in which they take so much pleasure and return to the wretchedness of the court where there must be eternal conflict between their desires and those of Mark. For it is made clear in the Thomas-Gottfried version that it is largely Mark's yearning for Isolde's beauty which brings about the return to court. When he sees her in the cave he cannot resist the desire to possess her again, even if this means a renewal of his torments. Thus even in Mark's own mind there is a conflict between society and his own desires. He is prepared to tolerate the affection which he knows exists between his wife and Tristan in return for the enjoyment of Isolde's beauty. But such a delicately balanced situation cannot long endure. The overt act, the one thing which Mark cannot allow, is his discovery of the lovers asleep in the garden. The fabric collapses, and Tristan must go.

His subsequent career, in Thomas' version, is a desperate attempt to find a means of living without Isolde the Fair. He does not spend his time in fruitless attempts at assignations—he returns to Mark's court only three times, once with Kaedin, to convince him of Isolde's beauty, once as a leper, and once, very briefly, for Kaedin to take revenge on Cariado, the noble who has accused him of running away. The entire stress in this part of Thomas' poem is on Tristan's efforts to live away from Isolde. He loves her intensely, and his apparent wavering in marrying Isolde White Hands is clearly due to identification of her with the true Isolde rather than to any love he bears her. Thomas never allows Tristan to consummate his marriage. He provides instead a motif which is unique to him, although Gottfried would presumably have used it if he had completed his poem—the hall of statues. Here Tristan attempts, in the most obvious manner possible, to provide a visual and tactile substitute for the absent Isolde. Here he can add to the love in his thoughts the admiration for physical beauty which only a visible object can bring. Yet in this there is an element of self-deceit. Kaedin can fall in love with Brangaene, whom he has never seen, as a result of gazing on her statue, but for Tristan the statue of Isolde, lifelike as it is, can only remind him of the real Isolde, who so far exceeds the beauty of any statue that to be reminded of her is agony. Thomas thus emphasizes the difference between love and sensual attraction. The difference was important, for him and even more for Gottfried. It was also a projection of the process of falling in love, for in lyric and narrative poetry the hero falls in love as a direct result of the visual impression made on him by his lady. Tristan does not fall in love in this way in any of the extant romances—but Kaedin and Mark do.

In many of the versions of the Tristan story, including that of Eilhart, Brangaene disappears from the narrative, and in several of the episodes in which she appears in the version of Thomas, another character, Camille, appears. Thomas, however, introduces a major event in the narrative in which Brangaene is the main character. There is an incident which appears, though not always with the same characters, in many Tristan stories, in the course of which she is called upon to spend the night with Kaedin while Tristan snatches a few hours with Isolde. In Thomas' version, Brangaene becomes very indignant both with Isolde, who has virtually treated her as a chattel, and with Tristan and Kaedin, who have been accused of cowardice by members of the court. The result is an outpouring of hate against Tristan and Isolde and a threat to reveal everything to Mark. No one could be surprised that Brangaene's equanimity should snap. She has been called upon to sacrifice her virginity to save Isolde's honor and has been almost murdered for her pains, she has been tossed to Kaedin like a bone to a dog and her revolt is long overdue. Yet in the end she does not revolt. Instead of accusing Isolde to Mark, she accuses Count Cariado of paying too much attention to Isolde and thus completely exculpates Tristan. She soon is formally reconciled with both Tristan and Isolde. Thomas' introduction of this episode is in accordance with his general procedure of attempting to motivate action by human considerations. Brangaene had every right to be angry with the lovers, for they had treated her very shabbily. The episode in which Isolde attempts to have her murdered must surely be one of the most unpleasant in medieval literature. It is hard to see why Thomas and Gottfried retained the episode unless they wished to throw some light on Isolde's behavior by doing so and the light they threw must inevitably be unfavorable. For Isolde is so obsessed with her love that she will toss to the wolves anyone who stands in her way or who may bring that love to an end. Thomas thus shows how brutal such a love could be and how it could break the lives not only of those who participated in it but also of those whose hearts were too tender to oppose it. Brangaene herself could, at any time, have destroyed the lovers but only in this one scene does she come close to doing so. The piled-up resentment almost breaks her loyalty, but not quite. She, like Mark, is unable to depart from the system of loyalties in which she has been educated. To her the love of Tristan and Isolde is an intrigue which satisfies the yearning of the lovers at the expense of Mark. Out of loyalty to them she is prepared to further the lovers' exploits. She does not appreciate the difference between the love of Tristan and Isolde and such an intrigue. The lovers' social position does indeed rest entirely in her hands, and if she had revealed what she knew to Mark that position would have been destroyed. She would have supplied to Mark the incontrovertible evidence he needed—and which he did not really want. In the end she is unable to bring herself to the ultimate act of disloyalty, just as Mark is unable to bring himself to the ultimate act of revenge. Both are oriented to a culture which is conditioned for love in a very different sense.

Thomas makes it very clear that he has no interest in the numerous amorous adventures of Tristan. He brings the story to a speedy conclusion after the Brangaene incident. The episode of Tristan the dwarf is an unmotivated and pointless incident which is inserted merely to provide a reason for Tristan's fatal wound. The summoning of Isolde, the incident of the white sail, falsely reported by Isolde White Hands as black, are not essentially different in Thomas' version from any other. Isolde finally, under the threat of her lover's death, breaks with Mark and with society and sails to Tristan—in vain. For now Tristan must pay the penalty for his failure to consummate his marriage, for his attempt to play with social convention while thinking of his relation to Isolde. The revenge of Isolde White Hands, like that of Brangaene, is perfectly understandable. She carries it out and Brangaene does not. Thomas studies the problem more deeply than Eilhart. In the Eilhart version, Tristan is wounded in the course of an amorous adventure of Kaedin, in which the latter is killed. Isolde White Hands tries desperately to cure Tristan—without avail. She does not know of Tristan's sending for Isolde the Fair until she learns— Eilhart says he does not know how—from the daughter of Tristan's messenger of the importance of the color of the sail. She deceives Tristan and he dies. Thomas tells the story much more plausibly. Isolde White Hands, with her marriage still unconsummated, hears the instructions which Tristan gives to Kaedin when he sends him to fetch Isolde the Fair. She is overcome by jealousy. The elements, too, conspire against the lovers. Isolde is delayed by contrary winds and storms and arrives when Tristan is already *in extremis*. Just as the sea had been guilty of bringing them together, so it is guilty of their ultimate separation. The wild and unpredictable element has triumphed.

Thomas makes no mention of the rose and thorn intertwined. The lovers are dead and their love is at an end. Their battle with society is over. Eilhart seeks another solution. Mark finds out—somewhat belatedly—that it was the potion which was guilty, not Tristan and Isolde. He pardons them, buries them in one grave, and mourns over them.

They were not wicked after all but the victims of powers beyond their control. Thomas does not believe this. His characters die as they have lived, at odds with society. They lose their lives because their love and the society in which they live are incompatible. There is no reason to think that Gottfried contemplated any other solution. For him, too, all attempts to conciliate "Tristan-love" and society were vain. His reasons for the incompatibility, however, were different.

# III

## THE PURPOSE OF THE POEM

WHEN GOTTFRIED BEGAN to write his own *Tristan,* he had before him the complete work of Thomas of Britain. It seems very unlikely that he was relying on memory or that he did not follow the Anglo-Norman text carefully, for the verbal reminiscences and the narrative correspondences are too close. He was also acquainted with Eilhart's version and possibly with the French of Béroul. His intention was to take the text of Thomas, whose narrative form suited his purpose, and remodel it to his own ends. No major changes were needed, since, as we have seen, Thomas' treatment envisaged the conflict between love and society which was to be Gottfried's own theme. It is doubtful in any case whether Gottfried was interested in the events of the narrative as such. They were to be used only as instruments of character delineation and as elements in a structure which could be variously interpreted.

Gottfried's method relieved him of the responsibility of finding and selecting narrative incident, but it was not without its disadvantages. Certain elements in the story used—or devised—by Thomas were even less in accord with Gottfried's treatment than they had been with that of Thomas and the question must be asked: Why did Gottfried retain them? There is, of course, no definite answer to the question, but one possibility suggests itself. To those who knew Thomas' story—and Gottfried suggests in his prologue that many of his readers might be acquainted with it—the effect of Gottfried's modifications would be even more impressive if the story told were precisely the same. Even such an unlikely incident as the attempted murder of Brangaene can attain significance if it occurs in a different cultural context and if the events preceding and following it are handled differently from those same events in the version of Thomas. The accidents of tradition have prevented modern critics from making such a comparison, since the very elements—stylistic detail and character analysis—which would be most important for a comparison are those most liable to be omitted or modified in the version of Thomas by Brother Robert. Yet such comparisons as can be made between the extant parts of the two authors indicate that Gottfried created a work completely different from Thomas' narrative.

No part of Gottfried's poem is more important than the preface, and since it is a categorical, if obscure, statement of his intentions, we must devote some time to it.[30]

The first four quatrains of the prologue could be interpreted as a humility formula, for they call for recognition of a man's values and of his good will. The quality of his work appears to be of less importance than the desire to do good. If a person intends to be of help to the world, his zeal should be recognized. Such an appeal could obviously benefit Gottfried himself; he may be calling on his audience to give him a favorable hearing, even though they may not agree with him. The idea of a personal appeal is reinforced by his dislike of those who attack things they really want and who demonstrate their own smallness of mind in so doing. But Gottfried has yet to mention his own work, or indeed the fact that he is writing one at all. His remarks apply to all men and in particular to men who have already "done something." The reference would thus seem to apply rather to those who have preceded him in writing of Tristan and Isolde and who have done their best with the material at their disposal. His own remarks would then appear to be the reverse of a humility formula, rather a recognition that even though he regards his own work as superior, he is nevertheless prepared to recognize the value of what his predecessors have done.

A slightly different note is struck in the fifth quatrain. The word *guot*, which has appeared seven times in the four quatrains already mentioned, is now for the first time opposed to *übel*.

Tiur unde wert ist mir der man,
der guot und übel betrahten kan,
der mich und iegelichen man
nach sinem werde erkennen kan.                    (17 ff.)

> Dear and precious to me is the man who can judge of good and evil,
> who can know me and all men according to their worth.

The exact meaning of *betrahten* is not clear. Probably "look on and judge" would be close. "Distinguish between" is perhaps too strong. At first sight the last two lines seem innocent enough in meaning—the man who knows good and evil is what I like. But if we look at the word-pattern, there is a strong implication that "guot" is to be equated with "mich" and "übel" with "iegelichen." It would seem that Gottfried is, after all, calling for recognition of his own superiority.

If this is the correct interpretation of his remarks, then the transition to the next quatrain is a natural one, for he states that poetical skill is directly dependent on the recognition it receives. The entirely factual, unadorned style of the earlier quatrains, with their deliberate interlacing and hence deliberate confusion of simple adjectives of description, is replaced by two visual metaphors—one of creation, one of flowering, which complement one another. This is Gottfried's first use of the flower metaphor in relation to poetry. He uses it constantly but most importantly in the so-called literary excursus which takes the place of a description of Tristan's knighting. In this passage of literary criticism it is made clear that Gottfried regards Hartmann von Aue, Bligger von Steinach, and to a large extent Heinrich von Veldeke as visual poets, and there is a strong presumption that he regards the writing of the romance in general as an exercise in visual imagery, superficial descriptions, and external appearances. The inner being is revealed rather by sound and the organized impact of music. *Lob*, "fame," will inspire poetry—but what kind of poetry? The visual kind, apparently, for it flowers. Furthermore, as the next quatrain says, unless honor and fame are attained by poetry, its chances of survival and hence of affecting anyone are small. Thus to gain fame, Gottfried's poetry, too, would have to conform to the visual, the flowering romance. Certainly Gottfried is at the mercy of those who criticize, as the next quatrain shows. For

> Ir ist so vil, die des nu pflegent,
> daz si daz guote zübele wegent,
> daz übel wider ze guote wegent:
> die pflegent niht, si widerpflegent.                         (29 ff.)

> There are many nowadays who follow the custom of regarding good as
> evil and evil as good. They are not acting but counteracting.

Note the emphasis on the *nu*—"today," "these days." These modern critics are bad, for they have no standards and damn what they should praise. Their actions are entirely negative, yet they obviously can be effective, for by withholding *lob* they deprive the poet of *ere*, "honor."

It becomes clear that Gottfried realizes that he is writing a poem which those who read romances—one can hardly call them critics—will find different and perhaps dangerous. He has called for works to be judged by their authors' intentions, he has professed his own tolerance— if somewhat ironically—and shown his realization that his work will be different. The double style which marks his poem throughout is already evident: the obvious line of humility and the request for a hearing are wrapped around a belief, implied if not expressed, that his work is not only different but better, that it is his work which is "guot." The flexibility of the words is astonishing. The expression "ze guote" in the first quatrain means "to the advantage of," "favorable to," and has no connotations of right and wrong. "Guot" in the second line is vague but means probably "pleasant," "something which is liked." The "guotes" in the fourth line may have the same meaning but may also be stronger, including that which is morally good. The important point is that the word in the first two appearances is directly dependent on an individual, in the second two it may refer to an individual effort but is far more likely to refer to the total of good in the world. In the second quatrain a new element is introduced. If a good man does something which is well intended and which does nothing but good to the world, anyone who does not receive his work does wrong. This is a far cry from the first quatrain, for it bases appreciation of a man's work on the assessment of the man's character. Even if the work is not good, the man should receive praise if he is well-intentioned. Thus good is not good if it is not appreciated, and a good man should be praised if his intentions are good. But how can we know a good man? Gottfried gives no answer—except to say that a man who can judge of good and evil is "tiur unde wert" to him.

The total effect of this highly ambivalent use of the word *good* is to say that, if we have decided that a man is good, we shall praise his work (even if it is not itself good) and that everyone should be judged according to his intentions. The irony is obvious. "If you decide I am a good man you will praise my work whether it is good or not (as you have praised that of other good men). I am prepared to praise anyone whose intentions

are good, whether his work appeals to me or not, and I would be obliged
if you would do the same for me." After all, "good" is a very personal
judgment—as lines 29–32 show.

Gottfried continues this theme in lines 33–36. The critic must appreciate art, not be jealous of it. Art is inconceivable without the faculty of
appreciation, but envy is not logical and destroys all art. Again the appeal
seems to be a *captatio benevolentiae*—but it may easily apply to other poets,
and to art in general. Gottfried's play on the word *tugent* is very similar to
that on the word *guot*. Its basic meaning here is "excellence of performance," and the way to the attainment of such excellence is indeed steep
and narrow, requiring much persistence and involving much danger of
falling and straying. Further, there will be critics who will not recognize
excellence of performance as virtue unless it conforms to their own narrow
ideas of what is excellent, and recognition will be hard to obtain. But
"tugent" has other meanings—"quality" and "virtue." The allusion to
the strait and narrow path of virtue is obvious, and the whole passage,
could very easily mean that virtue is a quality difficult of attainment—the
kind of virtue, perhaps, which will prevent critics from dealing with
Gottfried's work in a spirit of envy rather than a spirit of tolerance. Once
again the question is one of attitude: Can the critics attain the correct
degree of objectivity, can Gottfried attain the correct degree of excellence?
Now, in fact, Gottfried is quite convinced of the excellence of his work, as
he shows later in the prologue, and therefore if anyone is at fault, it must
be the critics. They must learn "tugent," even if the way is difficult.
Thus, as he says in lines 41–44, Gottfried has no desire to waste his time
when he knows he has something important to say. He is "gewerldet,"
experienced in the ways of the world, and now proposes to present himself and his work to the world, but that world, too, must be prepared to
approach the work in the right spirit; otherwise his whole effort will
be in vain.

It is significant that the initial letters *T* and *I* at the beginning of
lines 41 and 45 are the first letters of the acrostic which runs through the
poem, continuing wherever Gottfried introduces quatrains. Here, then,
is the true beginning, the definite statement, marked by the introduction
of the narrative rhyming couplet. The ironic questioning, the balancing
of author, audience, and critics, is over. Whatever the attitude, Gottfried
will proceed with his purpose so that his gift to the world may not be

wasted. He has undertaken a task for the world's delight—or perhaps because he loves the world—but, much more importantly, as a pleasure or solace for *edele herzen*. Now these two lines could easily be read, and indeed probably would be read, as referring to the world of polite society which was interested in romances, the very world, in fact, which Gottfried has been discussing in the earlier quatrains. Appearances are deceptive. Gottfried does not mean society or even polite society and the *edele herzen* are not simply nobles. They are an esoteric group and they have one characteristic in common—that they can understand Gottfried and the love of Tristan and Isolde as he presents it. The world with which Gottfried has communication is also the one which he understands, not rationally but artistically.

It is fruitless to attempt to determine what Gottfried means by *edele herzen* by referring to the etymology of the words or the usage of the separate words in contemporary Middle High German, nor is it of much more value to investigate the classical and Christian uses of *cor nobile* and similar phrases.[31] Doubtless Gottfried was aware of these uses, and they may have shaded his use of the term *edelez herz*, but essentially he was creating a term for himself, not two words but an expression, in much the same way as the term *schöne Seele* was used in the eighteenth century. The *edele herzen* are Gottfried's sympathizers, nothing more. If they understand, they belong to the company. Hence the general statement "der werlt ze liebe," for anyone in the world *can* appreciate Gottfried's work if he is rightly disposed. What follows is a narrowing down of this world, a statement of the conditions which allow a man or woman to join the *edele herzen*. They must reject the idea of love as total joy, in other words, the unambiguous world of the comedy-romance, in which sorrow, when it occurs, is a test to be surmounted, not a permanent part of existence. It is of the nature of romance that the surmounting of obstacles should lead to ultimate perfect joy, to the balance of social responsibility and sensual pleasure. Chrétien's Lancelot romance and the Tristan romances were exceptions, but the exceptions were more apparent than real, for Lancelot lived for the moments of love he could snatch with Guinevere. His love was not different in kind from that of Erec for Enid or Yvain for Laudine but only in the degree to which he could enjoy it. The immediate presence of the beloved and the sensual enjoyment of love were essential in all such love affairs, and there is no evidence that love meant anything more than the attainment of the favor of the beloved within the prescribed social conventions.

It is precisely this idea of love with which Gottfried disagrees. He does not believe that love can be entirely happy, not because he is thinking of lovers' tiffs and the squalls that disturb the blue sea of affection but because love in the sense that he understands it, the total merging of one being with another, is incompatible with society as it was constituted in the romances or in life. If real love exists—and he wrote the *Tristan* to prove that it could—then it is not a succession of halcyon days of enjoyment but a demanding power which forces its subjects to love whatever sorrow it puts upon them. Those who cannot understand this can gain little from Gottfried's poem. They should go away and read normal romances. Gottfried's world consists of people who know that love is always composed of joy and sorrow and that the lover can hardly tell which is which, so inextricably are they bound together:

> ir süeze sur, ir liebez leit,
> ir herzeliep, ir senede not,
> ir liebez leben, ir leiden tot,
> ir lieben tot, ir leidez leben:
> dem lebene si min leben ergeben.                              (60 ff.)

> Their sweet bitterness, their loving sorrow, their hearts' love, their yearning misery, their loving life, their wretched death, their loving death, their wretched life: let my life be devoted to that life.

This is not mere play with words. It is a visual and aural representation of the state of love and, further, a progressive representation, for the first states described are those of physical and emotional sensation, mixtures of love and sorrow such as any lovers could experience. The feelings are intensified in the second line and in the third and fourth move to a different plane, for here their love is equated with life itself, their death with sorrow, while in the fourth line death is lovely and life miserable. Does their love survive death and welcome it after a life of sorrow? Possibly, but this is not Gottfried's principal meaning. He is thinking rather of the fact that death was welcome because of the impossibility of continuing the struggle against the forces which prevented their loving and the example which their death provided to others who love and suffer. Death can be dearer and more significant than life to the true believer, and Tristan and Isolde are models for the true believers in love. The words thus involve the audience in their interlacing, for *liebez* and *leiden* can be their feelings as well as those of the lovers. To this life Gottfried will devote his own. The words mean far more than a mere dedication to the writing of a poem about Tristan and Isolde. They indicate a total devotion of the poet's life to the cause, a participation in the life of love which reaches its peak in the story of Tristan. Gottfried describes their experience, but he is also telling his own strivings and failures. This is not mere fanciful interpretation, for Gottfried tells us so himself in the scene in the *Minnegrotte*. His life is indeed given over to their life, and his world is theirs. He recognizes no other and with it he will live or die—or be saved or damned. The inter-action of life and death is expressed this time in the double meaning of the words *verderben* and *genesen*, for they can mean physical sickness or health—or spiritual damnation and salvation. The poet's whole being lives only for this "Tristan-love" and from it he has derived all guidance, all teaching, all direction.

The religious overtones in all this are very obvious, and it is not difficult to demonstrate that Gottfried is making use of the terminology of the mystics and in particular of that of Bernard of Clairvaux. The poet was certainly acquainted with the language and methods of mystical writing and he undoubtedly intended to shade his own presentation of the love problem by introducing reminiscences and overtones from the mystics.[32] It is, however, quite another matter to argue that he was presenting his own views in mystical language entirely and even less can it be stated that he wished that love to be regarded as mystical. Since it was an all-embracing phenomenon, the mystical element must be present, as must sensuality, sentimentality, cruelty, and play. But it is only one element, though an important one. The importance lies in the fact that the mystical element is conspicuously absent from the love described in the courtly romances which Gottfried rejects. Since love in such poems is based on the service-reward relationship, a mystical element was impossible. Mystical love, in a religious sense, meant the yearning of the human soul for union with God to such a degree that in ecstasy the soul felt itself becoming part of the divine. If such a relationship can be thought of in secular terms, it can mean only the complete and mutual absorption of one personality into the other, a mutual absorption, since neither of the lovers can be regarded in objective terms as superior to the other, even though each would claim that in yearning for the other he or she regarded the other partner as an object of veneration. Though such love may be expressed in mystical terms, it cannot be true mystical love. Gottfried used the mystical terminology as a modern writer might use Freudian terminology, as an accessible and widely if not universally understood system which would allow him to differentiate Tristan-love from the love described in courtly romances.

The real question at issue is how far we are to understand his use of such mystical terminology as implying agreement with or rejection of the Christian ideals with which it was associated. Critical opinion has divided sharply over this issue, and claims have been made that Gottfried intended his lovers to be bound together in a Christian sense or, on the contrary, to be bound by a force which seemed like Christian mystic love but was in fact an anti-Christian force which drove them into desperate sin. In my opinion, neither of these views can be justified from the text of the poem. Tristan-love is not Christian or anti-Christian but a-Christian. It exists in its own world, as Gottfried clearly says:

> *der* werlt will ich gewerldet wesen.
>
> It is of that world that I wish to be a citizen.

Gottfried is prepared to show the complete dedication of his hero and heroine to the cause of love by using a terminology which to his audience would indicate complete dedication to the mystic love of God. Each is completely absorbed, each is incapable of living in terms other than those proposed. Death is not physical annihilation but the absence of the beloved, life is not the beating of the heart but the certainty of being loved. The terms might be used of a Christian in his love for God; they can certainly be used of Tristan and Isolde in their love for each other.

The principle of love is sharing. Tristan and Isolde learn to share, to give up, to accept. Gottfried shows in his prologue that by sharing the experience of Tristan-love with his audience he can help them to overcome their own misery. He assumes in his audience a capacity to understand Tristan-love and a feeling of sympathy with the lovers. He assumes that they too suffer and that by hearing of even greater suffering—for it is always taken for granted throughout the poem that, although others may approach Tristan-love, they cannot attain it—they will be comforted. Again, the Christian parallel is obvious: no one can understand the sufferings of Christ, for He suffered for all mankind, but by hearing an account of those sufferings we may be brought to an understanding of those much feebler trials which we ourselves must undergo. The story of Tristan and Isolde will be at once a consolation and an inspiration to *edele herzen*. Even though they—and Gottfried himself—cannot fully participate in Tristan-love, they can come closer to understanding by vicarious participation through the medium of poetry. This is the task which Gottfried has set himself—to find the best means of poetic expression to attain this end.

Gottfried explicitly dissociates himself from those writers of stories who tell love tales merely to amuse. If a lover has any leisure, he will surely think of love, and love tales would make him unhappy. This view was standard with those who believed that love was a kind of madness. To effect a cure, it was necessary to occupy the lover with something else, not allow him to feed his sickness on the miseries of other lovers. Gottfried says he has only one objection to this point of view, but it is an objection which invalidates it completely:

> Swer innecliche liebe hat,
> doch ez im we von herzen tuo,
> daz herze stet doch ie dar zuo.
> der innecliche minnen muot,
> so der in siner senegluot
> ie mere und mere brinnet,
> so er ie serer minnet. (108 ff.)

He who has true love within him, even though it pains him to the heart,
that heart will stand fast. The more that deep inner love turns into
passion's glow, the more he will love.

This love is utterly different. It is not madness or passion but complete dedication. The word *innecliche* is decisive. There is no question of relief or cure. The true lover does not desire a cure or relief because he is not sick. Since joy and pain are both parts of the love experience, they are inseparable and to a degree identical. Gradually Gottfried moves from his logical justification for writing the poem to a rich if simple imagistic presentation:

> Von diu swer seneder maere ger,
> dern var nicht verrer danne her;
> ich wil in wol bemaeren
> von edelen senedaeren,

die reiner sene wol taten schin:
ein senedaer unde ein senedaerin,
ein man ein wip, ein wip ein man
Tristan Isolt, Isolt Tristan.                                    (123 ff.)

So he who desires a story of passion need go no farther than here. I
will tell him a tale of noble lovers who exhibited pure love: a man in
love, a woman in love, a man, a woman, a woman, a man, Tristan,
Isolde, Isolde, Tristan.

The seeker after a story need go no further. Gottfried will envelope him
in the story and make him part of it and join him with *edele senedaeren*—
not merely *edele herzen* but *edele herzen* in love, who can present a true
picture of what love should be. These are the lovers in abstract, but the
picture can be simplified—merely the juxtaposed *senedaer | senedaerin*—
and simplified still further—*ein wip | ein man*—so that it embraces the
masculine and the feminine entirely, juxtaposed and intertwined, and
reaches its highest fulfillment in Tristan and Isolde, those two, inseparable
and in their role as lovers indistinguishable as Gottfried by his reversed
repetition intends to show. By his use of nouns, Gottfried has moved the
reader from the literature of love to noble lovers to masculine and feminine
to Tristan and Isolde. This represents graphically what his poem will
be.

The whole discussion of the intention of the poem has taken place
between two rhyming quatrains, the first of which begins with the initial
*T* while the second begins with the initial *I*. The narrative portion between
the quatrains begins with an *I* and the one after the second quatrain with
the initial *T*. Again the two names are intertwined and reversed. The two
initials *T* and *I* are closely connected with Gottfried's own observations,
for the *I* in each case is the first letter of "ich" and the *T* is the first letter
of a verb of which "ich" is the subject. In launching and explaining the
purpose of his poem, the poet connects himself closely with his subjects
almost to the degree of identification. In telling their story he must to some
degree feel as they do. He is to a degree in the same position as Milton,
who must tell the story of the Fall from the point of view of one of the
Fallen—for since he is a man, he cannot help but be Adam's descendant.
Yet the poet must preserve an epic stance, the ability of the narrator to
comment on the actions and thoughts of his characters, to know more
than they know and to understand when they do not. Further, he must be

able to communicate to his audience what the lovers—and their opponents —feel in a way the lovers cannot do. Thus the author must be at the same time of the company of the *edele herzen*—otherwise he could not understand them—and yet at a distance from them in order to make their example clear to others.

It is this objective viewpoint which Gottfried now proceeds to study. For when he says that many people have written of Tristan but very few have written correctly, he is referring less to the subject matter than the method. The word *lesen* can, of course, mean either "read" or "write," and the ambiguity is intentional, for if the poet has done his work in the real fashion, how can the audience understand? Gottfried makes it clear that he is prepared to extend to his predecessors the charity which he claimed at the opening of his preface: he will assume that they had good intentions and he carefully echoes lines 5–8 in lines 141–45. They wrote in different ways for a different audience. The only person who has chosen the right way is Thomas of Britain. I do not believe that "in der rihte" refers only to subject matter but rather to the total treatment of the poem, to his "version." Thomas had indeed gone to the original sources, to "britunschen buochen," and passed on the information he found, but this is not all. If Gottfried merely accepted his version, why does he say that he began to search in Latin and Romance books and work hard to produce a poem that told the story as Thomas did? If he were referring merely to subject matter, these remarks would have no meaning, since, as we know, he departed from Thomas' version hardly at all in respect of the events of the poem. The Romance and Latin books refer to the other material in the poem, the use of mystical terminology, classical mythology, allegory, and the numerous changes which Gottfried made in treatment and style. Finally he put all of Thomas' "jehe," his statements and opinions, in a book for the delight of "edele herzen." Once again there is a play on the two meanings of "lesen." Gottfried has indeed read all the material in one book—that of Thomas—and from that point of view the search for material was vain. The other sense is more important. Gottfried has gathered together the fruits of his searches and combined them into *one* book and this—this alone—will provide his audience with pleasure. Gottfried believed that only Thomas of all those who wrote of Tristan had moved the story in the right direction, had used it to show the fundamental conflict between love and society. This was his "jehe," this was "die rihte und die warheit." Gottfried would continue "in siner rihte" but he would add to what Thomas had done. His writing is a free offering of his feelings and understanding of the work of Thomas.

We should note that Gottfried at this point is at some pains to stress the moral implications of what he has done. The word *guot* appears again, as it had in the early part of the preface, but its force is greatly intensified. It is "innecliche guot," as in line 108 "liebe" was "innecliche" and in line 111 "minne" was "innecliche." The word refers to the depths of the human spirit, not to the superficialities of the human comedy. It is not behavior but being, a fact which Gottfried emphasizes by a favorite device, the use of verbs coined from nouns:

> ez liebet liebe und edelt muot,
> ez staetet triuwe und tugendet leben                                   (174 f.)

> It makes love loving and makes the spirit noble, it makes loyalty lasting
> and life full of meaning.

*Liebe* by definition should not need intensifying nor should it be possible to increase the constancy of *triuwe*. Yet there is—in some works—a kind of love which is no love and a kind of constancy which is not constant. These are the words which mean nothing except in the context of romance comedy. Gottfried's poem will give them meaning and they will perform their own moral service. The qualities normally associated with the knight in the romance are important indeed but only in the context of true love. The matter is made, for Gottfried, almost painfully explicit:

> liebe ist ein also saelic dinc,
> ein also saeleclich gerinc,
> daz nieman ane ire lere
> noch tugende hat noch ere.                                             (187 ff.)

> Love is such a blissful thing, such a delightful duty, that no one has
> quality or honor without it.

Love alone makes true virtues and only the kind of love that mixes joy with sorrow and, more important, recognizes that sorrow is an essential ingredient of love, so much so that no one who has not suffered can say that he has loved.

It is for this reason that Gottfried uses the story of Tristan and Isolde in the sense that Thomas had imparted to it. Here can be seen the love he speaks of in a pure and recognizable form. The last lines of the prologue are extremely significant:

> uns ist noch hiute liep vernomen,
> süeze und iemer niuwe
> ir inneclichiu triuwe
> ir liep, ir leit, ir wunne, ir not;
> al eine und sin si lange tot,
> ir süezer name der lebet iedoch
> und sol ir tot der werlde noch
> ze guote lange und iemer leben,
> den triuwe gernden triuwe geben,
> den ere gernden ere:
> ir tot muoz iemer mere
> uns lebenden leben und niuwe wesen;
> wan swa man noch hoeret lesen
> ir triuwe, ir triuwen reinekeit,
> ir herzeliep, ir herzeleit,
> Deist aller edelen herzen brot.
> hie mit so lebet ir beider tot.
> wir lesen ir leben, wir lesen ir tot
> und ist uns daz süeze alse brot.
>
> Ir leben, ir tot, sint unser brot.
> sus lebet ir leben, sus lebet ir tot.
> sus lebent sie noch und sint doch tot
> und ist ir tot der lebenden brot.                        (218 ff.)

Even today we hear of their love, sweet and ever new, their deep loyalty, their love, their misery, their delight, their sorrow; and even though they are long dead, their sweet name lives on, and their death must live on forever for the good of the world, to give loyalty to those who crave loyalty and honor to those who crave honors; their death must be life ever renewed for those of us who live on. For whenever anyone today hears tell of their loyalty, the purity of their devotion, their hearts' love and hearts' sorrow, he knows it is bread for all lofty spirits. Thus their death lives on. We read of their life, we read of their death, and it is as sweet to us as bread.
Their life, their death are our bread. Thus their life lives on, thus their death lives on. Thus they live still, even though they are dead, and their death is bread to the living.

The emphasis in this whole passage is on the enduring meaning of the story of Tristan and Isolde. Gottfried is at pains to show that the fact that they are long since dead does not affect the issue. Their example will always live and do good to the world. Their death brings loyalty to those

who seek it, honor to those who seek honor. How can the lovers' death
achieve this? In itself it would hardly be conducive to either "triuwe" or
"ere" in the normal sense of those words in romance, since both Tristan
and Isolde are guilty of a breach of "triuwe" and lose their "ere" as a
result of their love. What Gottfried apparently means is that their loyalty
to one another and their attainment of a higher honor than mere social
recognition should act as an inspiration to other lovers. Their death
provides other lovers with life because it shows that such love is possible.
I do not think that Gottfried has in mind here any love after death, any
merging of souls in mortal extinction. He is thinking rather that the fact
that they were prepared to sacrifice themselves should inspire other lovers
not to be afraid to follow their example.

     Gottfried says that their death is bread to those of us who still live,
and such a metaphor inevitably raises the question of a comparison with
the Eucharist. If the dead Tristan and Isolde are thought of as bread for
other lovers, they seem to be a parallel to the body of Christ, dead in a
mortal sense but still living for Christians in the bread of the Eucharist.
Gottfried realized full well that his words would call forth such a comparison and that such a comparison, if taken literally, must be regarded as
blasphemous, since Tristan and Isolde would then be to followers of true
love what Christ is to Christians. It is impossible to decide how far
Gottfried wished to push the comparison. He undoubtedly wished to
stress the exemplary aspects of the lovers' story. As Christ had died for
all men, so Tristan and Isolde had died for lovers. As His life remained an
example to all Christians, so did theirs to all *edele herzen*. Yet the text
fails, to me at least, to give any indication that the word *brot* has any
mystical or eucharistic connotations. It is the *story* of the lovers which
provides the nourishment for other true lovers and it is through that story
that they are inspired. They live on the story because love is life and life
is love. It is purely to lovers, alive, here on earth that their story is important, because it will provide them with the strength to be true lovers. The
role of the poet thus becomes extremely important, for he alone can act
as the link between Tristan and Isolde and his audience. The name lives
and provides nourishment for lovers only because the poet makes it so.
It is the reading of the story which is the bread:

     wir *lesen* ir leben, wir *lesen* ir tot
     und ist uns *daz* süeze alse brot.                                      (235 f.)

We read of their life, we read of their death, and it is as sweet to us as bread.

The prologue closes—he that has ears, let him hear. This—and this alone —is the true story of Tristan and Isolde.

Gottfried's preface and prologue—lines 1–44 and 45–244—have a great deal of unity. The preface is written in deliberately ambiguous terms, as we have seen. It raises the whole question of the relation between artist and audience and between artist and subject. Gottfried denies that there are any absolute canons of excellence. What he does say is that a man must be judged by his intentions and his skill. But he soon makes it clear that he believes that there is a right and a wrong way to write the story of Tristan. The right way is the one which presents the story for the guidance of a select audience and which recognizes it as the story of whole love. Whatever their intentions, other writers have not succeeded in this task. Only Thomas of Britain has moved in the right direction, and even he is imperfect. It is clear that Gottfried, throughout these 244 lines, is thinking of the story of Tristan and Isolde as an artistic presentation, as something whose full effect depends not only on the love story but how that love story is presented. Whatever the "facts" of the narration, they are useless without the skill of the artist. Gottfried regards himself as an originator, writing for a new type of audience. His hero and heroine will also be presented in different fashion.

# IV

## ASPECTS OF LOVE

GOTTFRIED'S PRESENTATION of his hero and heroine would first of all change the significance of the lady. All courtly romances center, theoretically, on the lady, and she is the person who rules the conduct of the hero. Yet, in fact, the lady is usually a shadowy figure, little more than an abstraction, whose personality consists of a number of qualities and not of feelings or flesh and blood reactions to her lover. Even Chrétien de Troyes could not make of Laudine more than a psychological catalyst for Yvain, although his ability to portray a real woman is amply demonstrated by his characterization of Lunete. The ladies are simply beings who make knights function and even such a genius as Wolfram von Eschenbach found it hard to impart life to Condwiramurs.

Gottfried's conception of the feminine element of the love relationship is entirely different from that found in the courtly romance. He rejects totally the idea of love service and the subordination of the man to the woman and substitutes for it a partnership which is based on sexual attraction and recognition in the other of the fulfillment of a need. In such a relationship the need of the woman for the man is as great as the need of the man for the woman, and the concentration of the poet is not on bringing his story to the point at which the knight wins his lady—as he does in the first part of a conventional romance—or at which he achieves understanding of the place of love in society—the end of the romance— but rather on the exploration of the continuation of love and its ultimate fulfillment. It is only a slight exaggeration to say that Gottfried begins his study of courtly love where the authors of most romances end it. Sexual fulfillment is as important for the woman as for the man in Gottfried's view. It is not merely a question of a man's "winning" his lady but of their continuing to meet, love, and endure. Thus Gottfried was led to reexamine the whole problem of the active role of the female in the process of falling in love, a role totally neglected by his predecessors.

How conscious Gottfried was of the importance of an understanding of the way in which people fall in love is easily discerned by his differing treatment of the relations between Tristan's parents, Riwalin and Blanscheflur, and those between Tristan and Isolde. The portrait of Riwalin is given in entirely physical and visual terms. He comes to Mark's court because he is a young man in the full bloom of life who has heard of that court as a center of chivalry. He is greeted by the young king as fellow knight, a potential tournament-competitor. The day of the tournament is described in passages of glorious visual splendor. The month is May, the landscape is of that brightly colored beauty found only in the descriptions of the *paysage idéal*. And to add to this beauty, knights and ladies in glittering costume are scattered like stars on the grass. The whole scene is an "ougenweide," a feast for the eyes. And that is all it is, for there is no further perception and no depth. Riwalin is seen only in physical terms, and Gottfried is careful to show his physical attractiveness through the eyes of the ladies of the court. Thus Blanscheflur is only one of many who are attracted:

> "seht," sprachen si "der jungelinc
> der ist ein saeliger man:
> wie saelecliche stet im an
> allez daz, daz er begat!
> wie gar sin lip ze wunsche stat!
> .  .  .
> wie saelecliche stat sin lip!
> o wol si saeligez wip,
> der vröude an ime beliben sol!"
> nu marcte ir aller maere wol
> Blanscheflur diu guote,
> wan sin ouch in ir muote,
> swaz ir dekeiniu taete,
> ze hohem werde haete;
> si haete in in ir muot genomen,
> er was ir in ir herze komen . . .                    (704 ff.)

"Look," they said, "the young fellow is divine. How divinely all his

actions become him! What a perfect body he has! . . . How divine his
whole person! How happy the woman who can have her joy of him!"
Now the good Blanscheflur noted all their remarks, for she thought
highly of him herself whatever they might do. She had taken him to her
thoughts, he had entered into her heart.

The juxtaposition makes the point obvious. Blanscheflur is attracted by
the same qualities as the other ladies. Nor does her first approach differ
from the conventional statements of courtly romance. There is the arch
statement—"Sir, you have done me great injury"—and the conventional
reply—"What can that be?" This is *Cligès* over again, or the thoughts of
Lavinia in the *Roman d'Enéas*. There follow the usual self-torturings, the
musings whether this can be true, the conjuring-up of mental images of
the beloved. The only attraction can be physical, for Riwalin and Blanscheflur have hardly exchanged a dozen words, and the only doubt can be
whether the other partner is equally affected.

Gottfried is careful to make connections with the later scene in which
Tristan and Isolde first feel love for each other and he does so chiefly by
using the same simile of the bird on the limed twig. The emphasis in the
long descriptions of Riwalin and Blanscheflur as they realize that they
are in love is on change, on vague perception of something wrong, and
on loss of freedom. Each is concerned most with the effect on his or her
own behavior and misery. In this scene Gottfried uses the limed-twig
simile of the male, Riwalin, and the emphasis is on loss of freedom,
whereas in the potion scene it is of the female, Isolde, that it is used.
Riwalin is motivated by the unthinking physical forces of youth. In his
dealings with his overlord, Duke Morgan, he had already demonstrated
his lack of self-restraint, his dependence on impulse and personal inclina-
tion. In the sudden impact of the beauty of Blanscheflur, he felt that he
was subjected to forces which he could neither control nor shrug off, and
his physical reaction is well demonstrated by the figure of the struggling
bird, an insensate struggle against a force which it does not understand.
Both Riwalin and Blanscheflur are concerned with the effect on themselves,
their view of love is inward. The only concern each has with the other is
whether the feeling is mutual and whether their love will be successful.
Such sorrow as there is is sorrow for pain, for sadness, for inability to
understand, not sadness for the other's plight. Isolde's reaction (11,789 ff.)
is different. She too struggles against the power of love but her intention

is not to assert her freedom nor to wonder at her sorrow. She goes through none of the conventional "Can this be love" phraseology:

> diu versuchtez ouch genote,
> ir was diz leben ouch ande
> *do si den lim erkande*
> *der gespenstegen minne*
> und sach wol, daz ir sinne
> darin versenket waren . . .                              (11,790 ff.)

> She kept trying hard enough, and this life was wretched for her. When she recognized the birdlime of sinister love and saw clearly that her senses were sunk deep in it . . .

She recognizes the phenomenon, that she is plunged into "die blinden süeze/ des mannes unde der minne" ("the blind sweetness of the man and of love"). Her pondering is not about Tristan's response but about her own feelings. She does not know whether she, as a maid, has any right to these thoughts. She is very far from arch, very far from the sensuous day dreaming of Riwalin and Blanscheflur. It is not the attraction of Tristan's physical presence which concerns her but the reality of love itself. It is worth noting that the birdlime simile is used of the man Riwalin and of the woman Isolde. The man struggles against a force he hardly recognizes but which cramps his freedom, the woman against a force she knows all too well. Isolde knows that to yield to it means complete surrender. She will never be the same person again, while for Riwalin the question is whether he will have a mistress or not.

Gottfried has approached the problem of falling in love in two completely different ways. His first pair of lovers are motivated by the social conventions and by visual, physical proximity. The process of falling in love corresponds to the lyric formula—used by narrative poets too—of the image which is seen by the eye corresponding to the image of ideal beauty in the beholder's soul. Except for Riwalin's physical beauty, Blanscheflur has no impression of him and he has even less of her. The reader is invited, as he is by Chrétien de Troyes, to watch this spectacle of two people going through the agonizing of wondering whether their love is reciprocated, when he knows all the time that their puffings and blowings are part of a ritual which will end with mutual protestations of affection and happiness ever after. That, at least, is what should happen. That it does not is due to something unusual in the romance comedy.

The hero is really wounded to death—not with the conventional wounds from which a recovery is speedily effected, but with a deadly thrust which appears mortal. In Thomas' version the incident occurs in the tournament, but Gottfried, for whom tournaments were courtly exercises, prefers the verisimilitude of a real battle. Blanscheflur is thus forced to come to terms with herself. If she is ever to love Riwalin, it must be here and now, with no ritual, no pleasant words and shy refusals, but in the stark atmosphere of a death chamber with all attendants sent away and with a hero who is no longer the flashing knight of the tournament field but a feeble shell of a man who will soon cease to exist. Tristan is conceived in death and is to be born in sorrow. His parents embrace for what they believe is the first and last time. This is not the conventional pain of love but the true sorrow of human life and death. The incident is not without its ironies. Not only does Tristan's life spring from this union of death and life, but Riwalin recovers the life he had before—and gives death to the live Blanscheflur. He returns to that conception of life when he draws renewed strength from Blanscheflur's embrace and recovers from his wound. There follows an intrigue in true courtly fashion—"tougen minne" in the courtly sense, not in the sense in which they had practiced it on the night of Tristan's conception. What is far from clear in the whole affair is why Riwalin could not ask for the hand of Blanscheflur in marriage. He is a ruler, has lands, and obviously stands well with her brother, Mark. Why should there be such secrecy, such worry over a simple matter like this? It is, in fact, not at all clear that Riwalin wanted to marry her, until she revealed that she was carrying his child. When he is summoned back to defend his lands against Morgan, he shows no feelings for her except formal regret, certainly no intention of taking her as his bride. The comparison with the Dido-Aeneas parting is interesting. No grand passion is evident, none of the psychological tension one might expect. When Blanscheflur reveals that she is with child, the whole matter moves out of the sphere of love into that of honor. Her appeal is not based on love at all but on the shame she will have to endure if it is discovered that she has broken the rules of polite society. The appeal is shrewd. A cry of distress at love departed might have been turned aside, but when honor is at stake Riwalin has little choice. He takes her onto his ship and, when he reaches his home, marries her.

The whole incident is an ironic treatment of the difference between love in romances and love in real life. The reason that Riwalin does not take the obvious step of asking for the hand of Mark's sister is that he knew that the marriage of a king's sister was a political matter and that he could hardly expect Mark to give away his most important asset to a minor foreign ruler, merely because she happened to love him. So we have the ritual, the secret love, and finally the marriage which is performed to make an honest woman of Blanscheflur. The true love scenes, the only ones in the whole incident, take place when the social conventions cease to be important, when both participants feel that imminent dissolution frees them from the necessity of pretending. It is the imminence of death which enables Gottfried to show that life and death are a unity, just as joy and sorrow are a unity, and that true love lives in both.

Gottfried realizes that it would be less than artistic to posit a complete contrast between the love of Tristan and Isolde and that of Tristan's parents. All loves have something in common, and Tristan derives his being from Riwalin and Blanscheflur. The repetition of the trapped-bird simile represents the feeling of helplessness in the face of the power of love which all lovers feel, even though the reasons for that helplessness may be completely different. Lines are repeated or recalled from the earlier scenes in those which describe the awakening of the consciousness of love in Tristan and Isolde.

| | |
|---|---|
| als er des limes danne entsebet | . . . ir was diz leben ouch ande |
| und er sich uf ze vlühte hebet, | do si den lim erkande |
| so clebet er mit den vüezen an . . . | der gespenstegen minne |
| so der in senede trahte kumet | und sach wol, daz ir sinne |
| und liebe an ime ir wunder vrumet | darin versenket waren, |
| mit senelicher swaere, | si begunde stades varen, |
| so wil der senedaere | si wolte uz unde dan: |
| ze siner vriheit wider; | so clebet ir ie der lim an; |
| so ziuhet in diu süeze nider | der zoch si wider unde nider . . . |
| der gelimeten minne.        (847 ff.) | ir gelimeten sinne |
| | dien kunden niender hin gewegen |
| | noch gebrucken noch gestegen |
| | halben vuoz noch halben trite, |
| | Minne diun waere ie da mite. |
| | (11,791 ff.) |

| | |
|---|---|
| When he perceived the lime and started to escape, he was held by the feet . . . . [Thus when untrammeled | . . . This life was wretched for her. When she recognized the birdlime of sinister love and saw |

emotion] falls into a yearning mood
and love works its miracle upon it
with loving sadness, the lover wants
his freedom again; but the
sweetness of clinging love pulls him
down.

clearly that her senses were sunk
deep in it, she began to make
for firm ground, she was
determined to get out and away.
But the lime kept sticking to her,
it pulled her back and down . . . .
Her limed senses could not
move anywhere, over neither
bridge nor path, not even a half
foot or a half step, without love
accompanying her.

In spite of these resemblances and echoes, the process of falling in love is totally different for the two couples. Riwalin and Blanscheflur follow the conventional pattern of falling in love at their first meeting. Tristan and Isolde, on the contrary, show none of the accepted signs of love. Riwalin and Blanscheflur fall in love as a result of the visual impact of each upon the other, as Yvain does at his first meeting with Laudine. Gottfried does not emphasize—or indeed mention—the recognition by the male lover of the perfect qualities of the female, a constant theme of the lyric. He wishes to emphasize the instinctive sensuous physical attraction. His description of the first meeting of Tristan and Isolde is very significant:

sus wart sin harpfe dar besant.
ouch besande man zehant
die jungen küniginne.
daz ware insigel der minne,
mit dem sin herze sider wart
versigelt und vor verspart
aller der werlt gemeiner
niuwan ir al einer,
diu schoene Isot si kam ouch dar
und nam vil vlizecliche war,
da Tristan harpfende saz.
nu harpfeter ouch michel baz,
dan er ie da vor getaete . . .                                       (7809 ff.)

So his harp was sent for, and they also had the young queen summoned. She was the true signet-ring of love with which his heart was later sealed and set apart from all the world, except for her alone. And fair Isolde did come there too and looked closely at Tristan as he sat there playing his harp. Now he harped much better than he had ever done before.

It will be observed that there are no visual images in this passage; "nam
... war" is hardly visual, since it is closely connected with "harpfende"
and refers to the fact that Isolde sees a man harping—not Tristan or
Tantris but a musician. The first impact on her is that of a man of music.
Gottfried makes a further connection—the verb *besanden* is used both of
Tristan's harp and of Isolde. The comment on the meeting is made by
Gottfried in his capacity of omniscient observer. This girl is the true seal
of love. She will be Tristan's only love, the world will be well lost for her.
But there is no evidence that she is affected by her first meeting with
Tristan. There is no love at first sight, no visual impact, no recognition of
extraordinary qualities. The effect of her coming is to make Tristan play
better. The words could be insignificant—after all, he is hoping that a
piece of effective harping will cause her mother, the older Isolde, to cure
his wound—but Gottfried rarely hews to a purely narrative line. The
music which Isolde inspires is of a higher quality than anything he had
played before. He does not realize it, nor does Isolde, but the music he
plays will bring them together. It is to this purpose and no other that the
next scene is devoted, for Tristan and Isolde do not fall in love as a result
of visual impact but as a consequence of a developing common artistic
sensibility.

It is specifically stated by the queen that Tantris is to teach Isolde
what he knows over and above that which could be taught to her by her
tutor and the queen herself. There is an obvious irony in the words, an
irony reinforced by the queen's remarks that in *her* hands lies the power
of life and death for Tristan. The remark is true enough, both in the
physical sense in which the queen intends it and in its relation to the love
for Isolde of which no one is yet aware. Tristan is to teach Isolde a great
deal more than music and yet it is music that is to represent and bring
about the essential harmony between them. This is not a question of
singing lessons or elementary harping. Isolde has already been taught the
essentials of music which were regarded as suitable for a medieval princess
(7979 ff.). What Tristan has to teach is in part theory, the knowledge of
music gained from books, which in medieval education was regarded as a
superior branch of learning, and even more the ability to use her musical
skill to impress other people. Gottfried devotes two of the most significant
passages of his work to describing the impact of music on a courtly
audience. The first is that which immediately follows Tristan's arrival

at Mark's court, and it depicts in glowing terms the admiration of the court for Tristan's achievements. A great deal of their feeling is astonishment at the abilities of a fourteen-year-old boy, and Gottfried intensifies this aspect of the situation by describing a series of performances by Tristan, each slightly different from the one which precedes it, which calls forth further admiration from Mark and his courtiers. The audience believes it is admiring technical skill, as indeed it is, but it is also made clear that the audience is of a lower cultural level, unable to appreciate in full what Tristan is doing:

> ". . . mich lerten Britunoise,
> die waren uz der stat von Lut
> rehte liren und sambjut."
> "sambjut, waz ist daz, lieber man?"
> "daz beste seitspil, daz ich kan."
> "seht," sprach daz gesinde
> "got der hat disem kinde
> uf rehte wunneclichez leben
> siner genaden vil gegeben!"                                          (3680 ff.)

> ". . . Bretons from the town of Lut taught me to play the lyre and sambuca properly." " 'Sambuca?'—what is that, dear man?" "The best stringed instrument that I can play." "Look," said the courtiers, "God has given this boy a full measure of his grace for a life of true delight."

The gaping admiration of the would-be cultured in the face of supreme skill and learning was never better expressed, but this is not the whole story. The audience has long since been deprived of its powers of rational judgment by Tristan's playing:

> do begunde er suoze doenen
> und harpfen so ze prise
> in britunischer wise,
> daz maneger da stuont unde saz,
> der sin selbes namen vergaz:
> da begunden herze und oren
> tumben unde toren
> und uz ir rehte wanken;
> da wurden gedanken
> in maneger wise vür braht.                                           (3588 ff.)

Then he began to play sweet notes and such excellent music on the harp in the Breton fashion that many a man who stood and sat there forgot his very name, and his heart and ears began to play tricks and fool him and turn from their right path. There thoughts were expressed in various ways.

Boethius had long before this commented on the power of music to bring out and play upon specific aspects of character.[33] Tristan's music is such that it deprives men of their rational faculties. They are completely in its power and prepared to grant almost anything to the man who possesses such skill. It is worth emphasizing that they need not and probably do not understand the music in any rational or intellectual fashion. So far as an ordinary courtly audience is concerned, music of this power is an incomprehensible force—and it is this music, not that of Mark's court-musician or Isolde's tutor, which Tristan teaches to Isolde.

The most significant fact is that she was able to learn it at all. It is hardly likely that any others in the courtly audience could have done so and, as we shall see, quite certain that Isolde White Hands could not. Tristan did indeed teach her to play better, to understand new forms of music which had not yet reached Ireland from France and new theories which were being developed there. Yet the greatest gift he imparted was again an irrational and intangible one—the power to make an audience forget itself, its history, its prejudices, and hand itself over to the judgment of the musician. This was the power of Orpheus, of the Sirens, of the Muses, this indeed was true lyric poetry. In six months she attained a mastery of the irrational. This time it is the court of Dublin which sits in judgment, more formally than the court of Cornwall—one suspects the court of Gurmun was a stodgier court than Mark's—summoned by the king to hear his daughter perform:

nu gevuogetez sich dicke also,
ir vater so der was vröudehaft
oder alse vremediu ritterschaft
da ze hove vor dem künege was,
daz Isot in den palas
vür ir vater was besant;
und allez daz ir was bekant
höfschlicher liste und schoener site,
da kurzetes ime die stunde mite
und mit im manegem an der stete.                    (8036 ff.)

And it often happened this way, that her father felt merry or, when there were foreign knights with the king at court, that Isolde would be summoned

before her father in the palace and she would entertain him and many
other people with all the courtly attainments and pleasant ways she knew.

The result is extraordinary. No doubt the company had prepared itself
for an hour of boredom, but they soon found that they were wrong. Not
only does Isolde play superbly on instruments they hardly know but she
performs

> ... so vremediu notelin
> diu niemer vremeder kunden sin ...                                    (8059 f.)

... such strange notes that there never had been stranger.

They are swept away not only by her performance and skill but also by the
sight of such beauty producing such music. Their eyes cannot leave the
white fingers playing on the strings and producing such sounds. The effect
is hypnotic:

> durch si wart wunder gedaht,
> als ir wol wizzet, daz geschiht,
> da man ein solich wunder siht
> von schoene und von gevuocheit,
> als an Isote was geleit.                                              (8080 ff.)

Because of her, amazing thoughts came to them, for, as you know, that
sort of thing happens when anyone sees such miracles of beauty and
grace as Isolde possessed.

The admiration here is for beauty of sight and sound rather than for
technical skill, and the irrational nature of the reaction of the audience is
even more obvious. Isolde exercises a force like that of the Sirens or the
magnetic rocks which pull bolts from ships, forces which are not comprehensible but which divert ships and men from their normal course.
The description is full of words of uncertain motion—*ungewisser habe,
wankende, ündende, swebet, wiselose*—and so it is with men's minds:

> si sanc in maneges herzen muot
> offenlichen unde tougen
> durch oren und durch ougen.
> ir sanc, dens offenliche tete
> beide anderswa und an der stete,
> daz waz ir süeze singen,
> ir senftez seiten clingen,
> daz lute und offenliche
> durch der oren künicriche

hin nider in diu herzen clanc.
so was der tougenliche sanc
ir wunderlichiu schoene,
diu mit ir muotgedoene
verholne unde tougen
durch diu venster der ougen
in vil manic edele herze sleich
und daz zouber dar in streich,
daz die gedanke zehant
vienc unde vahende bant
mit sene und mit seneder not.                                        (8112 ff.)

She sang to the spirit of many a heart, both openly and secretly, through
their hearts and their eyes. The song that was performed openly in this
place and others was her sweet singing, the soft sound of her strings
which penetrated down deep into the heart, loud and clear through
the kingdom of the ears. The secret song was her amazing beauty,
which, in secret, slipped unawares through the windows of the eyes with
her sound of the spirit into many a noble heart and spread its magic
there, so that she captured their thoughts at once and, in taking them
bound them with desire and the misery of desire.

It is clear that Isolde has learned Tristan's ability to render men irrational
in their admiration, but she already possesses something which Tristan
cannot possibly have. She is a woman. The combination of her physical
beauty and musical skill acts upon her predominantly male audience in
an entirely predictable manner. They are all, at least while the music lasts,
in love with her. Gottfried deliberately uses the terminology of the lyric
"falling in love" *topos*—except for one very important change. It is
music penetrating through the ears which brings about their condition,
not the impact of physical beauty. The two are both present, but it is
music which is predominant and it is the *edele herzen* who are principally
moved. Love is thus an irrational force, but in its highest manifestation it
is stirred by music more than by physical beauty, although Isolde has
both. There is only one person who is apparently unmoved by Isolde's
beauty and newly acquired musical skills—her tutor, Tristan. He has raised
her to his own level, a level far above that of their contemporaries. She is
capable of loving him—in the fullest sense—but there is no evidence that
she does or that he loves her. Falling in love is not so easy for "Tristan-
lovers" as the romances might make it appear. Certain it is that Tristan
and Isolde achieve love gradually and that it is a changing process.

At this point it is instructive to digress briefly to compare the impact of Tristan's music on Isolde White Hands with that on Isolde the Fair. It is of the essence of the musical relationship with Isolde the Fair that it is mutual. Once Tristan has performed his duties as a tutor, Isolde has been brought to the point where she can participate with him in the performance of music and can share with him the harmonies which they both know. She does not do so in the scene of her performance at court because Gottfried does not wish to anticipate his climactic scene of harmony in the *Minnegrotte*. We are simply allowed to see that she can produce with music the same effects as her master. The impact of Tristan's music on Isolde White Hands is totally different. She is a passive listener, never sharing the performance, never aspiring to learn the music he provides. She is one of the audience upon whom both Tristan and Isolde can play and is totally confused by the music, for she believes that it refers to her and that Tristan is expressing love for her in his songs. The confusion is natural enough. Tristan himself is confused, for he is directing his music not to the trained and understanding Isolde the Fair but to an Isolde who is incapable of musical comprehension. Music fails to bring harmony and achieves only confusion. The scene is a brilliant example of Gottfried's ability to use his "objective correlative," music, in a negative fashion to show what disharmony can arise when a man and woman seem to have a basis for love and do not. Tristan's music has not changed. It is the ear of the audience which fails to respond, and Tristan, accustomed to the response of Isolde the Fair, cannot adjust to the situation.

The difference between the two Isoldes apparently lies in the fact that Tristan has taught Isolde the Fair something else beside musical skill, namely, *moraliteit*. This is not part of his formal instruction to her:

> under aller dirre lere
> gab er ir eine unmüezekeit,
> die heizen wir moraliteit,
> diu kunst diu leret schoene site:
> da solten alle vrouwen mite
> in ir jugent unmüezic wesen.
> moraliteit daz süeze lesen
> deist saelic unde reine.
> ir lere hat gemeine
> mit der werlde und mit gote.
> si leret uns in ir gebote

got unde der werlde gevallen
sist edelen herzen allen
zeiner ammen gegeben . . .                                    (8002 ff.)

As well as all this instruction he taught her a discipline which we call
*moralitas*, the art which teaches fine behavior. All women should
practice this in their youth. *Moralitas*, that sweet pursuit, is delightful
and pure. Its study is in harmony with the world and with God. In its
commandment it teaches us to please both God and the world. It is
given to all lofty spirits as a nurse.

"Moraliteit" thus seems to be a quality which accompanies the teaching
of Isolde, rather than a special subject. It comes "under aller dirre lere"
and it is an "unmüezekeit," the very word which Gottfried had used in
his preface to describe his own actions in writing his poem. By imparting
his knowledge and skills, Tristan had produced "moraliteit" in Isolde, the
quality which distinguishes *edele herzen* from all others. Gottfried has
deliberately chosen a word which, so far as we know, had not been used
previously in Middle High German, to identify a quality which had no
previous existence in literature. The word is almost certainly derived from
the Latin *moralitas*, which does not mean "morality" but "state of mind,"
"character." Boethius had noted in his work *De re musica* how the
*moralitas* of a person determines the effect which music will have on him
and this is an opinion with which Gottfried undoubtedly agrees,[34] but
the quality of *moraliteit* is not for him a mere disposition but a positive
quality, the quality which distinguishes *edele herzen*. It is not courtliness
or any social grace, nor is it recognizable by any external features. It is
simply a quality which raises men to a higher level, which gives them
qualities which bridge the gulf between the human and the divine.
Gottfried makes no effort at a close definition, for such exactitude would
defeat his purpose. Just as the *edele herzen* are the highest type of audience,
so *moraliteit* is the highest discipline. It alone prepares a person for the
highest type of love. The only formal connection which Gottfried makes
between it and any other discipline is to show its close bonds with music,
through which it is most exactly expressed, and its general affinity with
the arts. It is also closely connected with women rather than with men.
Gottfried never associates *moraliteit* specifically with Tristan, except in
his role as teacher, and with men only in so far as they are included in
the *edele herzen*. Yet *moraliteit* is clearly attainable by all persons of good

will. All men should strive for it, as they should for Tristan-love, but few, very clearly, attain it in full measure and those only through the medium of the arts.

Isolde is a different person after Tristan's instruction, but there is no hint of love between them. Gottfried goes to considerable lengths to show this. The passage which describes Isolde's accomplishments ends with the line "si kunde schriben unde lesen" ("she could read and write"), and in the same rhyming pair we have "nu was ouch Tristan genesen" ("and now Tristan was cured"). There could hardly be a sharper break and the effect is reinforced when Tristan pleads for permission to return home on the grounds that his wife will think he is dead. The wife appears to be Gottfried's own invention. Both Isolde the Fair and her mother show a very proper regard for preserving the marriage bond. The older Isolde speaks for both, gives Tristan a rich present, and dismisses him in the fashion appropriate for a servant who has performed well. His farewells are said in seven lines and in three more he is back in Cornwall. Isolde has not fallen in love with Tristan—but it is doubtful whether she could fall in love with anyone else.

Immediately upon his return to Cornwall, Tristan is asked about Isolde the Fair. His reply is a paean of praise of her beauty, a passage interesting in two respects. He deliberately compares her with Helen of Troy and states that she has replaced Helen as the paragon of female beauty, adorning the whole sex with her glory. This is not the usual romance statement that the knight's lady far exceeds all others—in fact, Tristan denies that there is any such competitive element. Isolde is so far above all others that she has beauty to spare for all her fellow women. The other aspect of the passage is less obvious but more important. Tristan, in describing Isolde to his courtly audience, concentrates entirely on her physical, visible beauty and even in this he avoids particularization. The rhetorical *topos* "description of a lady" is scrupulously ignored, a fact emphasized by the mention of Helen who, in the textbooks of rhetoric, was the personification of ideal female beauty. Tristan never even suggests the true virtues of Isolde, which were described at such length when he was her instructor. There is no reference to music or intellectual abilities. Tristan knows what will appeal to Mark's court.

Why does he launch this enticing description? The obvious structural reason is to lay the basis for the barons' plot to send him back to Ireland to obtain Isolde for Mark. As Gottfried makes clear, he had no patience with "swallows bringing hair" as a motivation for the events of his plot. Tristan's extravagant praise of Isolde certainly renders the barons' determination to obtain her for Mark extremely plausible and it is one more example of a facet of Tristan's character to which we shall have occasion to refer again, his thoughtless plunging into a situation in a spirit of bravado, a flying in the face of fate in the belief that he has the presence of mind to extricate himself from any situation by his superior cunning. Yet this is not all. We learn later (lines 8900 ff.) that Tristan was aware of a method of winning Isolde—a guaranteed way. It merely required him to kill a dragon, a standard procedure in romances for winning fair ladies. If he killed the dragon and took Isolde back to Cornwall, he would have scored some very nice points off the barons (as he had by his victory over Morolt) and he would have brought about the seemingly impossible feat of reconciling Ireland and Cornwall. Gottfried makes it quite clear that Tristan had no very definite ideas about how he was going to do this. He would, as usual, lie his way into and out of various situations, operating on an *ad hoc* basis. Clearly the killing of the dragon was to be the first stage.

It would be attractive to speculate that Tristan's praise of Isolde and his eagerness to return to Ireland indicate a desire to see her again, even if he is not in love with her, but there is no real evidence for this. He can admire her impersonally and does, but his motivation in returning to Ireland seems to be much closer to that which led him to attack Duke Morgan than to a desire to see his beloved.

In the whole of the wooing scene, there is a strong element of parody. Mark is to obtain Isolde as a result of a dragon slain by proxy, and the seneschal endeavors to obtain a similar favor by using the same dragon. Here is the medieval system held up to ridicule, for the fairest lady in the world barely escapes being handed over to a cowardly knight in exchange for a dragon's head and does not escape being handed over to a king she has never seen and who is middle-aged in speech and bearing if not in years. Love clearly has no place in arrangements such as these, and yet they are the normal way in which the sexes are brought together in medieval society. Isolde might easily have been handed over to the seneschal if Tristan had not been found—or if she had killed him. And here is the heart of this wooing scene.

It is difficult to see how Gottfried could have intended his audience to believe that Tristan had any love for Isolde when he was making such elaborate arrangements to hand her over to Mark, and it is equally difficult to escape the conclusion that Isolde was a mere pawn in Tristan's game of defeating the barons.

The turning point comes when Tristan is sitting in his bath and Isolde is idly turning over his armor and speculating on his fate:

ouch was er iezuo wol genesen,
lieht an dem libe und schone var.
nu nam Isot sin dicke war
und marctin uzer maze
an libe und an gelaze;
si blicte im dicke tougen
an die hende und under dougen;
si besach sin arme und siniu bein,
an den ez offenliche schein,
daz er so tougenliche hal;
si bespehetin obene hin zetal:
swaz maget an manne spehen sol,
daz geviel ir allez an im wol
und lobetez in ir muote.                                          (9990 ff.)

Now he was well recovered, his person fair and his color good. Isolde often looked at him and observed very closely his body and bearing. She kept stealing glances at his hands and features; she gazed at his arms and legs, where what he was keeping secret was made perfectly obvious; she examined him from top to bottom; whatever a girl is supposed to see in a man pleased her well in him, and she praised it in her thoughts.

The interesting thing about this passage is that it is the first time that Isolde has taken note of Tristan as a person. We have not been informed by Gottfried how Isolde reacted to Tristan as an instructor. We know only what she learned. Now she sees him as a man and her musings take the form of speculation on the ways of providence: How could a man of his caliber be condemned to the wandering life of a minstrel? he should be a ruler, a kingdom should obey *him* rather than the many weak rulers who abound. Now this statement is hardly a philanthropic contemplation of the injustice of fate. If Tristan were a nobleman, he would be able to marry Isolde, for he has already proved his title to her by slaying the dragon. So far as Isolde knows, he is the musician Tantris and as a lowborn man he can prevent the seneschal from establishing his claim but cannot claim Isolde for himself. She sums up her thoughts in these words:

> der so getugendet waere,
> der solte guot und ere han.
> an ime ist sere missetan.                                    (10,028 ff.)

A man with these qualities should have wealth and honor. He has not been fairly treated.

The expression "guot und ere han" is precisely that which is associated with "moraliteit."

Isolde has thus progressed beyond the mechanical acceptance of Tantris the musician, her master-of-arts, the dragon-slayer. She feels that he is a man to admire, and Gottfried conveys admirably the growing sense of trust in his knighthood and admiration for his qualities. This is no visual perception of his physical beauty but a slow awakening to his personality. There is no corresponding reaction from Tristan. The only sign of interest still is the description before Mark's court.

The discovery of the notch in the blade follows immediately upon this recognition of Tristan as a man. In one flash Isolde knows that he *is* a nobleman, heir to a throne, a great warrior—and that knowledge makes him at once eligible and utterly ineligible to marry her. He is no longer Tantris the musician but Tristan, the killer of her uncle. Gottfried represents her confusion in a passage which sounds ludicrous if it is interpreted as a piece of rational thinking:

> "hie wart min oeheim mite erslagen
> und der in sluoc, der hiez Tristan.
> wer gab ez disem spilman?
> der ist doch Tantris genant."
> Die namen begunde si zehant
> beide in ir sinnen ahten,
> ir beider lut betrahten.
> "a herre" sprach si wider sich
> "dise namen die beswaerent mich.
> ine kan niht wizzen, wie in si:
> si lutent nahe ein ander bi."
> "Tantris," sprach si "und Tristan,
> da ist binamen heinliche an."                               (10,096 ff.)

"My uncle was killed with this, and the man who killed him was called Tristan. Who gave it to this minstrel? He is after all called Tantris."

> Then she began at once to turn over the two names in her mind and examine the sound of both. "O Lord," he said to herself, "these names worry me. I can't think what it is with them. They sound very much alike." "Tantris," she said, "and Tristan, there is some strange connection."

Slowly, reluctantly she comes to the conclusion that this Tantris is in fact Tristan. It is her reluctance to believe it which causes her hesitation, not a deficiency of understanding. Here is the explanation of her instinctive belief that Tristan was something more than a minstrel—her attraction to him as a nobleman. This, then, is the man they have cured and supported.

> "ernert? erst nu vil ungenesen.
> diz swert daz muoz sin ende wesen!
> Nu ile, rich din leit, Isot!"                                    (10,137 ff.)

> "Healed? He will soon be unhealed. This sword shall be his end.
> Quick, Isolde, avenge your misery!"

Isolde's desperate confusion, her feeling for Tristan conflicting with her knowledge that she should avenge Morolt, leads her to rush at Tristan with the sword—but hold it suspended above his head. She cannot strike. Tristan's appeal is not, as it is in the version of Thomas, to her personal advantage. There he had told her that without Tristan's help she would be handed over to the seneschal. Here he appeals to her as a woman, with a woman's sense of taste. Her mother, who has even more reason for bringing about the destruction of Tristan, enters at this moment and her presence, not unnaturally, inhibits the younger Isolde. The sight of her daughter about to cut down her guest, naked in his bath, was not something calculated to inspire even a medieval mother. Yet, as Gottfried says, even if she had not been prevented by her mother and later by Brangaene, Isolde could never have killed Tristan:

> ouch was diu muoter ie da bi,
> diu durnehte künigin:
> er mohte sunder sorge sin.
> ouch waerer zuo den stunden
> in daz bat gebunden
> und Isot eine da gewesen:
> er waere doch vor ir genesen.
> diu süeze, diu guote,

diu siure an wibes muote
noch herzegallen nie gewan
wie solte diu geslahen man?                                    (10,230 ff.)

Her mother was there too, the skilful queen, and he did not need to
worry. And even if he had been tied in the bath at the time and Isolde
there alone, he would still have been safe. The sweet, the good woman,
had none of the bitterness or sourness of a woman's emotions. How
could she have killed anyone?

Isolde could never have killed him because her "wipheit" triumphs over
anger. The exact meaning of "wipheit" is left deliberately unclear. Tristan
appeals to her feminine honor but it is rather the fact that she is a woman
and he is a man which saves him. The key word here as elsewhere is
"genesen." Isolde the queen had cured Tristan from the physical wound
he had received from Morolt and again from the effects of the dragon's
tongue. Isolde the Fair plays upon the word when she says he will now be
"vil ungenesen"—undone, uncured—but nevertheless, as Gottfried says,
"er waere doch vor ir genesen"—he would always be safe from her.
Tristan's mother had "cured" Riwalin, Isolde the queen had cured
Tristan, but such cures led to a wound of much greater depth and intensity. Tristan is indeed "genesen" in the sense that he stays alive, but
Isolde's statement is nevertheless true. He is the victim of love.

It is hard to see how Gottfried could have written this scene, in a
form different from that in his source, if he had not intended it to be an
indication that Isolde had formed an affection for Tristan. Her speculation
about his status, the turmoil of mind which came upon her when she
discovered that Tantris was, in fact, Tristan, her inability to kill him,
her sense of hopeless sorrow at her fate, all point to such a conclusion.
All of which does not mean that she was conscious of her love for him.
It is here that Gottfried differs most sharply from the conventions of
romance. The love monologue always is on the theme "Am I in love—I
think so—but surely not—he cannot love me." It is the literary equivalent
of pulling petals from daisies and psychologically at about the same level.
The characters are all prepared for falling in love, they anticipate it and
expect it. Isolde is not so prepared and for her the loss of control and
reason which love brings is a shock which she cannot comprehend. She
who had been accustomed to sway the emotions of men now finds herself
at the mercy of forces beyond her control and understanding. Like Dido,

she had dedicated herself to one goal, only to find that her emotions rendered that goal impossible of attainment. Her confusion of Tantris and Tristan is but a graphic representation of her emotional turmoil. Tristan was to suffer a similar confusion later in his career when Isolde White Hands obscures his vision of love.

But for the moment Tristan shows no signs of affection. He is still the "spilman," playing out the game to the last, appealing to the woman-hood of Isolde the Fair and to the honor of Isolde the queen—not without a side reference to the seneschal from whom he alone can save them. His reference to "good news" which he can give them if he is spared is exactly timed. Each will interpret it in the way she likes best. Typically, it is the reasonable Brangaene who persuades the two Isoldes to hear his proposal. He is clever enough to keep the exact nature of it from them until assured of his own safety. The proposal itself is quickly made and quickly accepted. Only Isolde the Fair—who is not consulted and who gives no opinion—shows where her thoughts are by repeating to her mother the way in which she had discovered that Tantris was Tristan.

The succeeding scene of court pageantry shows us Tristan and Isolde for the first and only time as they appear to a courtly audience. They are both figures of glorious sensuous appeal, and Gottfried leaves no doubt that their beauty is such as to arouse sensual thoughts in all beholders. The scene is strongly and deliberately reminiscent of the court scene in which Riwalin and Blanscheflur appear for the first time in each other's presence. It is the moment for falling in love but there is no falling in love which is apparent to the reader. Only an increased awareness of the other, a realization of the other's physical beauty. For it is the image of Isolde for Tristan and of Tristan for Isolde that we see. This is no mere rhetorical description, with its head-to-toe catalogue of features, but the selection of detail by an eye dwelling lovingly on the body of a person really seen for the first time.

THE REVELATION OF LOVE

Gottfried's observation of the departure from Ireland is extra-ordinarily penetrating. Isolde's grief at parting from her parents is natural and understandable. She was being handed over to a king she had never seen and who until recently had been her father's deadliest enemy, at the

instance of a man she had every reason to hate and whose conduct throughout had been shot through with lies and deceit. Nor is her situation rendered any better by Tristan's attentions. He visits her cabin frequently,
ostensibly to comfort her:

> der gie wilent dar in
> und troste die künigin,
> da sie weinende saz.
> diu weinde unde clagete daz,
> dazs also von ir lande,
> da si diu liute erkande,
> und von ir vriunden allen schiet
> und vuor mit der unkunden diet,
> sin wiste war oder wie
> so troste si Tristan ie,
> sor suozeste kunde;
> ze ieglicher stunde,
> als er zuo zir triure kam,
> zwischen sin arme er si nam
> vil suoze unde lise
> und niuwan in der wise
> als ein man sine vrouwen sol.                           (11,545 ff.)

> Sometimes he went and comforted the queen as she sat there weeping.
> She wept and cried that she was parting from her own country, where
> she knew the people, and from all her friends, and sailing with a crew of
> strangers, she knew not where or how. Then Tristan comforted her as
> gently as he could. Every time he came to her as she was sorrowing, he
> took her in his arms sweetly and gently and in no other fashion than the
> way in which a man should take his lady.

Why does Tristan spend so much time in Isolde's cabin when she says
that she hates him? Why does he put his arm around her? What is the way
in which a man should lay his arm about his lady? The whole passage is
extremely ambiguous, for "man" can mean both "male" and "liege
man"; "vrouwe," mistress in both the social and the sexual sense; and it is
far from clear that there is any way in which a liege man may properly
embrace his future queen. Whatever Tristan's intentions, there is no doubt
about Isolde's interpretation. She is afraid of any contact with him.
The reasons she gives are perfectly logical—he murdered her uncle and
has taken her from her parents. Yet they are unconvincing. The first was,
so far as Isolde was concerned, a technical offense, and every medieval

princess could expect—if she was lucky—to be married to someone away from her own lands. Her scorn and anger are rooted in more personal emotion. Tristan could, after all, have exercised his rights as dragon-slayer for himself, married Isolde, and stayed in Ireland. This, perhaps, is behind Isolde's musings about his status. His duty to Mark prevents him from making such a bargain, but the evidence of attraction between the two grows stronger. Tristan haunts Isolde's cabin, and she shows an anger toward him which seems so excessive as to be akin to love. Her real complaint against him is that he has completely disordered her life. The charge is true, and it is against this emotional background that Gottfried introduces the *Minnetrank*, the draught of love.

The motif of the love philter is an invariable element in Tristan stories. We should beware of rejecting out of hand the statement in the narrative that the pair actually drank a love potion. Most people in the Middle Ages believed in the existence of love potions and in their efficacy —as apparently people still do, although they give them more sophisticated names—and there is no reason to think that Gottfried was any exception. The drinking of the potion is not a "mere" symbol or representation of the act of falling in love and being bound by love forever. It is an act in time which actually took place but which had a significance beyond its narrative function. Just as the *Minnegrotte* existed in time and space and yet could be visited by Gottfried who had never been to Cornwall, so the love potion can be drunk but still indicate the universal state of fidelity in love. Gottfried is applying here the techniques of exegesis which he had learned from the study of the Fathers and the Scriptures.

What does the love potion indicate? It indicates that the lovers are aware of being in love. Gottfried has already shown us that they were attracted to each other to an increasing degree and that Isolde, much more than Tristan, shows the symptoms of affection struggling with reason. Awareness of the other's presence was growing but not awareness of love. The conditions on board ship are also brought into play. Gottfried emphasizes the inevitable increase in intimacy which is brought about by the cramped quarters, the boredom, and the misery of long days at sea. Except for Brangaene, Tristan is the only person of rank on board. Isolde is no longer segregated in the women's apartments, watched over by her mother and her ladies-in-waiting. She shows how conscious she is of the rank question by twice addressing Tristan as "Meister," which could be a sarcastic reference to his position as her tutor or, more likely, to his being the captain of the ship. In either case it is an effort to lower his status, to make him think of the gulf between him and a princess. Isolde would hardly have brought up the matter if she had been uninterested.

Gottfried's exposition of the lovers' feelings differs markedly from the standard romance description, and it is here that we find his view of awareness of love. His characters do not "fall in love" because their love is an ever changing and ever intensifying phenomenon. In describing their feelings—which he does before letting them speak for themselves—he stresses two elements: the sorrow which love will bring and their total unity. Sorrow is, as we know, inseparable from Tristan-love, but it is only a part of it. Here it appears to be the whole. There is throughout this entire passage a sense of deceptiveness, of surface meaning differing from inner meaning, of action differentiated from its ultimate result. The little girl brings them what she believes to be wine and they drink it as wine:

> nein, ezn was niht mit wine,
> doch ez ime gelich waere:
> ez was diu wernde swaere,
> diu endelose herzenot,
> von der si beide lagen tot.                                      (11,672 ff.)

No, it was not filled with wine, although it looked like it: it was long-enduring wretchedness, endless misery for the heart, as a result of which both would die.

Wine, the stuff of life, is death and misery. Yet in terms of the romance which Gottfried is writing it is misery only for Tristan and Isolde in this life. For all lovers it is an everlasting joy. Brangaene, too, can perceive only the immediate effect, the death which must inevitably come to Tristan and Isolde if they commit adultery. She thinks, as she always does, only in social terms, of their physical death and her own loss of honor in not carrying out the task assigned to her by Isolde the queen. She flings the remains of the potion into the raging sea, a disturbing element back to its like, thus preventing any other person, and particularly Mark, from sharing it. She fears the deadly disorder which the potion has brought, an uncontrollable element in a well-regulated world.

Gottfried does not state that the potion binds the lovers forever, still less, as some versions do, for a specific number of years. His emphasis is on the complete unity and harmony which the potion brings about:

> si wurden ein und einvalt,
> die zwei und zwivalt waren e;
> si zwei enwaren do nieme
> widerwertic under in
>
> . . .
>
> mit liebe also vereinet,
> daz ietweder dem anderm was
> durchluter alse ein spiegelglas.
> si haeten beide ein herze . . .                                    (11,716 ff.)

They became one and unified now who had previously been two and
disparate; the two were no longer at odds with one another . . . they were
so joined in love that each was clearer than a looking-glass to the other.
They had one heart between them.

They had "become one flesh," even though they were not married and
could not be, yet there is much more than flesh involved. Their feelings,
their joys and sorrows, had now become one. Neither could feel without
affecting the other, but this does not mean that from now on there would be
no disagreement or misunderstanding between them. They would attain
their knowledge of true love only gradually. The harmony which had
begun with the teaching of music to Isolde has now developed to the point
at which the bodily union of the lovers becomes imperative. This is by
no means the ultimate ideal but a step along the way.

It is a step which both lovers are reluctant to take. Gottfried carefully
avoids describing an immediate union, which to him would have been
aesthetically distasteful and artistically impossible. The effect of the
potion is to make Tristan and Isolde realize that neither can live without
the other, but not to make them fall into each other's arms. Gottfried does
not have his lovers express their feelings in love monologues, as would
have been customary in romance. His Tristan speaks five lines of monologue, his Isolde none at all. Gottfried prefers to examine the lovers'
realization of their state by third-person description, for he is thus able
to use a series of metaphors and parallels which the lovers could not have
used of themselves with any degree of verisimilitude.

Tristan's resistance is based on feudal concepts of loyalty, and his
subjection to love is expressed by metaphors of the relation between a
liege man and his lord. For Tristan, Isolde is the princess whom he has

won for his uncle Mark. He is thus bound by a manifold sense of duty—
that of a nephew toward his uncle, of a younger man to an older, and in
particular that of a liege man to his liege lord. Tristan does not normally
show gratitude for what he receives, as his treatment of his foster-father
shows, but he feels close ties to Mark.[35] Any feeling of love for Isolde
inevitably implies the grossest possible injury to his uncle, and the word
*ere* here has a meaning far beyond "reputation." Tristan's hesitation is
based not on any doubts about the way in which he will be received by
Isolde, whether she cares for him or not—he never mentions his doubts
or thinks about them, unlike the standard lover of the romance—but on
his dislike of betraying a trust. The feudal metaphor continues. He has
now to choose between two loyalties, the well-established relation with
Mark and the new, yet fundamental, more powerful, asocial overlordship
of love, less tangible, governed by no known code, unpredictable and
indomitable. Here too there must be unflinching loyalty but it is a loyalty
which cannot be prescribed by rules and one more powerful than feudalism.
Gottfried has set up in his description of Tristan's agony the basic conflict
of his poem—that between society and love. He has also predicted what
the result will be:

e sis [Tristan and Isolde] ie wurden gewar,
do stiez sir sigevanen dar
und zoch si beide in ir gewalt . . .                                    (11,713 ff.)

Before they [Tristan and Isolde] were aware of it, she pushed her
victorious banners forward and drew them both into her power.

The struggle is between the individual and a greater power, but Gottfried
is careful to recall his motif of love as a snare, a force which cannot be
understood by the person trapped. He had used this figure of the uncom-
prehending Riwalin and he uses it of both lovers here—for Tristan a snare,
for Isolde a limed twig. Such a metaphor applies only to the earliest stage
of love. It has no relevance for its maturity.

The conflict within Isolde is one that might take place in any young
girl. She has forgotten her hate for Tristan, her championing of her dead
uncle, and her wretchedness at being torn from her home in the overwhelming attraction she feels for Tristan, and to her the only impediment is a
natural reluctance to take an irrevocable step. Gottfried takes care to
emphasize the sensual nature of the attraction, the constant pull of the

eyes to the other's body. If any part of love can be ascribed to the potion, it is this. The higher elements, the harmony, must be deferred until their bodily needs are satisfied and it is to the satisfaction of bodily needs that Brangaene and the lovers devote their attention for a considerable part of the poem.

Gottfried carefully avoids the normal romance-dialogue technique of having the lovers retail to one another the classic symptoms of love, so that they and their audience may be made aware of their state. Instead, he adopts what we may call the psychological-realistic technique of making them follow a course which would be familiar to anyone who had ever been in love and hence, by definition, to all *edele herzen*. They fall into conversation largely confined to recapitulating the events they have shared and thus bringing about a feeling of intimacy. Inevitably, Isolde accuses Tristan of running her life; inevitably, he asks how he has done so. They slip into a dangerous closeness of physical and verbal contact. Finally Isolde confesses the cause of her misery—*l'ameir*. It is ironical that Tristan, the master linguist and man of his tongue, should be so reluctant to accept the word in the meaning he most wants to hear, yet his attitude is entirely natural under the circumstances. His confusion is parallel to Isolde's over the names Tantris and Tristan and Tristan's over Isolde (the Fair) and Isolde (White Hands). The words jostle in his head but clear meaning does not emerge. He cannot believe his good fortune—that Isolde really loves him. What is obvious to Brangaene is not obvious to him. From now on the relations between the two slide inevitably toward physical consummation. It is worth noting that they know nothing of the love potion, and they swear Brangaene to secrecy in the belief that they are attracted by love and love alone—as indeed they are. Tristan and Isolde never blame the potion for their state, as they do, for example, in Eilhart's poem. They do not feel that they are victims of a ruthless power but participants in a glorious experience. Tristan's reaction to Brangaene's disclosure of the fatal nature of the potion is characteristic of the lovers' feeling at this time:

> "nu waltes got!" sprach Tristan
> "ez waere tot oder leben:
> ez hat mir sanfte vergeben.
> ine weiz, wie jener werden sol:
> dirre tot der tuot mir wol.

solte diu wunnecliche Isot
iemer alsus sin min tot,
so wolte ich gerne werben
umb ein eweclichez sterben"                                    (12,494 ff.)

"Now may God determine it," said Tristan, "be it life or be it death: it
has given me a sweet poison. I don't know what *that* death will be like,
but this one suits me well. If the lovely Isolde is always going to be my
death, I would like to sue for death everlasting."

Like most of the statements made in this scene, Tristan's cry of joy is
ambiguous and full of tragic irony. He is full of the joy of love attained,
full of the physical ardor of young manhood, and death is merely a word
to him. If this is death, let us enjoy it. He distinguishes between "that"
death, the ultimate death which Brangaene has promised will come, and
the present death which to him is a joke, an impossibility. He is to spend
a great deal of time in the rest of the romance in discovering what is meant
by death. Their love is death, just as it is sorrow, but it is manifesting itself
as life, it is sickness cured by Love the physician, a physician whose cures
are but a new sickness. The whole passage illustrates how little Tristan
and Isolde know of love. The *edele herzen* who are the audience know more,
for they have been told by Gottfried. Yet they really know less, for Tristan
and Isolde are those with the ultimate knowledge.

Gottfried prefers to describe the consummation of the love of Tristan
and Isolde by a series of metaphoric and graphic words rather than the
more realistic description used by some of his contemporaries—but not
Hartmann von Aue or Wolfram von Eschenbach. He pauses in the narrative to reflect on the nature of true love, just as at Tristan's investiture
he had been concerned with the quality of his hero's knighthood and its
relation to literary form. He points up the significance of what he is
about to say by the insertion of a quatrain, not one of those whose first
letter forms part of the intertwined names of the lovers but one which
belongs to the acrostic of his own name. The excursus leaves the lovers in
bliss while it meditates on the nature of love. The quatrain, as usual, is
ambivalent and difficult to interpret:

Ein langiu rede von minnen
diu swaeret höfschen sinnen:
kurz rede von guoten minnen
diu guotet guoten sinnen.                                      (12,183 ff.)

> A long discourse on love wearies minds trained at court: a short discourse
> on love that is good makes good minds turn to good.

Is Gottfried referring, as some critics think, to the crudities and inartistic
nature of long descriptions of love-making? Thus "höfischen sinnen"
would be those with delicate sensibilities and parallel to or identical with
the "guoten sinnen" of the last line, and the second pair of lines would
merely be repeating in a positive way what the first two had said negatively.
It is more likely that the quatrain is intended to look both backward and
forward, to the lack of description of the love scene and to Gottfried's
own remarks. If it does, the first two lines may mean that courtly audiences
are bored by long discussions of love but good (in Gottfried's sense)
minds may benefit from a short discussion of it—which is precisely
what he intends to provide. And in what way are we to understand "sinnen"—sense or senses? The choice, as usual, is left to us.

Gottfried's disclaimer of personal experience of love is made at two
critical junctures in the love story of Tristan and Isolde—here, at the
first uninhibited consummation, and at the highest point of that love, the
scene in the *Minnegrotte*. At both points the poet observes and comments
on their actions as one who understands but cannot participate. Here, at
this purely physical act of union, he merely denies any personal experience.
In the *Minnegrotte* scene, where the love experience is far more complicated, Gottfried claims personal knowledge of the aesthetic and emotional
elements which form an important part of the love complex but states
explicitly that he has never experienced its consummation. The difference
between the two statements reflects the progress of the poem.

The discussion of love proves, in fact, to be a discussion of the way
society treats love, and it is conveyed through an interesting series of
figures. The first is the soaring joy of love which is free from surveillance.
True love cannot exist in any atmosphere where it is constantly watched
and thwarted—and this, it will be remembered, is always the case in the
standard love situation in the lyric, whether it be the *canzon* or the *alba*,
and in such romances as *Cligès* and *Chevalier de la charette*. Gottfried is
indicating that *true* love can exist only when it is unfettered, and that
happy situation occurs only twice in the poem, here on the ship and later
in the *Minnegrotte*. At all other times the conventions of society intrude.

The second figure is that of sowing the seeds of bad love and expecting
true love to spring from such seed. Love is not responsible for the dire

results but those who sow—and who are they? Gottfried says "wir
saejen." Does he mean all men—or all contemporaries—or all authors?
This is not an exact parallel with the parable of the sower in the New
Testament. There the seed was good, and the soil upon which it fell varied.
Here it is the seed which is bad. It can produce nothing but weeds whatever
ground it falls on. The seed is false, not the seed of true love, and it brings
forth misery:

> wir buwen die minne
> mit gegelletem sinne,
> mit valsche und mit akust
> und suochen danne an ir die lust
> des libes und des herzen:
> son birt si niuwan smerzen,
> unguot und unvruht unde unart . . .                                    (12,237 ff.)

We cultivate love with minds made bitter, with deceit, and with cunning
and then look for pleasure of the body and the heart in her: but in that
way she produces nothing but pain, no-good, no-fruit, no-nature.

It is deception which is the root cause of unhappiness, and Gottfried
emphasizes the unnatural result by the three last words—*unguot, unvruht,
unart.* But who is being deceived? Surely it is the lovers themselves who
are guilty in deceiving Mark and the whole society to which they belong.
Their history from this point on will be a series of deceits which will
involve not only their own reputations but those of such innocent persons
as Brangaene. They will allow nothing to stand in the way of their sexual
pleasure. It is hard to see how Gottfried could sympathize with such an
attitude, and indeed he does not. The question is: Who is responsible?
This excursus seems to blame contemporary society rather than the lovers
in it. Society's conception of love is such that it cannot recognize true
love when it sees it but prefers to encourage hole-and-corner liaisons rather
than open and frank love. Deceit is of the very essence of "höfische Minne."
It would certainly not be difficult for Gottfried to produce literary evidence
for his views, and a whole segment of contemporary polite society was
prepared to accept the thesis, at least in theory, that true love consisted in
the secret passion of a married woman for someone not her husband.
Love is the most popular of subjects yet it is utterly debased. It is hard to
escape the conclusion that Gottfried is here referring to literature rather
than to contemporary life. In literature love is the commonest of all subjects
and is used merely as an excuse for gaining a reputation as a writer.

At this point Gottfried makes his sharpest figural contrast. He has just compared love to a poor peddler going from house to house to sell her wares and now he reverts to true love:

> Minne, aller herzen künigin,
> diu vrie, diu eine
> diu ist umb kouf gemeine!
> wie habe wir unser herschaft
> an ir gemachet zinshaft!
> wir haben ein boese conterfeit
> in daz vingerlin geleit
> und triegen uns da selbe mite.                          (12,300 ff.)

Love, the queen of all hearts, the free, the one alone, is up for sale to anyone! See how we have grabbed our profits from our mastery over her! We have put a miserable imitation in our ring and with it we deceive ourselves.

The figure of love as ruler, as dominant over all hearts, is a truism of courtly literature. Gottfried believes it, for he uses this figure over and over again. But it is clear that he thinks that most of his contemporaries use it without believing it. Love should be the mistress, the overlord, but we make her a subject of trade. The metaphor can, of course, be understood in several different ways, but one must be that the love story has become a source of profit. The result has been a mere mockery, a counterfeit of love. Such a reading is borne out by the reference to ancient love-stories. Everyone, says Gottfried, is prepared to admire such stories and wish he could have such an experience. Yet such a wish remains hypothetical, for no one is prepared to bring to such an experience the one essential ingredient—*triuwe*, complete loyalty. Without complete loyalty there can be no true love. What Gottfried means, surely, is that his society is prepared to admire in literature, that is, in fiction, what it cannot achieve in fact. Literature, to his contemporaries, consists of pretty stories which have no relevance to life. For Gottfried, literature is life. People must believe what they read and hear and relate it to life, and their own attitude to society must be that of the people they admire in literature. Tristan and Isolde are not mere figures in an old story but lovers whose experience is still relevant. For them society stood in the way of love, yet they loved. And so must it be for all true lovers.

> Ich weiz wol, Tristan unde Isot,
> die gebitelosen beide

benamen ouch ir leide
unde ir triure ein ander vil,
do si begriffen daz zil
gemeines willen under in.                          (12,358 ff.)

I know very well that Tristan and Isolde, that eager pair, relieved each
other of a great deal of misery and sorrow when they grasped the object
of the desire they both had.

This is indeed the only way to love. In his description of the lovers'
conduct Gottfried repeats many of the figures he has used disparagingly
of love among his contemporaries: Tristan and Isolde "give and take
willing tribute and profit from love and from each other with minds that
were faithful." Here is the same idea of love as payment but with the
addition that it was a source of mutual satisfaction, not a buying of
favors. Concealment is to be avoided. The concept of "tougen minne" is
alien to Gottfried's concept of love but so is the idea of a lady who will
not admit that she is in love. Lovers should declare themselves. Thus the
ideas of secrecy, of concealment, of false modesty are all mentioned in
connection with the lovers and are all rejected. Yet they are still present.
For however open Tristan and Isolde may be with each other, they must
conceal their love from society; however much they reject the idea of
paying tribute unwillingly, Isolde will still have to pay unwilling tribute
to Mark whenever he demands it; however much they deplore deceit,
they will be forced into the crassest deception to maintain their love;
and however free they may feel themselves to be, they will be in the power
of love for the rest of their lives. Pure love can exist only in a place with-
drawn from society—a ship on the sea or a cave far from courts. In society
it is debased and cast down, a victim of the prejudices of little men.

THE KING AND THE NEPHEW

Such is the process of falling in love according to Gottfried. There is
no such thing as falling but rather a gradual feeling of affinity which
develops into a new phase of love, a new phase of understanding which,
while it never neglects or underestimates the power of physical attraction,
moves beyond it to a harmony of body, soul, and spirit. In contrast to
this true love, the love toward which the *edele herzen* must strive, we may
glance at the love experience of King Mark. It will be remembered that
he had been most unwilling that Tristan should go to Ireland to fetch

Isolde. Gottfried goes out of his way to make the editorial comment that his determination to marry Isolde was caused not by Tristan's glowing description of her beauty but by his desire to set a goal for marriage which could not be realized. When Isolde arrives, however, he does not hesitate to accept her as his bride. Unlike the love-making of Tristan, the wedding of Mark is a massive social occasion. All the amenities are observed: knights summoned from far and wide and universal agreement that Isolde is just as beautiful as everyone had said. Gottfried disposes of the wedding ceremony with remarkable brevity—indeed, the most significant thing about it is the provision that Tristan should inherit if Isolde bore no children, an ironical twist—and proceeds to Mark's consummation. He is deceived; he "marries" Brangaene, not Isolde. Thus love abuses two innocent persons, Mark and Brangaene, in its efforts to remain untouched. Now it is true that Mark is not really deceived. To him brass was as good as gold and Brangaene's body served him as well as Isolde's, but the deceit is there, the opposition to the social system. If such is the conduct of love, society cannot survive. The abuse of Brangaene is worse, for loyalty is being rewarded by dishonor and not even by love; Isolde is afraid that her cousin, like many a substitute bride, will make use of her position to ingratiate herself with Mark. Isolde's love is at a stage where she can allow nothing to interfere with it, not even the honor of her cousin—or her own honor. Mark's love is a sad affair. He does not fall in love with anyone but merely enjoys such sensual pleasures as are offered. He is incapable of Tristan-love, incapable of being one of the *edele herzen*, yet he is an honest man, one of those for whom romances are written. He loves his wife in a perfectly decent way, even though he is unworthy of her and unable to understand her. Love for him is a sexual affair and an affair of social obligation, not one of *moraliteit*. He preserves this attitude throughout the poem.

There are two elements of conflict between uncle and nephew in the matter of Isolde and both bear on Mark's concept of love. The former and by far the more simple is the attraction of Isolde's beauty. Gottfried makes this clear not only in the consummation scene but even more when Mark comes to the hole which allows him to observe the lovers in the *Minnegrotte*. He has already been told of the naked sword between them and accepts it as a sign of innocence. (The audience knows the truth, for the sword is one more example of Tristan's technique of deceit when faced with the courtly world—he has heard the near approach of the hunt.) Mark's acceptance of the sign depends, however, on his view of Isolde's body. He is so overcome with its beauty, so desirous of possessing it again, that he is prepared to accept the sword as proof of innocence against all the evidence of reason. Throughout the poem this conflict is going on within him and his much disputed inability to believe the stories he is told about Tristan and Isolde and even the evidence of his own eyes is ascribed by Gottfried to this reluctance to cease to enjoy the pretty plaything he has in his possession. The only thing which drives him to fury and makes him reject Isolde is the sight of her rewarding Tristan with glances of love which he feels:

>     si begunden dicke under in zwein
>     ir ougen unde ir herze in ein
>     mit blicken so verstricken,
>     daz si sich uz ir blicken
>     oft und ze manegen stunden
>     nie so verrihten kunden,
>     Marke envünde ie dar inne
>     den balsemen der minne,
>     durch daz er nam ir allez war.
>     sin ouge daz stuont allez dar:
>     er sach vil dicke tougen
>     die warheit in ir ougen
>     und anders aber an nihte
>     niwan an ir gesihte:
>     daz was so rehte minneclich,
>     so süeze und also senerich,
>     daz ez im an sin herze gie
>     und solhen zorn da von gevie,
>     solhen nit und solhen haz,
>     daz er diz unde daz,
>     zwivel unde arcwan
>     allez zeiner hant lie gan.                           (16,493 ff.)

Their hearts and eyes were constantly entangled with one another because of the looks that passed between them, so much so that they often could not put those glances to rights before Mark perceived in them the balm of love, and as a result he knew everything. His whole attention was focused on them. He covertly saw the truth in their eyes over and over again and in nothing else—only in her look that was so truly loving, so sweet and tender that it struck him to the heart and caused there such rage, such spite and hatred, that he at once abandoned both this and that, his doubt and his suspicion.

There are two significant features of this passage. One is the importance of the visual impact for Mark, as for all of Gottfried's courtly characters; the other is that here, as hardly at all elsewhere, Mark flies into a real rage, not his usual reaction of sorrow tempered with personal misery. Here we have the raw reaction of a jealous man.

The second element of conflict in Mark's love for Isolde is his attitude to his nephew Tristan. In other versions this attitude is relatively simple, particularly after the wedding with Isolde, when it speedily develops into uncompromising hatred. Gottfried rejects this oversimplified motivation. His Mark is unable to shake off the spell which Tristan put on him at this first appearance. The king remains enslaved by his nephew's intellectual and artistic superiority and by the deep friendship formed after his arrival at court. One event after another binds Mark to him—his skill in the formalities of the hunt, his command of languages, his musical abilities, and to these is added gratitude. When all other members of Mark's court had failed him, a young untried boy defeated Morolt and would have paid for it with his life if he had not brought about his own cure by daring and skill. Again, after Mark had promised him the succession, Tristan relieved his uncle of embarrassment and crushed the aspirations of the barons by undertaking the apparently impossible task of bringing back Isolde as queen. Mark was intelligent enough to realize that without Tristan there would have been no Queen Isolde—and indeed no King Mark.

There is a queer paradox in the delineation of Mark's character. He speaks and acts like a middle-aged man, yet it is not hard to produce evidence from the poem itself that he was still quite young, perhaps thirty or a little more.[36] He is sententious, full of wise saws and Polonius-like advice, and toward Tristan he adopts a protective, fatherly attitude. Yet this attitude does not extend to making decisions, for Mark cannot make a decision. Up to the involvement with Isolde, it is Tristan who makes all Mark's decisions for him—to challenge Morolt, to go to Ireland, to marry Isolde. Mark is unable to operate when this advice can no longer be given and he falls into the hands of Tristan's detractors while still incapable of believing that his nephew whom he so much admires could possibly have betrayed him. Thus he is torn one way and the other in his love for

Isolde, overmastered by desire for her beauty, jealous of a nephew whose attractions far exceed his own, yet loyal to the memory of his warm relationship to that nephew before their harmony was disturbed by Isolde. Only when brought face to face with the fact that he is being deprived of the enjoyment of Isolde's beauty does this factor sweep aside all other considerations, as it does when he sees the lovers' behavior after Tristan's first return from exile or Isolde lying below him in the *Minnegrotte*.

Gottfried has elaborated the figure of Mark to serve as the most important representative in the poem of non-Tristan-love. In doing so he has avoided the stereotype of the *jaloux* on the one hand and that of the middle-aged incapable husband on the other. To have made Mark into a figure corresponding to Arthur in the Lancelot-Guinevere story would have defeated his purpose, for he does not wish the king to be a despicable figure. Mark represents a type of love which is not degrading or reprehensible in itself but which is imperfect, since it consists in physical attraction coupled with admiration for physical beauty. There is no other bond, and Mark's object is pleasure. He has the support and understanding of the courtly society which he represents, the society to which Gottfried refers at the beginning of his preface and of which he says that he appreciates its values but regards it as inadequate. But Mark's love for Isolde has another and perhaps more important structural function in the poem. By its very nature it represents the force of "huote," of surveillance which is so inimical to true love. Such surveillance is the attempt of society to protect its rights over what has been obtained, by purchase, negotiation, or otherwise. It is a constant theme in lyric poetry, where the defeat of the measures designed to protect the beloved is one of the principal objects of the lover. Such a treatment would be too crude for Gottfried. Although the lovers do indeed attempt to circumvent the barriers imposed on them by the fact that Isolde is married to Mark, since they would otherwise find it impossible to meet, they find no happiness in such clandestine meetings and are cheated of their desire. Only when the restraints of society are not present at all can they really love. Mark represents these restraints. He is incapable of true love—that is, Tristan-love—but he prevents it by taking to himself Isolde. This, in Gottfried's opinion, is the way in which society works, not because of the injustice of individuals but because of its organization. It watches over lovers and prevents them from the enjoyment of their happiness.

THE CREATURES OF THE COURT

Mark's essential nobility redeems him from the worst faults of his class. His personal attachment to Tristan gives him sympathy, if not understanding. There are, however, creatures of this society who have no such scruples and restraints. Each represents in a different way the attitude of the court to love when that attitude is determined by purely selfish motives. Such "love" in its lowest manifestation appears in the seneschal. He cannot even plead the excuse of sensual attraction, for he does not desire Isolde as woman but as heiress to the Irish throne. She is his by right of conquest, a woman bought for a dragon's head. The terrifying aspect of the case is not that a lady of Isolde's standing could be promised to an unworthy liar in exchange for services not rendered but that his scheme came so near to success. The two Isoldes, confronted with his claim, can only hope for a miracle—which happens. They find Tantris. What kind of a system is this which could sacrifice a woman capable of love in its highest form to a man utterly without affection or scruple and motivated only by greed? Only chance and Tristan's cunning avert the tragedy. The criticism is not of the seneschal, who is significantly unnamed and in all respects a cipher, but of the whole system. Traditionally the seneschal—often Sir Kay—represents courtly society at its worst, enforcing the so-called rules of that society with little regard for personal feelings or true morality. Sir Kay's conduct, especially in the works of Chrétien de Troyes, leads to his being ridiculed—but by a member of that society who represents its conventions in a higher form (Yvain) or by a person of superior morality (Perceval). Gottfried introduces a seneschal of a rather different kind—stupid indeed and without moral scruple but who nevertheless is shrewd enough to use a feature of both medieval romance and medieval politics, the bartering of a noblewoman for services received or expected. Gottfried makes quite sure that the point is driven home by inserting a scene in which these very considerations are formally presented. The steward claims in open court that it is love which has inspired him to overcome the dragon, a claim which deceives no one. The older Isolde waves it aside with the ironical statement that he deserves a good wife but merely killing a dragon does not entitle him to such a reward as Isolde.

> "truhsaeze dine minne
> die sint luter unde guot
> und hast so menlichen muot:

du bist wol guotes wibes wert.
swer aber so hohes lones gert,
da er sin niht verdienet hat,
entriuwen, deist ein missetat . . ."                                    (9834 ff.)

"Steward, your love is pure and good and you have a man's spirit. You
are worth a good woman. But if anyone desires such an extraordinary
reward—and hasn't deserved it—well, well, that is misconduct."

As she justly remarks, "You brought a dragon's head—so what?" This
is derision of well-established custom, and the steward is shocked—he
has already suffered so much for her love! Isolde's reply is that she never
gave him any encouragement, so why is he disappointed? The reply
again consists of *Minne* cliché: women can't be trusted, they love con-
tradictions and never love the men who love them. He knows all their
tricks and is not going to be deprived of his rights. Again the elder Isolde
turns his words against him in sharp irony. He seems to know more about
women than is right—but he is correct in one thing:

"du minnest, daz dich hazzet;
du wilt, daz dich niht enwil
diz ist doch unser vrouwen spil;
waz nimest du dich hie mit an?
so dir got, du bist ein man,
laz uns unser vrouwen art."                                           (9914 ff.)

"You are wooing someone who loathes you: you desire what does not
desire you. That's the way we women play games—why do you get
involved in it? Heaven's above, you're a man, aren't you? Let *us* behave
like women."

The words usually spoken with hope of contradiction are here deadly
earnest. Isolde is not for sale—and her mother leaves the steward dangling,
wondering what kind of man he will have to face in the judicial combat
he has demanded. The whole scene is a mockery of the service-reward
concept which appears in so much medieval lyric and narrative, for the
steward is gradually forced to concede that he wants Isolde as a reward,
not because he loves her, and that his claim rests entirely on his alleged
killing of the dragon.

The ultimate confrontation is designed to bring the steward to the
depths of degradation. The court is crowded and the ladies are a miracle
of loveliness. All eyes turn on them and the steward must surely think that

all this will be his. Again he states his case and seizes gleefully upon Isolde's apparent inability to produce her evidence, pouring scorn on her request that he drop his claim:

> "Truhsaeze," sprach diu künigin
> "sol dirre kampf unwendic sin,
> son weiz ich rehte, waz getuo:
> ich bin dar ungewarnet zuo.
> und zware woltestun noch lan
> uf solhe rede understan,
> daz Isot dirre maere
> ledic und ane waere,
> truhsaeze, zware ez kaeme dir
> ze alse guoten staten als ir."                                    (11,045 ff.)

> "Steward," said the queen, "if this combat cannot be avoided, I do not really know what to do; I am quite unprepared for it. But if you were prepared to give it up with the understanding that Isolde were completely free and exempt from the whole matter, steward, it would be as good for you as for her."

This is the sober truth, but the steward is not prepared to be merciful. That Isolde hates him counts for nothing in his plans.

> "ledic?" sprach der ander do
> "ja, vrouwe, ir taetet ouch also,
> ir liezet ouch gewunnen spil."                                    (11,055 ff.)

> "Exempt," said the other, "oh, yes, my lady, you would do just that, you would give up a game already won."

This is the point. He is betting, he believes, on a sure thing and will become king of Ireland. Slowly his position becomes clear as first Tristan is introduced and then the dragon's tongue. He is hoist with his own petard but even then tries to insist on his right to combat until his supporters drag him away. The farcical insistence on the letter of the king's promise in complete defiance of morality and the desire to possess Isolde as a political chattel are a vicious parody of the common convention of epic poetry and courtly romance in which the lady is a reward for services. For if Erec can win Enid because she is the lady who will help him gain the sparrow hawk and if Yvain can win Laudine by killing her husband, why should not a seneschal take Isolde in exchange for a dragon's head? He had no love for her and sought only political advantage—but as

Isolde herself says to Tristan, he might have learned. The portrait of the seneschal is the severest but by no means the only attack on men who think of love in purely social terms.

## THE CONFLICT OF MINSTRELS

It is Tristan's bravery in fighting the dragon and his skill in handling an unusual situation which have led to the discomfiture of the claimant to Isolde's hand. He displays very similar qualities in dealing with another "lover," Gandin, the minstrel. The Gandin episode could clearly be omitted from the narrative without disturbing the structure or affecting the development of the love between Tristan and Isolde. Yet it has a definite relevance to the picture of love at court or in the romance which Gottfried wishes to present. On the surface the Gandin episode is merely one more example of the "rash boon" motif: a stranger appears at court, performs some service which gives great pleasure to the sovereign, and is told he may name any reward he chooses. He often asks for the queen. Poor Guinevere must have trembled every time a minstrel appeared at court, for no amount of sad experience seems to have taught Arthur not to swear rash oaths. The incident in Gottfried's poem is far from being a mere episode of this nature. Gandin is a musician, a man of real technical accomplishments, who has lived in Ireland and obviously admired Isolde, but he is also a knight, known to be such by the queen, who has chosen to come to the court of Cornwall without any knightly weapons, carrying only a rote, a musical instrument regarded as less distinguished than the harp. He has come to Cornwall because of his admiration for Isolde and, as events show, has a clearly formulated plan for abducting her. The parallels with Tristan's visits to Ireland are clear. He too was a knight who chose to appear with a musical instrument only and to rely upon his musical skill coupled with deception to win his way. Gandin provokes curiosity by the incongruity between his knightly appearance and his carrying of the rather ludicrous instrument, not, like Tristan, by the beauty of his performance. This ludicrous element persists as he refuses to lay aside his instrument when seated at the high table where a musician would never under normal circumstances be accepted. Tristan, an unrecognized knight, had played first and through his playing gained acceptance. Gandin refuses to play until he has been promised a reward. In other words, he behaves like the lowest type of minstrel, even though he is a knight and although Mark's request that he play is clearly more politeness than a real desire to hear him.

> der künec der hovebaere,
> Marke der tugende riche
> der bat in offenliche,
> ob er iht rotten kunde,
> daz er in allen gunde
> daz si vernaemen sin spil.                                    (13,184 ff.)

> Mark, that courteous and well-bred king, asked him before them all whether, if he had any skill on the rote, he would be kind enough to let them hear him play.

The language is formal, and the description of Mark casts him in his role of "courtly king." The reply is crude and in sharp contrast with Tristan's behavior on similar occasions:

> "herre, ine wil,
> ine wizze danne umbe waz."                                    (13,190 f.)

> "My lord, I will not unless I know my reward."

Mark's reply is a routine assurance that he can have a present:

> "welt ir iht, des ich han,
> daz ist allez getan:
> lat uns vernemen iuwern list,
> ich gib iu, swaz iu liep ist."                                (13,193 ff.)

> "If you would like anything I possess, agreed. Let us hear your accomplishments; I'll give you whatever you want."

Mark is doing what any king in such a situation would do. He is relying on the honor of the knight-musician and assuming that he will ask for a reasonable reward. Gottfried does not describe Gandin's playing, except to say that the court enjoyed it. There is no description of its effect, such as invariably accompanies the playing of Tristan or Isolde. It should be noted that Mark has not sworn any oath and at first he refuses utterly to hand over Isolde; but Gandin makes it a matter of honor, insults Mark by calling him a liar if he does not keep his word, and challenges him to fight for Isolde. What he has gained by cunning as a minstrel he proposes to keep by fighting as a knight. Mark can find no one prepared to fight Gandin (Tristan is away hunting) and as for himself:

> noch Marke selbe enwolde
> niht vehten umbe Isolde ...                                   (13,249 f.)

And Mark himself had no desire to fight for Isolde.

A pitiful figure indeed, who will not even fight to defend what another has won for him.

There are several parallels here: the cowardly seneschal who is clever enough to claim Isolde but not clever enough to keep her or bold enough to fight; the winning of Isolde by music, as Tristan had done; the cowardly Cornish nobles who would not fight the Irish Morolt as they will not fight the Irish Gandin and who, without Tristan, are helpless. But most important is the situation of Isolde. She is once again the victim of a convention which makes a mockery of love and honor. Just as her father had promised her to the killer of the dragon and thus, but for the intervention of Tristan, would have handed her over to a liar and coward, so Mark, by a similar thoughtless act, would have handed her over to Gandin. Yet Mark is more to blame. Isolde's father could be said to have sacrificed his daughter for the salvation of his country, and there would normally have been the assurance that the man who could kill such a monster would be at least brave and noble. The seneschal perverts the convention by his lies—as Gandin perverts the convention by his cunning and the fear he inspires in a king who, in spite of his noble professions, is not man enough to defend his wife. In either case society is to blame by setting up conventions whose effect is to hand over women against their will to any person who knows how to use or abuse such conventions.

Yet there are features about Gandin's attitude which differentiate him very sharply from Mark and the seneschal and bring him closer to Tristan. He relies on skill in music to effect his first claim to Isolde, he uses his cunning to think up a plan, he is adept at finding the weakness of his opponent. Like Tristan, he combines his skills as minstrel and knight to achieve his ends, although his music is in no way comparable to that of the lovers. Most importantly, Gandin is motivated by affection for Isolde. Whereas the Irish seneschal sought only material gain in his attempts to win her, Gandin has traveled from Ireland with a plan which involves seizing Isolde for her own sake and for that alone. Gottfried makes this clear at once:

> der ritter unde der amis
> was er gewesen manege wis
> und ouch ze manegem male
> und kam ze Curnewale

durch ir willen von Irlant.
nu bekande ouch sin zehant:
"deu sal, messire Gandin!"
sprach diu gevüege künigin.
"merzi," sprach Gandin "bele Isolt,
schoene und schoener danne golt
in Gandines ougen!"                                        (13,127 ff.)

He had been [Isolde's] knight and escort in many ways and on many
occasions, and it was on her account that he had come from Ireland to
Cornwall. She recognized him at once: "God preserve you, Sir Gandin,"
said the courteous queen. "Thank you, fair Isolde," said Gandin,
"beautiful and more beautiful than gold in Gandin's eyes."

Gandin is inspired entirely by motives of attraction to Isolde (the use of
French in the greeting is significant), and he is prepared to go to great
lengths to win her. His attitude is admirably portrayed in the scene in
which Tristan effects the rescue. He is too delicate to force himself on her,
is acutely distressed by her weeping—but in spite of her obvious misery
will not give up his plan to take her to Ireland. He wishes absolute possession and is annoyed even at the thought of Tristan's touching his lady to
put her on his horse.

Isolde has been abducted by a knight behaving like a minstrel. She
is rescued by a knight who is a musician and who uses his skill to defeat
his counterpart. Tristan's conduct is strikingly parallel to Gandin's own
in playing for reward—but there is a difference. Tristan is clever enough
to declare himself a compatriot of Gandin and to obtain a promise of a
definite reward. His playing has its usual effect on Isolde, far different
from that of Gandin, but the purpose is different. Tristan is declaring his
affinity with Isolde by playing his music, but his purpose is to gain time.
He succeeds and is able to trick Gandin by setting Isolde before him and
riding off with her while pretending to carry her through the water to the
ship. (There is a remarkable anticipation here of Tristan's carrying Isolde
at the ordeal of the hot iron.) One minstrel has tricked the other and once
again Isolde has been brought back from Ireland to her husband Mark by
Tristan's skill and courage. Gandin is left in despair—but it is a noble
emotion, not the snarling defeat of the seneschal. Gandin loved Isolde in
his way and was prepared to play the minstrel to win her but he was no
match for the true musician. Gottfried implies strongly that Tristan and
Isolde took their pleasure as they returned to court. Once again one

must ask why they returned, after Mark had proved himself so utterly incapable—and once again the answer is that both were still in the grip of those courtly conventions whose validity Gottfried denies. Tristan remarks to his sovereign on returning Isolde:

> wer gesach ie mere künigin
> durch rottenspil gemeine sin? (13,447 ff.)

> Who ever saw a queen made common property by a performance on the rote?

This is, indeed, the moral—a noble lady exchanged for a song.

Gandin was a nobleman inspired by noble motives but there are creatures at Mark's court whose conduct is the result of urges of a lower nature. Two persons, Marjodo—also a seneschal—and the dwarf Melot, seek the destruction of Tristan and Isolde because they are thwarted and jealous. Marjodo had become Tristan's friend only because he hoped through him to gain access to the queen. When he finds that she loves Tristan, his one thought is to hurt the lovers. Melot is a twisted personality who fits well into the plots made to entrap them. Here we have the lowest manifestation of *huote*, of surveillance, inspired not by any feelings of honor but merely to bring about the punishment and destruction of those happier than themselves. Such persons are the worst phenomena of "courtliness," those inspired by the basest of motives, who are themselves incapable of love and cannot understand it in others.

DECEIT AND FRUSTRATION

The love of Isolde White Hands for Tristan, with its fatal consequences, and the love of Kaedin for Brangaene would undoubtedly have been used by Gottfried as parallel illustrations of the love theme, but the unfinished state of the poem does not permit any but tentative judgments. The relationship with Isolde White Hands is best discussed as part of Tristan's own love story. It seems likely that Gottfried would have used Kaedin's pursuit of Brangaene to show a knight of great honesty of purpose who had been brought up to think of love as falling into two categories—marriage, which would be for social reasons and to which he urged both his sister Isolde and his friend Tristan, and amusement, which is what he seeks from Brangaene. In Thomas' version he recognizes that she is marvelously attractive indeed but far inferior to Isolde. Nevertheless as a bedfellow she will suit him admirably. He makes no pretense of being in love with her—as Gandin was with Isolde the Fair—nor has he the ulterior motives of the Irish seneschal. Like Tristan's father, Riwalin, he pursues pleasure where he finds it and does harm only by accident.

Gottfried shows these secondary love-incidents as relatively static. The attitudes of the Irish senschal, Mark, Gandin, Isolde White Hands, and probably Kaedin are fixed because they spring from characters and a convention which lack originality or variety. Each is capable of seeing and appreciating only one facet of the many-faceted jewel called love, and thus they each contrast in one way or another with the true love of Tristan and Isolde. For it is important to realize that this love is extremely mobile, changing its nature from one scene to another and, above all, developing. We have already seen how the ground was prepared for that love in the instruction given by Tristan to Isolde and how the tensions and proximity of life on the boat led to physical attraction and to sexual fulfillment. The pursuit and enjoyment of sexual love is the lovers' only concern for the period of their stay in court before Tristan's first exile. Consequently their life takes on the character of an intrigue in which they, aided by Brangaene, match their wits against the forces of surveillance, Mark, Marjodo, and Melot. This is the courtly game of love, the deliberate sacrifice of personal honor and loyalty to pleasure, and it is unworthy of true love. Its only justification is the fact that Mark himself is unworthy of Isolde and that he has stooped to conspiracy with the basest creatures of his court. Brangaene is a central figure in these intrigues, but it must be remembered that her loyalty is to the two Isoldes, not to Mark, and that she feels an obligation to allay the lovers' misery by bringing them together.

The attempts of Tristan and Isolde to win love by deceit are singularly unsuccessful. A series of trivial accidents leads to Marjodo's discovery that Tristan has gone to visit the queen. The thought of being alone with Tristan and under his official tutelage is enough to make Isolde give an unguarded answer to Mark's inquiry about the proper protector for her while he is away on a pilgrimage. (It may be remarked that before Marjodo's news, Mark himself would never have thought of anyone else but Tristan in this connection.) It is Brangaene who instructs Isolde in the correct course—deceit, false tears, pretended despair at Mark's impending departure. Part of this deceit is slander and protestations of hatred of Tristan. Mark's doubts are silenced. He believes what he wants to believe, but not for long. Her obvious reluctance to let Tristan depart brings back all his suspicions until, again instructed by Brangaene, she uses her charms to lull them once again. The series of episodes is entirely unedifying, each side trying to take advantage of the other with the body of Isolde as the prize. Gottfried remarks with suitable irony:

den truhsaezen Marjodo
den haete er aber mitalle do
zeinem lügenaere,
doch erm diu waren maere
und die rehten warheit
von ir haete geseit.                                        (14,229 ff.)

So as a result of all this he regarded the seneschal Marjodo as a liar, even though he had in fact given him the actual facts and the exact truth about her.

Now it is a seneschal who speaks the truth and the lovers who are liars. The conflict between love and society has reached the point where all values are reversed.

The deception continues with the conflict between the lovers and Melot. The dwarf is enlisted by Marjodo, but his motivation is spite. He envies Tristan's beauty and success. The plot is in essentials the same as Marjodo's—to put Tristan and Isolde into a compromising position where they can be observed by Mark himself. It is the differences which are important. Here for the first time we find Mark issuing direct orders that Tristan shall not be allowed in any place where he may see Isolde. Thus the lovers experience the misery of separation and anticipate what is to be their fate later in the poem:

Er unde Isot, si beide
si triben die zit mit sorge hin.
triure unde clage was under in
in micheler unmüezekeit.
si haeten leit unde leit
leit umbe Markes arcwan,
leit, daz si niht mohten han
keine state under in zwein
daz si geredeten in ein.
ietwederem begunde
von stunde ze stunde
herze unde craft geswichen

bleichen unde blichen
begunde ir varwe unde ir lip:
der man bleichete durch daz wip,
daz wip bleichete durch den man
durch Isote Tristan
durch Tristanden Isot . . .                                      (14,306 ff.)

He and Isolde both lived through a time of misery. Sadness and grief
were their constant companions. They had sorrow in two forms, one due
to Mark's suspicion, the other because they could never find an
opportunity to converse with one another. Hour by hour each began to
lose spirit and strength and their color and appearance began to flag and
grow pale: the man grew pale for the woman and the woman for the man,
Tristan because of Isolde, Isolde because of Tristan.

The passage is a fascinating example of Gottfried's stylistic technique and
will be discussed at the appropriate occasion but here it is sufficient to
observe that the emphasis is on *leit*—misery—not that intermingling of
pleasure and sorrow which is the result of true love, and on the bodily
manifestations of that sorrow. The lovers have not yet learned to live with
physical separation nor to recognize that there is a love which can overcome it. Hence their efforts are still directed to allaying Mark's suspicions
and to contriving methods by which they can defeat his ban on their meeting.
Thus their deceit continues, for by a lucky accident Mark's effort at surveillance is discovered and they are once again able to "prove their innocence" by a lying dialogue which convinces a man only too ready to be
shown that his suspicions are ill-founded. Nevertheless their love has
moved a step forward. For the first time they have experienced separation.

The motif of separation is continued in the next—and final—episode
of struggle and deceit. Tristan has been restored to favor and he, like
Brangaene and Melot, is sleeping in the same room as Mark and Isolde.
Yet he is as far separated from her as if he were miles away and Melot's
plot to trap him consists of the simple strewing of flour about her bed.
Tristan is now faced with his eternal problem. He desires Isolde but to
attain her he must sacrifice his honor and hers. He tries to overcome the
obstacle by deceit and physical prowess and apparently succeeds—except
that the blood flows from a vein which has been bled. The pattern is
consistent. It is an accident which gives him away and yet he is not
obviously guilty. The flour was untrodden, and the blood in Isolde's bed
*could* have come from Isolde's own wound. Suspicion there is but no

certainty, and for a person of Mark's temper, decision is hard. The lovers are caught in deceit and cannot escape from its toils.

Thus the lovers progress, under the pressure of physical desire, through the corruption of Brangaene and the deception of Mark to a sordid contest between their type of deceit and the craftiness of Marjodo and Melot to an attempt at the justification of their love by the ultimate deceit—that of God himself.

### THE ULTIMATE DECEPTION

The ordeal by hot iron has been much discussed as an indication of Gottfried's own attitude toward Christianity. It is much less important in this regard than for the light it throws on the attitude of the lovers to the morality of the court and to contemporary morals in general. A careful examination of the text will make this clear.

Mark's move to resolve his doubts is the first of a strictly legalistic nature.[37] His earlier suspicions had been founded on hearsay, on the statements of subordinates, all of whom had ample reason to envy Tristan and hence to slander him. Mark himself had never caught the lovers *in flagrante delicto*, in spite of the traps he laid. The evidence of the blood in the bed, however, is sufficiently strong to prompt him to take further action. His appeal to his lords is, legally, the correct thing to do. He is now having the matter judged in open court by the wisest men in the realm, but it is important to remember that this is in no sense a trial. Mark himself makes it clear that he wishes for the advice of his nobles in respect of certain rumors:

> und seitin, wie diz maere
> da ze hove ersprungen waere
> und vorhte harte sere
> siner e und siner ere . . .                                    (15,283 ff.)

> And he told them how this rumor had sprung up at court and that he
> was very concerned about his marriage and his honor.

Until these rumors are cleared up, he says, he will withdraw recognition from the queen not legally but as a person. In other words, some device must be found to settle the rumors and the onus is now on Isolde to demonstrate her innocence. It will be noted that no charges are made against her or Tristan (who has presumably left the court). It is the king's honor which is at stake here. The advice of the lords is perfectly sound:

Mark should call a formal council of both secular and religious nobles whose decisions would carry far more weight than mere advice but who would still not constitute a court.

The assembly takes place immediately after Whitsun, an ironical reversal of the usual courtly springtime, and we hear the views of only one of the lords, the Bishop of the Thames, presumably the senior cleric of England in Gottfried's view.

> Uf stuont der vürsten einer do,
> die bi dem rate waren,
> an witzen unde an jaren
> ze guotem rate wol gestalt,
> des libes edelich und alt
> beidiu grise unde wise;
> der bischof von Thamise . . .                                    (15,342 ff.)

One of the princes at the council stood up, a man well qualified by age and knowledge to give advice, dignified in appearance and old, both advanced in years and wise—the Bishop of the Thames.

The irony is clear. He had the qualifications for wisdom and looked the part—but was he really wise? The reader must judge by what follows, for now we move from the sphere of courtly intrigue to the judgments of God. The bishop's speech is a fair and balanced appraisal of the situation. He emphasizes the weakness of the case against Isolde—the lack of firm evidence and in particular the failure of any member of the court to challenge Tristan directly. Anyone can slander them, but proof is a different matter. Yet, having said this, he has to admit that it is impossible for the court to continue in this state of suspense and he advocates that Isolde be formally summoned to clear herself.

As so often in Gottfried's poem, there is a strong element of tragic irony in his speech. The reader knows that Tristan and Isolde are guilty and that the "slanders" are in fact the truth. The bishop tries to tell the court that Isolde may well be innocent because of the fact that all persons love hearing and spreading spicy rumors and his statement is perfectly justified—but in this case wrong because all the rumors fall short of the truth. We can absolve the lovers of guilt only if we accept that the morality of the court is wrong and that they are justified by a higher morality which love imposes. The courtly morality is now to be reinforced by that of conventional religion.

When Isolde is summoned before the assembly, it is the bishop who addresses her and sets the court's request before her. Again he points to the fact that it is allegations that are to be refuted, not evidence, and he invites her to clear herself. The emphasis is on the fact that she is not on trial. In terms of the story, however, the emphasis is on the fact that all depends on the kind of explanation which Isolde can give—or, if we put it more bluntly, how successful her lies will be. The situation thus reverts to the norm—lovers versus court and love maintained only by deceit— but it becomes much more crass as the deception involves not only the courtly supporters of Mark but the whole of the lords spiritual and temporal, men who are honest seekers after truth and who wish to maintain the honor both of the court and of the royal pair. Isolde's reply is a masterpiece of evasion. She condemns those who accuse her by saying that she is suffering the fate of all those in high places—but she offers no evidence to repudiate the charges against her. Her technique is to force her opponents to declare their policy so that she can make her reply. The reply comes from an unexpected quarter—Mark himself. With brutal and unusual decisiveness he asks her to prove her innocence by the ordeal of the hot iron. He has thus moved the examination of Isolde to a new plane. She is no longer called upon to explain her conduct but to place the question of innocence or guilt in the hands of God. The thoughts which Gottfried ascribes to her show her perplexity. There is nothing in her mind but the impossibility of escape from sorrow. Furthermore, she cannot even discuss the matter with Tristan:

> Isot beleip al eine da
> mit sorgen und mit leide;
> sorge unde leit diu beide
> twungen si harte sere:
> si sorgete umbe ir ere;
> so twanc si daz verholne leit,
> dazs ir unwarheit
> solte warbaeren.                                    (15,534 ff.)

Isolde remained there all alone with her care and sorrow; care and sorrow both tormented her constantly. She worried about her honor, and the secret anxiety tormented her that she would have to bring her deceit into the open.

The repetition of the words *twingen* and *sorgen* makes clear her sense of being trapped. To deceive Mark is one thing, to deceive God quite another.

> si begunde ir swaere beide lan
> an den genaedigen Crist,
> der gehülfic in den noeten ist
> dem bevalch si harte vaste
> mit gebete und mit vaste
> alle ir angest unde ir not.
> in disen dingen haete Isot
> einen list ir herzen vür geleit
> vil verre uf gotes höfscheit . . .                                    (15,544 ff.)

At this point she turned over both her difficulties to Christ the merciful who helps in trouble; with prayer and fasting she commended all her anxiety and misery to Him most strongly. In these matters Isolde had worked out in her heart a trick which stretched God's courtesy very far.

The contrasts in this passage are shocking. Isolde commends herself to Christ, "a very present help in time of trouble," with prayer and fasting. The attitude is commendable and precisely what is called for by the situation. Unfortunately it is only a part, and that the least important part, of Isolde's plan. While praying for Christ's help, she does not rely on it but works out a ruse of her own which will require Christ's polite acquiescence. He will have to bring Himself down to the level of deceit which the lovers have been practicing—the use of the term *höfscheit* is significant —if He is to cooperate, and Isolde's ruse cannot succeed unless He does cooperate, for Isolde's intention is to swear an oath that is false. It will be technically correct, for she will swear that she has lain with no man but her husband and the pilgrim who accidentally lets her fall and in the process lies in her lap. The pilgrim is Tristan, summoned by Isolde to play his part but not, so far as we know, informed of the details of the plan.

Isolde manages the scene beautifully. The pilgrim's disguise, like all her actions, is designed to create in the audience a feeling of sympathy for her humility and acquiescence in God's will. She gives away her worldly finery, dresses very carefully for the part, and prevents her attendants from punishing the clumsiness of the "pilgrim." Gottfried leaves no doubt that all this was done with the intention to deceive, not in a spirit of true humility:

> diu guote küniginne Isolt
> diu haete ir silber unde ir golt,

ir zierde und swaz si haete
an pferden unde an waete
gegeben durch gotes hulde,
daz got ir waren schulde
an ir niht gedaehte
und si zir eren braehte.                                    (15,643 ff.)

Good queen Isolde had given away to obtain God's grace her silver, her
gold, her jewelry, and all the horses and clothes she possessed so that
God would not reckon her real guilt against her and would restore her to
honor.

The offer comes very near to bribery. Her dress, too, while expressing
her contrite state, is calculated to win sympathy by more direct means:

ir ermel waren uf gezogen
vaste unz an den ellenbogen;
arme unde vüeze waren bar.
manec herze und ouge nam ir war
sware und erbermecliche;
ir gewandes unde ir liche
des wart da dicke war genomen.                              (15,661 ff.)

Her sleeves were pulled up right to the elbow; her arms and feet were
bare. Many eyes and hearts noted how sad and pitiful she looked. Her
clothing and body both were the objects of close scrutiny.

The piece is a neat variation of theme, for Isolde had last attracted attention in this way when she appeared in full regalia at the court of Ireland—
with similar results. All now depends on God's cooperation. The seneschal
Marjodo, recognizing, perhaps, that some deceit was planned, tries to
frame the oath in such a way that she could not twist it but by now she has
won enough sympathy to be able to suggest her own form of declaration
and have it accepted. As a statement it is literally true but morally wrong.
She picks up the hot iron, carries it, and is not burned. The only conclusion
is that God is on her side and is prepared to help her.

What kind of a "Christ" is this who can be twisted around in such
cavalier fashion? Gottfried's scornful remarks appear at first reading to
be the rankest blasphemy:

da wart wol goffenbaeret
und al der werlt bewaeret,
daz der vil tugenthafte Crist
wintschaffen alse ein ermel ist:
er vüeget unde suochet an,

da manz an in gesuochen kan,
alse gevuoge und alse wol,
als er von allem rehte sol.
erst allen herzen bereit,
ze durnehte und ze trügeheit.
ist ez ernest, ist ez spil,
er ist ie, swie so man wil.
daz wart wol offenbare schin
an der gevüegen künigin:
die generte ir trügeheit
und ir gelüppeter eit,
der hin ze gote gelazen was,
dazs an ir eren genas.                                             (15,733 ff.)

There it was revealed and confirmed to all the world that Christ who is so
full of virtue is as easy to turn as a windblown sleeve. He fits and clings
as closely as you want Him to, as pliantly and as well as He by rights
should do. He is ready for any heart to direct Him to honesty or deceit.
Whether it be serious or a game, He is just as you want Him to be. This
was perfectly obvious in the case of the supple queen. She was saved by
her deception and her doctored oath that went off to God, so that she
preserved her honor.

The emphasis of the passage is on "accommodation," "pliancy." Isolde
has worked out everything—is she not "diu gevüege künigin"?—and
Christ is willing to fit in with her plans. It will be noticed that there is no
word here of religion but there is an ironical use of the religious word
genas. Her honor was saved but there is no word of her soul. This Christ
has nothing to do with religion in any true sense. He is the creature of
the courts, as much a conventional figure as the seneschal and as bound to
formalities as a seneschal is. If anyone can devise a form of words which
fulfills the conditions and keeps to the rules, this Christ has no option but
to agree. Seen in this light, all the references to Christ are full of irony.
Isolde turns to "the Christ who is a help in time of trouble," the one
who is "full of qualities," not necessarily virtuous. This is the Christ of the
courts, of trials, of the hierarchy. He is as much a part of the courtly scene
as Mark and Marjodo and can be treated in the same way. He cannot, of
course, be deceived as they can and He has greater power, but if the rules
are observed He must play along. He is not concerned with morality but
with convention, and if society chooses to decide questions of right and
wrong by ordeals or hot iron, then society must abide by the result.

It is worth remarking at this point that the "deceit" of God is the ultimate example of the way in which love forces Tristan and Isolde not only to deceit but to conduct which by any standards is criminal. The most horrible example is the attempted murder of Brangaene. It is easy enough to explain the presence of the incident in the Tristan story by reference to the common motif of the substitute bride who usurped her mistress' place, but Gottfried's poem is far too sophisticated for such an explanation. He—and Thomas of Britain—could have omitted the incident without any loss to the story. The only possible explanation of Gottfried's use of it is that it illustrates the determination of Isolde to let nothing, even the life of her closest associate, stand in the way of her love for Tristan. (There is no mention that Tristan himself was involved in the plot.) Her whole action is, of course, illogical, for the murder of Brangaene must surely have aroused some comment and at the end of the episode she is at the mercy not only of Brangaene but of the two hirelings, who must have been stupid indeed not to have understood the references Brangaene made to the shifts which were white and later stained. Whatever the explanation, the scene makes brutally clear the ruthlessness of Isolde in defending her love.

The quality of this love begins to change after the ordeal. By far the most important manifestation of this change is the separation of the lovers. Tristan has fled into exile after the ordeal and from now on the normal condition of the lovers is separation. This separation gives their love a completely different quality, for sensual indulgence is no longer possible nor does it occupy the lovers to the exclusion of all else. Their love manifests itself in sympathy for the other partner and in constant consideration for the other's misery. The episode in which Tristan disposes of Urgan li vilus is remarkable less for the brutal realism of the conflict than for its motivation. Tristan is to dispose of a monster—admittedly a human, not a dragon—not in order to win a prize for himself, as the seneschal had hoped to do, but to gain for Isolde a consolation for his own absence. This consolation is the dog Petitcreiu and the peculiar nature of this little beast should be noted. It is a remarkable visual phenomenon, a thing of many colors which the eye finds it hard to grasp:

daz vremede werc von Avalun
sach man ez widerhaeres an,
son wart nie kein so wise man,
der sine varwe erkande:

> si was so maneger hande
> und so gar irrebaere
> als da kein varwe waere.                                    (15,838 ff.)

If anyone looked at this strange work from Avalon against the grain of
its coat, he could not tell its color no matter how clever a person he was.
It was so shifting and so deceptive, as if it had no color at all.

It is not hard to see the resemblance between this exciting but intangible
visual impression and that made by Isolde when playing before the court.
Such a vision defies rational comprehension. There is a further reminiscence of some significance. The description of Petitcreiu begins:

> daz was gefeinet, horte ich sagen,
> und wart dem herzogen gesant
> uz Avalun, der feinen lant,
> von einer gottinne
> durch liebe und durch minne.                               (15,806 ff.)

It was a work of magic, I am told, and had been sent to the duke by a
goddess from Avalon, the land of fairies, as a mark of love and affection.

The combination of incomparable visual beauty and ineffable music is
of supernatural origin—and the language in which it is expressed is
remarkably similar to that which describes the work of an author who
combines visual and musical beauty:

> sinen sin den reinen
> ich waene daz in feinen
> ze wundere haben gespunnen
> und haben in in ir brunnen
> geliutert und gereinet . . .                               (4699 ff.)

I think the fairies spun his clear argument in wondrous fashion and
purified and cleansed it in their fountain.

But the charm of Petitcreiu lies not in his colors, glorious though they are,
but in the music which comes from the bell hung around his neck:

> so süeze was der schellen clanc,
> daz si nieman gehorte,
> sin benaeme im und zestorte
> sine sorge und al sin ungemach.                            (15,856 ff.)

So sweet was the sound of the bell that no one ever heard it without all
his sorrow and pain being taken from him and totally banished.

The music given by the bell is not defined except by its effects. It gives a tone, not a melody, but it is capable of taking away the pain of separation from Tristan. By drawing Tristan's spirit into a harmonic relation, it takes away misery, but it should be emphasized that lack of misery is not the happiness of love. The music of Petitcreiu's bell can merely remove unhappiness, not give happiness. Tristan is now prepared to endure misery if he can remove it from Isolde, but she, who is wiser in the nature of true love, refuses to accept such a solace when she knows that Tristan must remain miserable. Such pleasure in music is not the shared harmony which is the basis of their love but the deadening of pain by sound. She rejects it because it is not mutual, leaving behind only the visual—and, for her, ineffective—beauty of the little dog.

The brief period of Tristan's acceptance at court is remarkable for two things: the absence of any planned deceit and the ultimate acceptance by Mark not so much of the lovers' guilt as of the inevitability of their love. The enforced separation of the pair makes them more eager for each other's company and Isolde's success in the ordeal of the hot iron has removed suspicion, but Gottfried makes it clear that the situation is by no means as it was before the ordeal. The desperate struggle for sexual satisfaction which marks the earlier scenes is replaced by a cooler and more realistic appraisal of the situation and by an attitude to love which gives evidence of the higher qualities shown during the Petitcreiu episode:

> wan sos ir state under in zwein
> niht wol mohten gehaben inein,
> so duhte si der wille guot,
> der gelieben dicke sanfte tuot:
> der trost und der gedinge,
> wie man daz vollebringe,
> dar an daz herze danne lit,
> daz gibet dem herzen alle zit
> lebende lust und blüende craft.
> diz ist diu rehte trutschaft,
> diz sint die besten sinne
> an liebe und an der minne:
> swa man der tat niht haben müge,
> da nach als ez der minne tüge,
> daz man ir gerne habe rat
> und neme den willen vür die tat.                    (16,411 ff.)

For when they could find no opportunity to be alone together, they

thought the intention sufficient, something which often consoles lovers.
Hope and confidence that one will achieve what one has set one's heart
on always gives the heart joy in living and blossoming strength. This is
real affection, this is the best attitude to love and attraction. Whatever
one cannot love in a way that is worthy of love should be gladly sacrificed
and the will taken for the deed.

Love can flourish and even give pleasure when fulfillment is impossible,
and indeed it is the characteristic of true love that it can exist on such
terms. Gottfried does not say, however, that his lovers were prepared to
accept the intention for the deed if the deed were possible. The highest
love still consists in the complete absorption of one personality in the
other, which is not possible at Mark's court.

The word *arcwan*, "suspicion," rises constantly to the surface of
Gottfried's narrative in all these scenes. It first appears in relation to
Brangaene's services to the lovers and in a negative context:

> daz tribens [the lovers and Brangaene] alse lise,
> daz nie nieman dervan
> dekeinen arcwan gewan                                           (12,962 ff.)

They did it so unobtrusively that there was not the least suspicion.

Suspicion becomes positive when Tristan realizes that Marjodo has seen
that he has visited Isolde (13,629) and it then spreads to Mark. From now
on Mark and *arcwan* are constantly linked:

> in leideten beide
> der zwivel unde der arcwan,
> den er haete und muose han:
> er arcwande genote
> sin herzeliep Isote . . .                                      (13,753 ff.)

Both doubt and suspicion tormented him, which he had and could not
help having: he was deeply suspicious of Isolde, his heart's love.

There is no escape from *arcwan* for Mark, or from its consequences for
the lovers. *Arcwan* and *zwivel* ("doubt") dominate the courtly scene and
particularly its representative, Mark himself. Gottfried makes this clear
in his disclosure of the king's state of mind (13,749 ff.). The word occurs at
each crisis of the relations between Mark and the lovers:

> "ir griffet aber morgen wider
> an iuweren arcwan als e."                                       (15,020 f.)

"But tomorrow you will take up your suspicions again."

—and suspicion is put aside (15,030). But the incident of the blood in the bed revives it (15,237). Suspicion continues into the trial scene (15,388) but at the end is gone:

> al sin herze und al sin muot
> diu waren niwan an si geleit
> ane aller slahte valscheit.
> sin zwivel und sin arcwan
> die waren aber do hin getan.                    (15,760 ff.)

His heart and mind were set wholly on her with no trace of deceit. His doubt and suspicion had been put away.

Suspicion returns when Mark observes the love in the lovers' glances and this time there is no question of the production of evidence of deceit but of the sheer physical impact of jealousy:

> daz was so rehte minneclich,
> so süeze und also senerich
> daz ez im an sin herze gie
> und solhen zorn da von gevie,
> solhen nit und solhen haz,
> daz er diz unde daz,
> zwivel unde arcwan
> allez zeiner hant lie gan:
> im haete leit unde zorn
> sinne unde maze verlorn                         (16,507 ff.)

It was truly loving, so sweet and full of yearning that it went to his heart and caused him so much rage, so much envy and hatred that he was at once rid of doubt and suspicion. His misery and hate had lost all sense and proportion.

This is the point at which cunning and deceit cease to be of significance and the epoch of the clever lovers and the suspicious husband has no further significance. Mark now has to face the definite knowledge of love between his wife and his nephew, not because of reports from Marjodo or Melot but on the evidence of his own eyes. And this will be the situation from now on. Mark sees for himself and must make up his own mind. His reaction at this point is to state that he can no longer watch them and that they must leave the court. This is, of course, a punishment, exile, but it means that the lovers can, for the first time, be together without interference. The powers of court and convention are now pushed aside for the first time in the poem and they are abandoned at the instance of their most important representative, Mark himself. The lovers now have the opportunity to fulfill their love without interference and thus to realize its fullest potential. Here, if anywhere, is to be found Gottfried's view on the true love.

The episode of the grotto of love is the most carefully constructed of all the scenes in the poem, for it is here that Gottfried's treatment of love reaches its climax. It is at one and the same time an incident in the story of Tristan and Isolde and an allegorical treatment of the highest form of love. Although the lovers are naturally the center of the scene, they are the human part of a total representation of the phenomenon of love, exemplary figures in a picture of love's harmony. It is anachronistic to speak here of the conceptions of microcosm and macrocosm, yet the cave of lovers is a microcosm which corresponds to the macrocosm of universal harmony—and so is every pair of Tristan-lovers in a similar situation anywhere in the world. The imagery used by the poet to depict his ideal love is worthy of detailed study.

First he takes care to emphasize the remoteness of the grotto from all contemporary civilization. Spatial separation is indicated by the barren land which the lovers must traverse for two days before reaching the cave and by the great wild forest which stretches without cultivated land below the mountain in which the cave is hollowed:

> aber umbe und umbe hin ze tal
> da stuonden boume ane zal ...                          (16,733 f.)
>
> von disem berge und disem hol
> so was ein tageweide wol
> velse ane gevilde
> und wüeste unde wilde.
> darn was dekein gelegenheit
> an wegen noch stigen hingeleit ...                     (16,761 ff.)

> But all around and down the slope stood countless trees.... For a full
> day's journey from this mountain and cave there stretched rocks without
> cultivated fields, wasteland, and wilderness. There was no way of
> reaching it by roads and paths.

Such separation in space is only an indication of the spiritual separation which is indicated by the leaving of Brangaene at court and the sending back of Curvenal, Tristan's old tutor. The courtly attendants are no longer with them, and of the trappings of courtly life only the dog Hiudan and the crossbow, the symbols of the hunt, remain. The separation in time is more subtle. The cave of lovers was something created before the Christian era, something long unknown but rediscovered by Tristan in the course of a hunt:

> daz selbe hol was wilent e
> under der heidenischen e
> vor Corineis jaren.
> do risen da herren waren,
> gehouwen in den wilden berc.
> dar inne haetens ir geberc,
> so sir heinliche wolten han
> und mit minnen umbe gan.
> und swa der einez vunden wart,
> daz was mit ere bespart
> und was der Minnen benant:
> la fossiure a la gent amant ...                              (16,689 ff.)

This same cave had been hewn into the grim mountain in pagan times, before the reign of Corineis, when giants ruled. Here they had their hiding place when they wished to be private and make love. And whenever a cave like this was found, it was barred off by a bronze door and a dedication set on it: la fossiure a la gent amant.

Love is a pre-Christian phenomenon and the expression "vor Corineis jaren" is intended to indicate a period even before Cornwall became a kingdom.[38] The giants, too, are symbols of remote antiquity, of a time before history began, as they are in the Old Testament ("And there were giants in the land," Genesis 6:4). These men of times long past shared with Tristan and Isolde the need to escape from society and devote themselves to love in secrecy, and the caves they found were marked for all time as devoted to love by the addition of a bronze door and a superscription in the universal language of love. Time disappears when lovers enter this cave, for it is devoted to love and separated from all the transient features of human society.

The cave itself is not a natural hollow in the rock but the work of human hands. Its form shows the harmony and proportions of a temple devoted to love and is illuminated by the pure light of heaven, and its door divides the initiated from the uninitiated. The landscape is that of eternal spring but the description is not the spring *topos* of the Riwalin episode. We were told that when Riwalin visited the court of Mark it was indeed May and springtime. There is no indication that it was spring when Tristan and Isolde left the court. In the area of the grotto it was always spring, as it was in the Fortunate Isles and the kingdom of Phaeacia. These are not two different landscapes, as Gottfried is at pains to indicate by carefully effected similarities in his descriptions, but one of them is in time and one out of the reach of time. The description of the eternal landscape of love is Gottfried's, not the vision which the lovers see. At this point we are given merely the slightest indication of the suspended situation in time and space.

The reader is brought back abruptly to the courtly situation in time and place by the brief description of the arrangements made by the lovers to cover their retreat. Curvenal spreads the story that they are in Ireland, in the other courtly world. In other words, he continues the courtly deceit but this time merely to allow the lovers to move out of courtly society altogether. He and Brangaene are to ensure that the courtly world does not intrude on the world of the grotto. The transition to the grotto world is effected by Gottfried's own discussion of the relation between the maintenance of physical existence in the normal world and the life of the lovers in the cave. He states specifically that the lovers had no material food. They fed upon the light from the eyes of the other and needed nothing else. Such a situation could arise only in a world removed from time where material needs were suspended. There is an element of parody in the lovers who go without food because of their great love, but such an element is incidental. Tristan and Isolde needed no food because they no longer belonged to the world of time. Nor do they need company. Company is the presence of society and its demands and conventions, a presence with which love is completely incompatible. Gottfried reinforces his argument by direct reference to King Arthur and his court, the apogee of company and courtliness. His presence and that of all his court, so much admired in most romances, were vastly inferior to the society of two people. For true lovers Arthur's court is to be avoided, not sought after. The great ceremonial feasts of that court are insignificant compared with the intense emotion of two lovers alone.

By his disquisition on spiritual and material sustenance, Gottfried has bridged the gap between the courtly world and the cave of lovers. He now proceeds to describe that cave in its timeless and enduring aspects by a timeless and enduring technique, that of allegory, which makes universal all experience. The fact of the cave's existence is revealed in the kind of ambiguous terms which Gottfried loves:

> durch welher slahte meine
> diu fossiure in dem steine
> betihtet waere, als si was.
> si was, als ich iezuo da las . . .                                     (16,925 ff.)

> . . . what the meaning was when I fashioned the cave in the rock, as it actually was. It was, as I have recounted . . .

What is the precise meaning of "betihtet"? Fashioned, indeed, but whether in fact or in words is not certain, and the uncertainty is increased by the juxtaposition "waere—als si was—si was" and the rhyming groups "als si was" and "als ich las." Had Gottfried merely read of the cave? Was it in the end a fiction? We might think so, if Gottfried did not tell us in line 17,100 that he *knew* all this, for he had visited the cave frequently. Once again the poet calls our attention to the fact that he is writing an exemplary story, that his words are intended to create a world in which all lovers can find solace and not merely to tell a pleasant story of two fictional lovers. Each of the elements in his cave has an existence for Tristan and Isolde as part of the surroundings in which they reach the highest phase of their love, but those same elements exist as eternal verities in the total experience of love for all men.

The qualities represented by the physical features of the cave are abstract and largely moral virtues: *einvalte*, "simplicity," in the sense of "straightforwardness" or lack of complications; *craft*, "power"; *hohe muot*, "aspiration," the exaltation given by the power of love; *staete*, "constancy" or persistence in love. *Wisheit*, "wisdom," and *sinne* (the senses or good sense), represented by the cedar bar, show the eternal wisdom of love which surpasses all other knowledge, while the bar of ivory shows *kiusche* and *reine*, "chastity" and "purity," the qualities which distinguish true love from gross passion. Such are the qualities of love guarded by *guote andaht*, "good thoughts," the correct attitude, perhaps, or good intention, and the golden key of *linge*, "success," and illuminated by the qualities of their social milieu, *güete*, "goodness," *diemüete*, "humility," and *zuht*, "proper behavior," the quality which comes from good breeding. It will be obvious that many of these qualities are those so often mentioned as characteristic of "courtly love" both in the lyric and in the romance. Gottfried never denies the importance of these qualities, but closer examination soon shows that the virtues are not merely social but are to be applied between the two lovers only. Isolde's love for Tristan can hardly be called chaste in any conventional sense of the term. It is chaste only because Isolde has no love for anyone but Tristan, even though marriage forces her to give her body to Mark. Love must be without deceit:

> einvalte zimet der minne wol,
> diu ane winkel wesen sol;
> der winkel, der an minnen ist
> daz ist akust unde list.                                    (16,933 ff.)

Simplicity is right for love, since it should have no angles. Any angle connected with love is cunning and sharp practice.

Yet the lovers have just passed through a long series of episodes of which deceit was the principal characteristic. They have not practiced this deceit against love, however, but against the forces which are kept out of the cave by the brazen door. Gottfried in describing the temple in which love flourishes endows it with what he considers the universal qualities of love but makes it clear that these qualities apply to love between two persons, not to the relation of those persons with their milieu. For in the cave of lovers there is no milieu but the lovers' two hearts.

The allegory has another and larger dimension which it derives from the use of allegorical and exegetical interpretation of the Scriptures and in particular of the allegory of the church building in terms of the *Ecclesia Dei*.[39] The fact that the individual parts of the cave are allegorized in a fashion similar to the parts of the Christian church is much less important than the fact that the parallel allegory is made at all. For just as the Christian allegory can be valid only through the assumption that an *Ecclesia Dei*, a unity of Christian souls in God, exists in eternity, so the allegory of the cave has validity only if a community of lovers exists in the spirit of love. As the church in which Christians worship represents in its parts the qualities and virtues which bind the souls of the worshipers with God and each other, so the cave of love symbolizes those qualities which the lovers—and we would not be wrong to call them *edele herzen*—share with each other and derive from universal love itself. In a church the light from the windows falls upon the altar, in the cave upon the crystalline bed which is in the middle of the grotto and in which love reaches its full consummation, as the Christian ceremony reaches its highest significance in the Eucharist. For just as the Eucharist is transformed from physical to spiritual substance, so love, though expressed in physical terms, is transformed in the crystalline bed into a higher form. Yet as the Eucharist depends upon the original bread and wine, so the love of Tristan and Isolde depends upon physical union.

Gottfried's own role in this allegory is that of an interpreter and prophet. The cave is seen through his eyes, not those of the lovers, who never speak during the whole scene. He speaks not merely as would an omniscient narrator, in the third person, but as one who has actually been in the cave and experienced it. This interpreter's role is important, for it makes of the poet one of the elect, who was thought worthy to open the brazen door not once but many times but who in spite of his knowledge and understanding never slept in the crystalline bed. The poet remains the priest, the seer, the interpreter, not the participator—or the martyr. And it is here that we must examine the role of Tristan and Isolde themselves. For they are above even the general community of lovers for whom the cave exists.

The lovers are described as the "getriuwe massenie," the persons who are at home here. They are perfectly attuned to the sights and sounds of the cave and enjoy them from morn to eve. As the sun rises to its zenith, so they approach the climax of their love:

so giengen si zer linden
nach den linden winden,
diu bar in aber danne lust
uzen und innerhalp der brust.                                    (17,169 ff.)

They went to the linden tree for its soothing breezes. This brought them delight, both in their hearts and outside them.

They approach the linden, the tree of love, which brings them joy—a clear reference to the association between ideal love and ideal spring. Their occupation is the telling of tales of unhappy love, at first sight a strange occupation for two lovers who have been left alone for the first time and who have reached the highest manifestation of their love. The stories, however, concern those whose love has foundered on the

opposition of society—Phyllis of Thrace, Byblis, Dido—and it is the fate of
these, so similar to their own, which Tristan and Isolde are bewailing.
Up to now the lovers have been in the open air and have participated in
the love phenomena of the world of sight and of nature. Later they withdraw into the grotto itself to commune with one another in a different
fashion:

> Sos aber der maere denne
> vergezzen wolten under in;
> so slichens in ir cluse hin
> und namen aber ze handen,
> dar ans ir lust erkanden,
> und liezen danne clingen
> ir harphen unde ir singen
> senelichen unde suoze.                                    (17,200 ff.)

But when they wanted to forget such stories, they slipped away to their
retreat and took up again the delights they knew so well. They played on
the harp and sang their songs both sad and sweet.

The word *vergezzen* is important. The lovers are deliberately dissociating
themselves from these conflicts of lovers with society and withdrawing
into a shrine where no hint of such conflicts penetrates. Here the disharmony of the outside world, the discord between the desires of the lovers
and the conventions of the world in which they must live, can be safely
ignored, and the lovers can indulge in that harmony of sight and sound of
which they alone are capable. It will be observed that there is a marked
difference between the musical accomplishments of the lovers here and
those described on earlier occasions. When Tristan played at the courts
of Cornwall and Ireland, and Isolde played before her father's court, all
the stress is on the effect of their playing on the members of their audience.
There is no such description here. The stress is on the performance and
particularly on the mutuality of their efforts. The singing and the harp
playing are inextricably joined, so that it is impossible to tell what contribution to the harmony each of the two lovers is making. So perfect is
their unison that the cave can be rededicated to their love. The cave, which
was only one of many caves given over to love by the giants, has been
made into a special shrine of harmony. "La gent amant" has taken on a
completely new connotation. It no longer signifies merely those who love
but a special group of lovers, "*la* gent amant." Tristan and Isolde are the

culmination of all the devotions to love which had been made in the cave
since time began:

> swaz aber von der fossiure
> von alter aventiure
> vor hin ie was bemaeret,
> daz wart an in bewaeret.
> diu ware wirtinne
> diu haete sich dar inne
> alrerste an ir spil verlan:
> swaz e dar inne ie wart getan
> von kurzewile oder von spil,
> dazn lief niht ze disem zil;
> ezn was niht von meine
> so luter noch so reine,
> als ir spil was under in.                                    (17,225 ff.)

All the ancient stories ever told about the cave were made real in them.
The true mistress of the place now realized her sport to the full. Any
amusements and games that had taken place there before never reached
this height. In its spirit it was not so clear and pure as theirs was.

Not only does their love mark the supreme hour of the cave of lovers but
it also marks the supreme hour of the lovers themselves. Here and here
only can they devote themselves entirely to each other:

> si taten niht wan allez daz,
> da si daz herze zuo getruoc.                                 (17,240 f.)

They did exactly what their hearts demanded.

Love completely separated from society reaches complete fulfillment.

The amusements of the lovers, those things which fill the day, consist
of music, which is the harmony of their love, and hunting. This hunting
is very unlike that which forms the staple amusement of the medieval
court. There is no ceremonial, no yelping pack of hounds, no breaking up
of the stag, no eating of the deer's flesh. The hunt is a simple expedition
by the two lovers with a dog trained not to give tongue and a crossbow to
do silent execution. This is a sharp contrast with the noisy and colorful
hunting ceremonial by means of which Tristan had first introduced
himself to Mark's court, yet it brings the reader back to the reality of the
story, to the present state of the lovers. Unusual though their hunt is, it
is still a hunt and it leads almost imperceptibly to another lover and
another hunter of a very different kind.

Mark, too, was suffering the misery of deprivation and wished to console himself with the chase. He mounts a hunt with full panoply of hounds and men and is led by a strange hart in the direction of the cave. Once again a hunt is bringing Tristan and him together. His approach has been heralded with all the clamor of dogs and sounding of horns that accompany a king's hunting retinue, and Tristan and Isolde are brought back to the realities of their position. Once again they experience the aural and visual delights of their landscape and retire to their crystalline bed— but with a sword between them. They return to the world of compromise and deceit.

Mark cannot enter the cave. His impression of it is entirely a visual one derived from his view through the window, as his view of Isolde is entirely one of external beauty. Just as he had been moved to send the lovers away by the sight of Isolde's beauty offered to Tristan, so now he is moved to an altogether irrational forgiveness by his yearning for Isolde's beauty as it lies before his eyes on the crystalline bed. His doubts are resolved not by any argument but by "der minnen übergulde,/ diu guldin unschulde" ("the superiority of love, the golden innocence"):

> diu zoch im ougen unde sin
> mit ir gespenstikeite hin,
> hin da der osterliche tac
> aller siner vröude lac.
> er schouwete ie genote
> sines herzen wunne Isote,
> diun geduhtin ouch da vor und e
> nie so rehte schoene me.                                        (17,553 ff.)

It drew his eyes and senses with its magic to where the Easter day of all his joy lay. He kept gazing at his heart's delight, Isolde, who had never seemed to him before so beautiful as now.

He devours her with his eyes and demonstrates once again his appetite for Isolde's beauty and his total lack of understanding of her nature.

Does Gottfried imply that the lovers would have lived on forever in the cave if they had not been discovered? Here they had secured at last that separation from the court which alone could allow them to find love in its fullest sense. They had taken care to cover their tracks by giving out that they were in Ireland, they had left Brangaene and Curvenal to report any danger. They have even achieved a degree of withdrawal which enables them to live without physical sustenance. Yet one has the feeling that such an existence could not continue indefinitely. In time the hunt will catch them. To continue such an idyll would imply that love can exist by a deliberate withdrawal from society, that the forces of social convention can be kept at bay by imitating a hermit and living the life of a recluse. Gottfried does not condemn such a life. On the contrary, he regards it as the highest human experience. It is simply that society, jealous of true love, will perpetually break in.

It is clearly impossible for the lovers to stay in the cave once they have been discovered. Mark can order his wife back to court and dismiss Tristan—or even kill them both. That he does not do so is due to Isolde's beauty—but separation is inevitable. They naturally rejoice that their honor is restored and that they can lift up their heads again but the price they have to pay is only too clear:

> die vröude haetens aber do
> vil harter unde mere
> durch got und durch ir ere
> dan durch iht anders, daz ie wart:
> si kerten wider uf ir vart
> an ir herschaft als e;
> sin wurden aber niemer me
> in allen ir jaren
> so heinlich, sos e waren,
> nochn gewunnen nie zir vröuden sit
> so guote state so vor der zit.                          (17,696 ff.)

> But the joy was far more on account of God and their honor than for any other reason. They went back the way they had come to the glory that had been theirs. But never again in all their years would they be so private as they were then, nor did they ever again have such a good opportunity for their delight as they then had.

This is the fact, simply stated, which has been made more elaborately in the allegory of the *Minnegrotte*: only away from society can true love flourish. Once again the scene is dominated by Mark, the doubter, the waverer, and life becomes a series of pointless compromises. Once again the lovers find themselves beset by constant surveillance, and Gottfried interrupts his narrative to point out the stupidity of any attempts to control love by such means. His discussion, which will be examined in more detail elsewhere, points out the total ineffectiveness of attempts to control a woman's love by supervision. A man who is held to his lady only by lust will often delude himself that she loves him merely as an excuse to hold her, although the evidence of her love for another is clear before his eyes. No one can blame the woman who revolts against such treatment. Indeed, it encourages the daughters of Eve in the characteristic they have inherited—the yearning for forbidden fruit. The finest women rise above such temptations of their own accord by bestowing themselves on one person whom they truly love and thus subject the desires of their body to the service of honor.

Gottfried's discussion is remarkable in its acceptance—or apparent acceptance—of the Church's tenet that the daughters of Eve were by their very nature prone to sexual adventure and the lusts of the flesh. He is even more remarkable in his rejection of the conventional solution to the problem, that they should be subjected to perpetual supervision to prevent them from sinning. Indeed, the concept of sin is not relevant to his argument. The only determining factor is the woman's honor, and here he uses the term *ere* in a manner far different from its normal significance. It is the woman's own concept of dignified and noble behavior which is meant, not compliance with conventional standards of behavior. It was with this latter form of "honor" that Isolde had been concerned when she urged Brangaene to take her place in the marriage bed and when she had gone to such lengths to deceive Mark. All that is past. True honor consists in the giving of love where love has meaning. Mark is no longer being deceived, for he is the victim of that very bodily desire which is ascribed to the daughters of Eve and has no one but himself to blame for his deception. In Gottfried's view only the woman herself can make the decision where her love should go, not her parents, her husband, or society itself. Gottfried is not advocating adultery but the freedom of women to love the man of their choice. He despises promiscuity as deeply as any Puritan but not on the same grounds. Not religion but a woman's own delicacy should forbid it.

Gottfried states and Isolde recognizes that her situation is impossible in medieval courtly society, but she also knows that her love no longer depends entirely on the physical presence of Tristan. Mark's discovery of them actually in bed together, firmly locked in each other's arms, puts an end to doubt, to any hope that Tristan can remain close to his beloved, and to a chapter in their love. The whole essence of their love as it must now be appears in Isolde's reply to Tristan's hurried and somewhat conventional farewell. Refusing to give him at once the farewell kiss he asks for, she addresses him for the last time in Gottfried's poem in a speech of brilliant intaglio whose meaning and substance are reflected in the constantly shifting images of unity and separation, life and death, joy and sorrow and unending love. She brushes aside the question of her ever forgetting Tristan—they have suffered too much together for that. She knows too that it is to Tristan that she has dedicated her whole being and has no fear that her own love will ever be shaken. Her worry is that there may be some other woman who will enter his life while they are apart:

> "nu sehet, daz mich kein lebende wip
> iemer von iu gescheide,
> wir ensin iemer beide
> der liebe unde der triuwe
> staete unde niuwe,
> diu lange und alse lange vrist
> so reine an uns gewesen ist."                                    (18,300 ff.)

"See that no living woman ever separates me from you to prevent us from being ever faithful and ever new in our love and constancy, that love which has been so enduring and for so much time has been pure within us."

After giving him a ring, the traditional token of remembrance, the unending circle, she interweaves images which make unity of separation and life of death:

> "gedenket an diz scheiden,
> wie nahen ez uns beiden
> ze herzen und ze libe lit.
>
>          .   .   .
>
> wart Isot ie mit Tristane
> ein herze unde ein triuwe,
> so ist ez iemer niuwe,
> so muoz ez iemer staete wern ..."                               (18,315 ff.)

"Think of this parting and how deeply it affects us both in heart and person. If ever Isolde was one heart and bond with Tristan, it must be always new, always enduring."

The variations of *iuwer* and *iu* appear over and over again—"iuwer lip,"
"iuwer leben"—but these really belong to the other:

> "ein lip, ein leben daz sin wir
> nu bedenket ie genote
> mich, iuwern lip, Isote.
> lat mich an iu min leben sehen,
> soz iemer schierest müge geschehen,
> und sehet ouch ir daz iure an mir
> unser beider leben daz leitet ir.
> nu gat her und küsset mich:
> Tristan und Isot, ir und ich,
> wir zwei sin iemer beide
> ein dinc ane underscheide."                              (18,344 ff.)

> "We are one life, one body. Think always on me, your very life, Isolde.
> Let me see my life in you as soon as it may be and you see yours in me.
> You have both our lives in your power. Now come and kiss me: Tristan
> and Isolde, you and I, are both one and inseparable."

Isolde produces no high-flown sentiments, merely the simple statement that
each does not exist without the other. The force of her declaration lies
in the fact that it is made at a time when physical separation is inevitable
and when there is no foreseeable possibility of their ever again being
together. So far as Isolde is concerned, their love is now assured even if
they are physically separated forever. Tristan has made no such declaration
and his testing is yet to come, for Gottfried makes it clear that Isolde has
understood the basis of true love, but Tristan, her instructor and companion
in harmony, is still subject to the pressures of society.

LOVE IN ABSENCE

To this problem the rest of the poem is devoted. Tristan is unable to
forget Isolde or to live without her but he is also unable to satisfy himself
with the spiritual and emotional attachment which Isolde enjoys. Her
position is very different from his. While Isolde is compelled by her
marriage to Mark to submit to his love-making and thus participate
physically in an act of love while desiring to abstain, Tristan is obliged to
remain celibate in every sense if he is to remain faithful to Isolde.

His meeting with Isolde White Hands is almost a parody of the first
meeting with Isolde the Fair. After his victory over the giant Urgan li

vilus his standing at the court of Kaedin is very much like that at the court of Mark and the court of Ireland:

> Hie mite was aber Tristande
> da ze hove und da ze lande
> vil lobes und eren uf geleit.                          (18,949 ff.)

At this Tristan was loaded with praise and honor at court and throughout the land.

It is at this stage that he is thrown into the company of Kaedin's sister. For Tristan it is inconceivable that he should love any other woman than Isolde. She is interwoven into his thinking and feeling and had urged him to give no other woman a place in his heart. But before him there is another Isolde, beautiful and attainable. Tristan does not love her but he cannot ignore her, life is lonely and wretched and she is attractive. Gottfried's masterly portrayal of his emotions hinges on the name, for the name is the person and one Isolde must share the characteristics of the other. It is, of course, foolish for Tristan to think that he can assuage his yearning for the absent Isolde by allowing his glances to stray to the one who is before him. Beauty is personal and gazing upon the beauty of Isolde White Hands will not bring back the beauty of Isolde the Fair. With whatever loyalty to his own Isolde he looks on Kaedin's sister, it is the new Isolde who is attracting him. He is torn this way and that not because he really confuses the two but because he cannot reconcile his loyalty with the physical attraction which draws him to Isolde White Hands, and he consequently tries to rationalize his conduct by thinking of the one in terms of the other.

Tristan's dilemma is ironical, for he is faced with a situation totally different from that which he faced with Isolde the Fair and one far more conventional and favorable to the progress of his love. At the court of Ireland he was at first known as a poor minstrel of unusual talents, only to be revealed as the mortal enemy of the Irish royal family who is nevertheless in a position to bring misery to Isolde the Fair. He is at once Isolde's tutor and her dependent, and their love manifests itself slowly in music and harmony as well as physical attraction. At Kaedin's court Tristan is a famous warrior to whom his host is much beholden, and it is both natural and socially desirable that Tristan should be attracted by Isolde. Kaedin is perfectly prepared to encourage any moves which one of them may make in the direction of the other, and it would be the easiest thing in the world for Tristan to take Isolde as his bride—as did in fact happen in Thomas' version and certainly would have done so in Gottfried's had he finished his poem. The attraction of the pair is depicted very much in the manner of courtly romance—the eyes which respond, the coyness, the questioning. But the irony lies in the fact that the surface relationship between the two, which conforms to the ideal picture of courtly love, has no real relevance to the true state of affairs. Tristan does not ask himself whether Isolde White Hands loves him, nor does he torment himself with the impossibility of winning her but rather with the resemblance between his own Isolde and the lady who is near him, while Isolde White Hands deludes herself that his attention to her springs entirely from admiration. Thus on the one occasion in the poem when love is possible in a conventional situation, it is vitiated by the fact that Tristan's love is already committed to Isolde the Fair. His lady is only too ready to receive his advances, but when they are made it is from reasons which are totally different from those she anticipates. Here the lady needs to worry whether the man really loves her, while the man makes motions which do not mean what they appear to mean.

The difference between the love which appears in gesture, form, and outward appearance and that which really exists between two persons in harmony—in other words, the difference between the love which Gottfried has just described as the manifestation of the highest qualities of a woman and love which is no better than lust—is admirably illustrated in the intellectual and musical relationship between the two Isoldes. Isolde the Fair and Tristan invariably share their musical and intellectual experiences, once Tristan has imparted to her the skill and knowledge which make such participation possible. Isolde White Hands is of a very different type. She is utterly passive, receptive, incapable of a positive contribution:

> dor an der megede gesach
> ir senelichez ungemach,
> daz sich daz üeben began,
> do leiter sinen vliz dar an,
> daz er ir vröude baere:
> er seitir schoeniu maere,
> er sang ir, er schreib unde er las;
> und swaz ir kurzewile was
> do zuo was er gedanchaft:

er leistir geselleschaft,
er kürzet ir die stunde
etswenne mit dem munde
und underwilen mit der hant
       .  .  .

so daz gesinde in ein gesaz,
er unde Isot und Kaedin,
der herzog und diu herzogin,
vrouwen und barune,
so tihteter schanzune,
rundate und höfschiu liedelin
und sang ie diz refloit dar in:
"Isot ma drue, Isot mamie,
en vus ma mort, en vus ma vie!"
und wan er daz so gerne sanc,
so was ir aller gedanc
und wanden ie genote,
er meinde ir Isote . . .                                    (19,183 ff.)

When he saw that the girl was continually suffering from the miseries of
love, he turned all his attention to entertaining her. He told her pleasant
stories, he sang to her, he wrote and read and gave attention to keeping
her amused. He kept her company, he whiled away the time for her,
sometimes by singing, sometimes by playing. . . . When all the court was
sitting together, he and Isolde and Kaedin, the duke and the duchess,
ladies and barons, he composed *chansons*, *rondeaux*, and courtly songs
and always added this refrain:

> Isolde my dear, Isolde my love,
> in you my death, in you my life.

And since he so enjoyed singing it, everyone thought and was firmly of
the opinion that he meant their Isolde.

The resemblances between this description and those in which Tristan
and Isolde the Fair are involved are obvious—and so are the differences:

sit gie diu junge künigin
alle zit ze siner lere:
an die so leite er sere
sinen vliz und sine stunde;
daz beste daz er kunde
so schuollist, so hantspil,
daz ich niht sunder zalen wil,
daz leite er ir besunder vür,
daz si nach ir selber kür

ze lere dar uz naeme,
swes so si gezaeme.
Isot diu schoene tet also:
daz allerbeste, daz si do
under allen sinen listen vant,
des underwant si sich zehant
und was ouch vlizec dar an,
swess in der werlde began.                                    (7962 ff.)

After that the young queen went to him for instruction every day. He
devoted much time and attention to her. He put before her in turn his
best attainments in academic learning and the playing of instruments,
which I will not list in detail, so that she could make her own choice of
what instruction suited her best. So the fair Isolde did this: she mastered
the very best that she could find among his skills and pursued
conscientiously anything that there was to be done.

Both passages show Tristan conscientiously at work ("leite sinen vliz")
but with Isolde the Fair he was teaching her "daz beste, daz er kunde" and
she "tet also daz allerbeste daz si do under allen sinen listen vant." With
Isolde White Hands the purpose is entirely entertainment—*vröude,
schoene maere, kurzewile*—a very different purpose and one suspiciously
close to the activities which Gottfried damns with faint praise in his
preface as being characteristic of love which seeks nothing but joy.
Tristan's music is being debased, and this is pointed up sharply in the
court scene. Tristan sings, Isolde White Hands listens. She learns nothing
from him and clearly understands nothing, for she and the whole court
think that Tristan is playing his music for her and fail to grasp the essential
point that Tristan's music is mutual and not mere performance. The effect
of the music of Tristan and Isolde the Fair, both singly and together, is to
deprive the audience, even a courtly audience, of its powers of reason and
to hand the lovers over to the irrational powers of love.

arme unde riche
si haeten an ir beide
eine saelige ougenweide,
der oren und des herzen lust:
uzen und innerhalp der brust
da was ir lust gemeine.
diu süeze Isot, diu reine
si sang in, si schreip und si las;
und swaz ir aller vröude was,

das was ir banekie.
si videlt ir stampenie . . .
si sang ir pasturele,
ir rotruwange und ir rundate,
schanzune, refloit und folate
wol unde wol und alze wol:
wan von ir wart manc herze vol
mit senelicher trahte,
von ir wart maneger slahte
gedanke und ahte vür braht.                              (8048 ff.)

Rich and poor, they both found in her a delightful feast for the eye and a
pleasure for the ear and heart. Their pleasure was the same within and
without their breast. Sweet and glorious Isolde, she sang to them, she
wrote, she read; and what gave them all pleasure was a delight for her.
She fiddled her *estample* . . . she sang her *pastourelle*, her *rotruange*, her
*rondeau*, her *chanson*, her refrain, her *folate*, well and well and all too well;
for as a result many a heart was full of yearning emotion and many
thoughts and ideas flourished.

The resemblances to Tristan's performances are clear, even to the mention
of a particular type of song and the virtual repetition of a line ("er sang
ir," etc.), but Gottfried dwells on the richness of her performance and
even more on its effect:

. . . so was der tougenliche sanc
ir wunderlichiu schoene,
diu mit ir muotgedoene
verholne und tougen
durch diu venster der ougen
in vil manic edele herze sleich
und daz zouber dar in streich,
daz die gedanke zehant
vienc und vahende bant
mit sene und mit seneder not.                           (8122 ff.)

The secret song was her amazing beauty which in secret slipped unaware
through the windows of the eyes with her sound of the spirit into many a
noble heart and spread its magic there; so that she captured their thoughts
at once and in taking them bound them with desire and the misery of
desire.

These effects are similar to those Tristan produces when he first sings at
the court of Mark, but his performance before Kaedin and Isolde is only

a shadow. Superficially it is the same, but the audience does not consist of *edele herzen* and his own singing suffers in consequence. All he does is to convey to an audience which cannot appreciate his artistry his longing for his love—which that audience promptly interprets as a love song addressed to Isolde White Hands. Each audience reacts only according to its nature, and Kaedin and his sister are affected only as courtly beings of a lower order. They are deprived of their reason in quite a different way.

It will be noted that in the descriptions of the relation between Tristan and Isolde White Hands there is no mention of *moraliteit* or of any accomplishments possessed by her other than physical beauty. It is on that basis only that Tristan is attracted to her—and by the fact that she is called Isolde and is close to him every day. There is no question of her taking the place of Isolde the Fair or even of her acting as a substitute. She can function, as Tristan realizes, only on the lowest plane of love, that of physical intercourse. He feels that his yearning for Isolde the Fair can be in part assuaged by physical love for another and believes, or pretends to believe, that Isolde's case is by no means as desperate as his own, because she has Mark as bed-companion. If Tristan believes this, he has not understood Isolde's love for him and has forgotten that throughout their love experience she has had to endure the treatment from Mark which he now regards as a partial recompense for his own absence. His confusion is total, his music unable to convey its true meaning, his love wavering. In spite of the fact that he was the instructor of Isolde the Fair, he does not grasp the essential nature of the love when faced by physical separation.

From now on Gottfried would presumably have traced the growing realization on Tristan's part that there was no life without Isolde the Fair and from this Tristan would move to a limbo of living with Isolde White Hands while still making plans for clandestine visits to Isolde the Fair. Thence would follow a slow decline and death while waiting in vain for the arrival of the only person who could give him back the gift of life.

We have traced the development of the love between Tristan and Isolde as far as Gottfried carries it. That development flies completely in the face of the conventions of the courtly romance. There is no sudden falling in love, no sudden recognition, no breathing sighs or tortured monologue. Love comes about only because two persons of high perceptiveness and artistic potential are brought together in a situation where the male can instruct the female and prepare the ground in which love can grow. The instruction makes Tristan-love possible but does not ensure that it will happen. The development of their love is hindered and, in any conventional fashion, prevented by factors which are of the essence of courtly life: the need to avenge a kinsman (Morolt); loyalty to an uncle (Mark); the need to marry the dragon-slayer, whoever he may be, provided that he is "noble"; the need to take back Isolde to Mark, because honor demands it, even though Tristan could have married her and become the heir to Ireland.

Love in the physical sense comes about when close proximity in the ship and Isolde's beauty so work on Tristan that he can take advantage of Isolde's loneliness and misery—and of the subconscious attraction to him of which she had already given evidence. The overwhelming necessity for physical love blinds the lovers to the higher aspects of love, which find expression in music. They are engaged in a continuous series of conflicts with courtly convention which manifest themselves in Marjodo, Mark, Melot, and Gandin. The lovers try desperately to deceive in order to live. They even sink to attempting to deceive God. Only in the grotto, far removed from the court, can their love find its true expression and there the physical takes its proper place in the total harmony of true lovers.

The discovery of the grotto ends this life and, I have no doubt, the lovers' life together. Although for Isolde love in separation is possible, for Tristan it is a sore trial, and his attempt to find a substitute in Isolde White Hands must surely have led to a tragic end.

# V

## THE MILIEU

THE ORIGINAL TRISTAN material was essentially the story of a warrior ruined and destroyed by the impact of a love affair which ran counter to the mores of the society in which the lovers moved. The warrior basis remained, and so did the conflict with society. The changes came in the attitude to love. For earlier warrior-epics love was at best an incident, at worst an impediment to the fulfillment of a hero's destiny. In the romance this attitude appears to have altered, for love is the central and decisive theme. Yet closer examination soon shows that the knight must remain essentially a warrior, for love cannot be gained without chivalric prowess nor retained without proof of ability in combat. If we examine the extant romances before Gottfried's, we find that they center at least as much on the abilities of the hero as warrior as on his prowess in love. For Enéas, his victory is the key to the attainment of his love. Erec's life is determined by the development of a feeling of responsibility in the use of his knightly power, as Yvain's is by the acquisition of knowledge that adventure is more than winning prizes in tournaments and love more than mere physical attraction. In these romances and in the *Lancelot* the hero is engaged much more in demonstrating his ability as a fighter than as a lover, even though his actions may be motivated by love. The romance, as has often been pointed out, is concerned with types and the hero-type in the romance is the warrior in love in various forms. In all cases the romance is concerned with the problem of making compatible the determination of its hero to excel as a fighting man and his bond to a lady whose attitude to his chivalric achievements may vary considerably. In every case, however, the hero cannot be thought of apart from his prowess. Only in *Cligès* is success at arms thrown into the background, and there the intention is obviously to discredit the whole idea of "love at court." There is no example, except *Cligès*, of a romance in which the hero is not the most successful of all warriors, a match even for Gawain, the paragon of virtues and the essence of courtly prowess in all its forms. The hero's very existence depends on his ability to defeat all opponents and his success in matters of love depends at least as much on his military virtues as on his personal attraction.[40]

Tristan's love has no connection with his ability as a fighting man. He is never called on to defend Isolde's honor in fight or to use his skill as a warrior in defense of any female. Quite the contrary. The parts of his existence are carefully separated and his skill in battle is often more of an impediment than an assistance to his love plans. The medieval romance is unthinkable without a knight as its hero, for he is the embodiment in medieval culture of the mythological hero who defies all odds to return to his wife, to win his lady, to return from the dead to the living. Quite apart from his mythological connotations, the knight-hero had the important advantage of being easily identified with contemporary ideals. Medieval society was essentially a society organized for war, and the romance appears to reflect that society and its respect for armed force, until we realize that no romance hero ever fights in a real war. He is simply carrying out a series of rituals which have to do with armed combat but he very rarely engages in a battle. His encounters are individual tests of courage, of a highly formalized nature, not battles in any real sense. His fights follow a highly predictable course of charges with the lance and sword-fighting on foot, of much noise and many wounds whose healing follows with speed and neatness and never a touch of gangrene. If by any chance the hero is gravely wounded—not by another knight but by some creature beyond the pale—he rises miraculously from the dead at precisely the correct moment. His combats, moreover, are essentially concerned with private rather than public morality. He is maintaining his own honor, or that of his lady, or the innocence of a persecuted victim, not, like Beowulf, the safety of his whole people, or, like Roland, the honor of his king. The romance, in other words, formulated its own rules of fighting, rules which bore as little resemblance to the realities of medieval warfare as the tapestries of the capture of Troy did to Bronze Age combat.

Such formal description of personal combat had the advantage of not distracting the reader from the aim of the romance: the presentation of easily identifiable types in fixed situations under circumstances which would allow the audience to draw the correct moral conclusions. The object of the romance was not to give a realistic description of life at a medieval court but to show ideal types functioning in a milieu whose standards were well known and therefore predictable. The interest consisted in the shifting relationship of the hero to these standards and his achievement of fulfillment in relation to them. Certain moral values were particularly extolled at this ideal court—honor (*ere*), best explained as reputation among the right people; generosity (*milte*); loyalty (*triuwe*); constancy (*staete*); balance (*maze*), the ability to strike a mean between various virtues; good conduct (*zuht*), the ability to behave well in polite society; and inevitably bravery (*tapferheit*)—but it is unlikely that an actual code of courtly behavior either existed or was thought to exist by writers.[41] These virtues were extolled but it does not follow that they were in all cases pursued or observed. Perhaps the most pervasive of all ideas is that of *dienst* and *lon*, service and reward, the idea that anyone who performed a service was entitled to a reward, from his overlord or from his lady. Such, indeed, was the theoretical basis of love and marriage. Service to or for the lady must be followed by her acceptance.

It is clear that the Tristan romances depart sharply from these ideals. As we have seen, Eilhart von Oberg sees Tristan as a warrior lost. Thomas and Gottfried, however, use the formal background of the romance as a milieu in which the hero and heroine, far from realizing their full potential, are crushed by a society whose tenets they cannot obey. Gottfried's courtly milieu is largely a so-called ideal society which proves to be incapable of sustaining ideal love. Thus the standard romance situation of an Arthurian milieu as a background for the development and maturity of love is denied and with it the whole basis of the romance, that the knight, the member of the warrior caste, is the only type capable of full individual development. In view of this denial it may be thought surprising that Gottfried used the courtly milieu at all and still more surprising that he does not seem totally unsympathetic toward it. The matter deserves a close analysis.

## THE COURT AND ITS VALUES

The court which plays the role of greatest significance in the poem is that of Mark. Of Arthur's court it may be assumed that it is the center of civilization in any work in which it appears, but Mark's court has to be established in this role by Gottfried himself. We see it first through the eyes of Riwalin, a man who has just been through a period of sustained warfare with his overlord, Duke Morgan. Warfare, be it noted, with real battles and dead men, cities devastated and populations despoiled, not the individual combats and mock battles of the romance. Riwalin wishes to enter the new and pleasant world and he has heard of Mark's court as affording the best introduction to this ideal world:

> er haete vil gehoeret sagen,
> wie höfsch und wie erbaere
> der junge künic waere
> von Curnewale Marke
> des ere wuohs do starke ...                                    (420 ff.)

> He had often heard it said how courtly and honorable Mark, the young king of Cornwall, was and how his fame was increasing.

Mark's titles and possessions are listed with unusual and rather unnecessary detail and then:

> ouch saget diu istorje von im daz,
> daz allen den bilanden,
> diu sinen namen erkanden,
> kein künec so werder was als er.                               (450 ff.)

> History also says of him that there was no king more worthy than he in the opinion of all the neighboring lands who knew his name.

This is the king from whom Riwalin is to learn "niuwe ritterschaft" ("the new knighthood") and to polish his manners.

> sin edelez herze seite im daz:
> erkante er vremeder lande site,
> da bezzert er die sine mite
> und würde selbe erkant dervan                                  (460 ff.)

> His noble heart told him this: if he learned the customs of foreign lands, he would improve his own thereby and would thus gain recognition.

Riwalin's information is deficient on one very important matter. Mark, if Gottfried's later account, given in his own person, is to be believed, was not an independent king at all. As a boy, he had been defeated in war and made subject to Gurmun, king of Ireland, and when Tristan comes to court later it is painfully obvious why. Mark is a feeble and irresolute king and utterly unfitted to challenge anyone. His court is a place of beauty indeed but it is not really a place where a knight would learn to be a man, although he might learn to make pretty speeches.

The whole description of the court relates at first to ceremony and festival. No individuals appear except Mark, Riwalin, and Blanscheflur. We are offered only the surface sheen, the May morning and guests star-scattered on the grass, the perfect atmosphere for mindless love. Mark is "der guote, der höfsche hohgemuote" ("the good man, the man of courtesy and fine sensibilities"), the center of all this. As we have already seen, the course of love between Riwalin and Blanscheflur follows the course to be anticipated in such an atmosphere of purely visual impressions. We hear nothing of any Marjodos, Melots, treacherous barons, or conniving seneschals, for the simple reason that Riwalin is unconcerned with such matters. He sees at Mark's court only what he wants to see, not the reality of a weak king but the dream-picture of an idealized court. Into this picture his love affair—a purely verbal one—fits very well, until reality intrudes in the shape of an invasion and war. Mark fights and wins (for the only time in the poem), but Riwalin in aiding him is struck down by a wound which seems mortal. This intrusion of the real world leads to the conception of Tristan, in anguish and sorrow, not in the artificial world of the court of Mark.

This first introduction is thus Riwalin's concept of a courtly world—glamor and visual beauty—which takes no note of the realities of Mark's position and never seeks to probe below the surface to find out whether there are real virtues beneath the glitter and whether the court has any true values. Tristan's introduction is of a different kind. Riwalin had come to Mark's court of his own free will because he thought he would find there a culture superior to his own. The impression he makes is due to his bearing as soldier—an occupation not stressed at the court of Cornwall. Tristan comes to the court by accident, and his impression of it and upon it is totally different from those made by his father. He is from the first superior to all its members in the very graces of civilized life in which they claim to excel. Young though he is, he makes the experienced huntsmen feel like babies in his presence, not because he is a better hunter (we never learn how good he is), but because, in a court devoted to ceremonial, he proves to have more detailed, up-to-date, and exotic knowledge than the so-called experts. Hunting is throughout the poem closely connected with love. It is while Tristan is away hunting that Gandin abducts Isolde, while hunting that he discovers the *Minnegrotte* which Mark in his turn discovers while on a hunting expedition. The chase was the most characteristic occupation of the nobleman, except fighting and preparing for fighting, and it was attended by more detailed ceremonial than any other pursuit. Tristan is not only horrified at the lack of knowledge of such ceremony among Mark's attendants but quick to use his own skill to make for himself—a fourteen-year-old boy—an honorable place at court. His use of his skill in languages and music, the very things of which Mark is proud, is of the same order. He has moved into a highly influential position as an adviser to Mark not through the physical accomplishments of his father, Riwalin, or through his birth, which is still unknown, but through polite arts, the very things his father came to learn. Mark's court can teach him nothing, nor is he of the quality which can be assimilated to or molded to its conventions. On the contrary, he exercises such a control over the courtiers' senses with his music that they must obey him.

Tristan is thus perfectly capable of being a "courtly knight" in the narrow sense and of excelling if he becomes one. But there is no mention of any love affair or relations with women. Normally in a romance we meet its hero at a turning point in his career—where he is a full member of Arthur's court, equipped in every way and endowed with every quality, except that he has no lady. Tristan not only has no lady but is unconcerned with the matter. There is no evidence of his being affected by the beauties of the Cornish court, as his father had been. Unlike most romance heroes, he does not rise above the values of the court but is superior from the very start.

Yet there is an element in which he has to prove himself—that of physical combat—and it is in this sphere that the indictment of the courtly conventions is particularly strong. However important the role of love in the life of a knight, his fate rested in the last resort in the strength of his arm. None of the romance heroes would have won their ladies (again with the possible exception of Cligès) unless they had defeated several opponents in combat. The conditions of these combats were strict. With a worthy opponent (Yvain and Esclados li ros, Erec and Guivreis), nothing but straightforward blows with spear and sword was allowed. With such lesser breeds as giants, dwarfs, dragons, and seneschals, more latitude was allowed but there was still a sense of what was fair. The ideal single combat probably bore little relation to real battle conditions.

Tristan's battles have little in common with these fanciful struggles. His revenge on Morgan is a masterpiece of duplicity but hardly an epic of chivalry. He wishes to obtain lawful recognition of his title to his father's lands from Duke Morgan, who claimed overlordship. He must have known that he would not get it, firstly because it was to Morgan's advantage not to give it and secondly because his title was legally dubious, for different local laws took different views of the legitimacy of a child conceived out of wedlock but born after a marriage of the parents. Tristan prepares himself well by moving with men whose arms and armor were concealed against a man on a hunting party and hence in civilian clothing. When Morgan rejects his claim with scorn, he challenges him— again in the certain knowledge that his demand would be rejected, for if Morgan declared him illegitimate, he also declared him incapable of participating in a judicial duel. Tristan's reply is to cut him down in cold blood. Needless to say, a romance hero would not behave in this way and even today the solution strikes us as drastic in the extreme. Yet it is logical, for if he were declared illegitimate, he would have no further recourse to legal methods and could obtain his father's possessions, to which he had a valid claim in local law, only by force of arms. He chooses the brutally simple path of striking down his enemy by a surprise blow, effective enough perhaps but hardly moral and certainly not courtly. Nor is his subsequent leadership in the struggle with Morgan's men particularly inspiring. Only the faithful Rual, anticipating trouble, saves him from a humiliating defeat and certain death. Tristan has fought as his nature determined—to remove an enemy by the most direct method. But there is no chivalry in his behavior.

The battle against Morolt is not dissimilar, but the circumstances under which it is undertaken are very different. In essence it is not a romance-style combat at all, since Tristan is fighting not for his personal honor in any sense but for the salvation of his adopted country. Morolt's challenge is quite unlike, say, that of the Green Knight in *Gawain and the Green Knight* or that of the Red Knight, Ither, in the Perceval stories, since it constitutes a threat not to individual honor but to the whole kingdom. Mark himself does not suffer if he hands over the tribute to

Morolt. Indeed, he has already paid the tribute on three previous occasions, but the tribute then consisted of material goods. Now Ireland demands thirty boys from Cornwall and the same number from England, and there is every indication that Mark intends to send them without demur and certainly without fighting, for when Tristan comes back from Parmenie he finds the noblemen drawing lots to pick who should go. This is the glorious court of Cornwall, the model of chivalry, unable to save its own young men from being handed over as tribute. It is easy to forget in view of the subsequent events that Tristan was not only a new knight whose experience of armed combat was limited to his not very successful attack on Morgan but also a mere boy, not more than eighteen years of age, a most unlikely savior of his uncle's name and realm. Nor does he thrust himself forward as a champion. He tries a formal speech of persuasion of seventy-one lines to shame the lords of the land into resistance. He urges them to pick one man to fight Morolt. The result in this court is predictable:

> "A herre" sprachens alle do
> "ja ist disem manne niht also:
> ime kan nieman vor genesen"                                    (6135 ff.)

> "Ah, sire," they all said, "it's not like that with this man: no one can survive a fight with him."

Tristan's next technique is to offer himself, with considerable stress on his youth and inexperience. His offer is accepted without hesitation, and, in spite of Mark's entreaties, Tristan pursues the affair, not immediately by challenging Morolt to battle but by another long speech which is carefully designed to confuse the whole issue. He argues that the tribute was originally imposed by force and should have long since been repudiated now that Cornwall has recovered its strength:

> als ist daz michel unreht,
> als ir noch hiutes tages seht,
> an in begangen iemer sit
> und waere zware lange zit,
> daz si der grozen swacheit
> mit wige haeten widerseit . . .                                (6285 ff.)

> So, as you see today, a great injustice has been inflicted on them ever since, and they should actually have resisted it and their servitude by war.

It is no doubt true that King Mark should have bestirred himself and thrown off the Irish yoke, but the fact remains that he had not done so, and Tristan's subsequent attempt to persuade Morolt that the matter should be settled by war between the two countries at some future date is a transparent attempt to defer the matter. Morolt says with some justice that he did not come to fight a war, since he had assumed the tribute would be paid, and Tristan's ingenious rhetoric is brought to nothing. He must, in the end, fight Morolt. But he has made several things clear—the craven nature of Mark and his barons, the fact that Ireland cannot expect mere acceptance of Cornwall's servile position, and above all the essentially immoral position of Morolt. Legally the right is no doubt on Morolt's side, but Tristan has shaken his faith in the morality of his stand, particularly since he had obviously given the matter little thought. Tristan's frequent calls on God to defend the right, his assumption of the role of David in a contest against the giant champion, can only shake Morolt's confidence.

Mark is distressed at the danger to Tristan but not distressed enough to take his place. Instead, he provides superb accouterments and it is here that we are presented with the visual picture of "Sir Tristan" which should have been presented at the description of his knighting. It may be remarked also that it is at this point in the story that the description most resembles that of his father, Riwalin, for in the eyes of the court he is a warrior. Love's dart on his helmet marks the difference. The psychological assault on Morolt continues. The combat is to be fought on an island, and Tristan pushes away one of the boats which bring them there. Only one will be needed to take the victor back. Gottfried goes to elaborate lengths to deal with the problem of Morolt's traditional strength—the strength of four men. No doubt there was once some connection between Morolt's strength and that of the numerous sun-god figures whose strength grew as the sun rose in the heavens but such connections are irrelevant here. Gottfried is ironically comparing his hero, assisted by God, Justice, and Determination, with the legendary strength of Morolt. Tristan has all the divine powers on his side, for his cause is morally if not legally impeccable. Yet at first his companions do not seem to have been of much help. Morolt is a powerful enemy and an experienced fighter and he gives Tristan little rest. Gottfried's descriptions of battles do not follow the generalized, idealized pattern of Arthurian romance. They are full of very pertinent detail, detail which would be of great interest to a courtly audience and which belies the idea that Gottfried, the bourgeois, knew nothing of knightly matters. Tristan receives the blow which is to be of such fateful consequence for him because he is an inexperienced fighter.

sus gienger in mit slegen an
biz erm mit slegen an gewan,
daz Tristan von der slege not
den schilt ze verre von im bot
unde den schirm ze hohe truoc,
bis er im durch daz diech sluoc
einen also hezlichen slac,
der vil nach hin zem tode wac . . .                              (6919 ff.)

So he went at him with blows until with his strokes he forced Tristan to push his shield out too far to meet the rain of blows and thus hold his guard too high, until he dealt him a vicious blow through the thigh which afterwards came near to killing him.

He just does not know how to handle his shield properly. But the wound he receives would, in a normal romance, be cured overnight. The problem lies in the fact that the sword is envenomed. Knights in romance do not fight with poisoned weapons, and Tristan had every right to be furious when he heard from Morolt that he could be cured only by Morolt's sister, Isolde, queen of Ireland. His answer is to employ tactics which, though not so base as Morolt's poisoned sword, are something less than chivalric. He knocks down Morolt, horse and all. Morolt gets up and, against all the rules of chivalry, makes a deliberate cut at Tristan's horse. Tristan goes down and, as he does, Morolt rushes to recover his helmet which Tristan has knocked off. He grabs it, runs to his horse to try and ride down Tristan—and has his hand slashed off by his opponent. A second later Tristan strikes him a terrible blow on the head and leaves a fragment of his sword in Morolt's skull. Morolt totters—and Tristan taunts him as he staggers and then strikes off his head. It would be hard to imagine a contest which departed more widely from the courtly tradition. Fought far from admiring crowds, with no ladies fluttering their kerchiefs, with a poisoned weapon and a deadly wound and a finish in which there is a scramble for position, a desperate blow, and an abrupt conclusion, it is probably far closer to a real thirteenth-century fight than anything in Chrétien's work. Tristan wins not because he is a better knight or even a better warrior but because he is a little more quick-witted, more ready to take advantage of an opportunity—in a word, more cunning. The battle is, in fact, closer to a realistic fight than to a literary contest. One of the contestants dies miserably, the other receives a wound which, unlike the normal wounds of heroes, does not heal within a few days but continues to plague him and drives away all the courtiers by its appalling stench. Gangrene would produce the same effect. Tristan is really wounded, not touched with red paint. Gottfried has depicted for his readers a political struggle with a real fight for a real objective. Its results are not merely the personal development of the hero but a total change in the relations between Cornwall and Ireland, between Tristan and Mark's courtiers, and ultimately between Tristan and Isolde.

Tristan never fights to defend Isolde. There are versions of the story in which he saves her from lepers by the power of his sword, but in Gottfried's version there is no connection between Tristan's martial prowess and his love for Isolde, although his next encounter with a human adversary is undertaken with the object of providing her with solace for his absence. Gilan, his host, owns the magic dog Petitcreiu, and it is to secure this animal that Tristan himself makes use of the rash boon, which Gandin had operated so effectively to Mark's disadvantage. His battle with the giant Urgan li vilus is a series of variations on the battle with Morolt. (It should be remembered that Morolt also possessed the strength of four men.) Urgan, because of his invincibility in battle, forced Gilan to pay tribute if he wished to lead a quiet life and was engaged in collecting it when Tristan was at court. Like Mark, Gilan has a splendid court and enjoys a quiet life—at the expense of martial ability. From this Tristan proposes to rescue him, but his motivation is quite different from that which had prompted him to challenge Morolt. He is now an experienced fighter and an exile. He wishes to be rewarded and is determined to obtain Petitcreiu for Isolde. Urgan is prevented from driving his tribute—animals, not men, as befits his status—and reacts as crudely as might be expected. He uses the normal weapon of his type, the club, but it is of steel not wood. The giant himself recalls the fight with Morolt with the interesting accusation that Tristan had fought him "umb niht," for no good reason. Presumably he shares Morolt's view that the whole matter of tribute had been settled and fighting was pointless.

The combat which ensues is as unchivalrous as its predecessor. No giant in a romance ever obeys the rules and it comes as no surprise when Tristan's horse is killed (as it is in all his combats) but Tristan's own behavior is unpleasant: he blinds the giant first in one eye and then the other, he cuts off his hand, and he ends by pushing him over a precipice to his death. Hardly an edifying spectacle and one which is made more effective by the parody of Yvain's pursuit of the Black Knight into his castle in desperate eagerness to obtain "proof" of his victory. It may be added that there are also reminiscences of the killing of the dragon—the destruction of the horse, the removal of a part of the victim as proof of victory, the offer of a princess and half a kingdom as reward. The whole description comes close to parody and lacks the deadly seriousness of the fight with Morolt. It is the last individual combat which Gottfried describes but there is a brief description of the war in which Tristan aids Kaedin, where the emphasis is not on individual combat but on the grim face of war on the countryside, burning cities and sacked towns.

Tristan's other feat of arms is, of course, his fight with the dragon. The incident was, by Gottfried's time, an essential part of the Tristan story, but its treatment could vary a great deal. The dragon might be described as normal. It has the common attributes—size, loathsome appearance, cliff-dwelling habits, and the ability to produce smoke and fire at will. It inevitably has a lien on a king's daughter, although not, in this case, because she is to be offered to it as a meal but because anyone who kills it will have her as wife. The combination of the dragon's prowess and the lady's beauty—a neat combination—kills thousands of eager knights whose passing causes little lament. The seneschal is more circumspect. He makes a careful survey of every attempt by other unfortunates but is careful never to become personally involved:

und alse ie man ze velde reit
durch gelücke und durch manheit,
so was ouch der truhsaeze da
eteswenne und eteswa
durch niht, wan daz man jaehe,
daz man ouch in da saehe,
da man nach aventiure rite,
und anders was ouch niht dermite,
wan ern gesach den trachen nie,
ern kerte belderichen ie.                                    (8953 ff.)

Whenever people rode out into open country to try their fortune and manhood, the seneschal was always somewhere around for no other reason except to make sure that he was seen where men rode out on adventure. There was no other purpose to his behavior, since he never saw the dragon without most gallantly turning his back.

The seneschal is accumulating information for future use, for he is well informed on the niceties of court life. Tristan's battle with the dragon follows the usual pattern of fine spear thrusts, scorched horses and shields, and ultimate victory. Just as he does later with Urgan, Tristan pursues the dragon to its lair and then has to dodge quickly to escape its dying wrath. Tristan wins and obtains the necessary token of victory, the dragon's tongue. It should be remembered that he has no idea what he can do with it, for any man from Cornwall who is revealed as such will suffer the death penalty. How then can he, dragon's tongue or none, win Isolde for Mark? As usual, he relies on the inspiration of the moment and hopes that a solution will present itself with time. His act in pushing the tongue close to his chest is uncharacteristic, for he must have known its poisonous nature—yet this uncharacteristic action is in fact the direct cause of his ultimate success.

The description of the approach of the seneschal to the dead dragon is one of the funniest scenes in the poem and the more so because it is a parody of the approach of the hero and his victory. The seneschal hears the noise of the monster from afar—and waits for it to die away; he calculates that there will be little to do but finish it off, and when he sees the dead body he almost falls off his mount, reins about so quickly that he collapses with the horse, and then runs off on foot. Accepted procedure was to advance boldly toward the sound, spur one's horse toward the monster, dismount because the horse was burnt from under one, and continue on foot toward the dragon. And all this the seneschal does (except for the scorching of the horse) once he is sure that the dragon is dead. His subsequent behavior conforms to this mockery of adventure—his slashing of the dead body, his boasting account of his prowess, his claim to Isolde's hand.

The real interest in the dragon episode lies, of course, not in the fight or even the parody but in the subsequent negotiations at court. We need not repeat the discussion of how this episode reflects on the court's attitude to love. What is significant is the light it casts on the relation of courtly procedures to the truth. Except for the accident of the discovery of Tristan by the two Isoldes, the seneschal's treachery and his fictional dragon-slaying would have been every bit as effective as the real thing. The verbalization, the reporting, the support from relatives and friends are more important than bravery in combat. Of two of the fights which occur in this work it may be said that the victory gained is less significant in the long run than the injuries inflicted: the wound received from Morolt is more important for Tristan than his victory, the dragon's poisoned tongue more important than its slaying, for each brings Tristan to Isolde. Only the fight with Urgan achieves its purpose, although the winning of Petitcreiu proves useless, since Isolde refuses the animal's solace. The victories in war gained in supporting Kaedin do lead to Isolde—the wrong Isolde and misery. It is hard to escape the conclusion that Gottfried rejects the connection between success in combat and success in love, for the relationship between Tristan and Isolde is not only totally independent of such success but affected rather by events in the combat which might be regarded as harmful. Furthermore, the combats themselves are of a kind far removed from the idealized "clean" encounters of courtly romance. They are either realistic, cruel fights or parodies of the romance variety—and it is more often Tristan's quick wit that saves him than the strength of his arm. Tristan is a brave man, braver in fact than any person we encounter in the poem, but his character emphasizes the feeble nature of most courtiers and the insignificance of fighting in any study of love.

The courts which Gottfried describes are singularly lacking in prowess. Mark is incapable of fighting his own battles, Gilan needs Tristan to rid him of the menace of Urgan, Kaedin, though by no means incapable, is grateful for Tristan's assistance. Of the court of Ireland we know little, since it is used purely as a background for the acquaintance of the two lovers and has little character of its own. Only one court—if such it can be called—demonstrates truly noble qualities, that of Rual li Foitenant. But Rual is a minor figure in society, a liege man, not a liege lord. He has no court in the technical sense and is depicted always as essentially a man of family rather than a ruler. The only court which is described in detail is that of Mark, and it may be assumed that Gottfried's views on the function and character of a court, particularly a literary court, are to be found in his treatment of Mark's court.

We have already noted how Riwalin arrived at Mark's court and how that court was concerned with essentially visual and superficial qualities. Tristan's impact upon it reveals its qualities even more. The hunt was an occupation of great interest to noblemen and its usages were highly formalized. Tristan is fortunate enough to meet the hunt from Mark's court at a crucial point at which he can demonstrate his superiority. It will be noted that the superiority is entirely verbal and formalistic. Tristan never proves that he is a better hunter than the others but that he knows more of the ceremonial connected with hunting. It is on this basis that he is accepted with acclamation at Mark's court and offered the position of master of the hunt. In this and all other respects he proves himself superior not only to the court but to its leader. Mark, as we have seen, is not an old or even a middle-aged man and yet he is no match for the boy who comes to his court. He defers to his judgment in every way, admires him, allows him to negotiate with Morolt and ultimately win a bride for him. In doing these things he proves himself incapable of leading and his court is shown to be inferior in breeding, ceremonial, and, most important, courage. Yet one observation must be made. Although Mark is inferior to Tristan in every way and realizes that he is, he remains kind and gentle. He never attempts to deceive his nephew except when he believes—quite correctly—that Tristan is deceiving him. Even then he acts at the urging of characters who, for Gottfried, represent more accurately the true nature of courts.

Those persons who constitute a court, as distinct from the sovereign and his consort, do not come well out of Gottfried's poem. Only a few of them are dignified by a name—Marjodo and Melot—and the Irish seneschal is known by his office. For the most part they are "barons," a nameless and faceless crowd. Yet they wield great influence. John of Salisbury had already commented on the evil nature of courtiers, and their petty jealousies and greed were proverbial. Gottfried's barons would have fitted this picture well. When Tristan comes to Cornwall as an unknown friendless boy, they are loud in their praise:

> "a Tristan, waere ich alse duo!
> Tristan, du maht gerne leben:
> Tristan, dir ist der wunsch gegeben
> aller der vuoge, die kein man
> ze dirre werlde gehaben kann."                                    (3710 ff.)

"Oh, Tristan, if only I were like you! Tristan, you may well live happily! Tristan, you have been given your choice of all the attainments that any man can have in this world."

But at this stage there is no competition. Dissatisfaction soon makes itself evident. The lack of rejoicing when he returns from Parmenie is due to fear of Morolt, as their happiness is when he returns victorious from the fight. It is on his return from Ireland that jealousy begins to mount. Whatever his age, Tristan is a boy-wonder no longer but the most effective man at court, proven in battle and proven in resource—and Mark's proclaimed heir. Tristan's gifts alone were bound to create envy, but his successes and the thought that he would one day be their lord were even more important considerations. The courtiers follow a pattern which can be found in history—accusations of magic and witchcraft to explain unusual abilities and success. The accusations are veiled, and no names are mentioned. Gottfried conveys very well the atmosphere of intrigue which puts Tristan in fear of his life and produces nothing but soothing words from Mark. Tristan has no trouble in turning the tables on the courtiers, whose envy is equaled only by their cowardice, but he does so, as with Morolt, only at the risk of his own life.

The court thus establishes its primary characteristic—envy of those superior to itself. The characteristic which is expressed in general terms about the barons becomes more personal as the story progresses. The Irish seneschal, envious of men truly brave, determined to exploit courtly conventions for selfish ends, is the ultimate manifestation of the true courtly spirit and has not even the courage to defend his lack of principle in combat. It is more usual for the court to work in secret, manifesting its envy and hatred by spying and denunciation. Marjodo is a steward, Melot a dwarf, and thus they both have a traditional label of spitefulness. That their efforts to ruin Tristan are not successful is due less to their lack of persistence than to good luck and Mark's desire not to be convinced.

It will be noted that Gottfried never describes a good man, knight or not, at Mark's court. A few subordinates, like the huntsman and the musician, are neutral figures whose purpose is merely to provide foils for Tristan. Everyone else may be assumed to belong to the envious majority who have no grace, skill, or courage of their own and who envy those who have these qualities. We are told very little of the court of Ireland, but the steward is presented as an exception who finally excites the disgust of even his own relatives. The court of Duke Morgan we know only as an organization for war. It would seem therefore that Mark's court is what Gottfried regards as a normal court in peace and that its principal characteristics are cowardice, envy, and indecision—a far cry from the courtly virtues of Arthurian romance.

Mark is far from blameless in this matter. A court reflects the values of its leader, and Mark proves in the struggle with Morolt that he lacks both courage and decision. As the story progresses Gottfried identifies him more and more closely with *arcwan* (suspicion), *zwivel* (indecision), leading to *nit* (envy) and *haz* (hatred). Mark is thus guilty of several of the deadly sins but this fact is less important than the corruption of his character by courtly influences. His previous open nature is darkened by suspicion and the atmosphere at court. It should not be forgotten that it was the envy of the barons which forced Isolde upon him as his wife and that he is therefore guilty of weakness in the face of these influences. Sympathy for his plight as a cuckold is tempered by the thought that the situation is of his own making.

Gottfried goes to some length to show that the attitude of the court to the love affair between Tristan and Isolde is based not on moral judgments or religious grounds but on hatred and envy. He has already established the court's attitude to Tristan before there is any question of Isolde's being brought to Cornwall. He further establishes Mark's unworthiness as a husband in the substitution of Brangaene and his failure to recognize the superior qualities of Isolde. Marjodo is motivated in his denunciation of Tristan not only by jealousy of his fame but by a frustrated desire to possess Isolde himself. No one at court makes the slightest effort to save the queen from Gandin; the ordeal by hot iron is clearly a desire to strike at Isolde through the religious authorities and once again Gottfried makes it clear that for Marjodo and Melot revenge, not justice, is the driving force:

> Nu waren da genuoge
> so grozer unvuoge,
> daz si der küniginne ir eit
> vil gerne haeten uf geleit
> ze schaden und ze valle.
> diu bitter nitgalle,
> der truhsaeze Marjodo

der treibez sus unde so
und manege wis zir schaden an.                                    (15,681 ff.)

There were plenty of people there of such crudeness that they would
gladly have imposed an oath on the queen which would have led to her
destruction and downfall. That bitter gall of envy, Marjodo, kept
working this way and that to destroy her in any possible fashion.

The passage should be read in close connection with Gottfried's comment
on the whole proceeding. He regards it as a perversion of religion in the
service of treachery, envy, and hatred.

Tristan must live in this hotbed of intrigue and counter its effects.
Great emphasis has been put on the *list*, the skill combined with cunning,
which he employs, on the lies he unblushingly tells in order to manipulate
a situation to his advantage, on his apparent rejection of courtly and
religious values.[42] There is much substance in these charges and we shall
have something to say about them later. Yet it must never be forgotten
that, of those who surround Mark, Tristan alone has any true concept
of loyalty to his sovereign. He is the only volunteer to fight Morolt, the
only person to pursue Gandin. Most important, it is loyalty which alone
stands in the way of his yielding to his love for Isolde:

Tristan do er der minne enpfant,
er gedahte sa zehant
der triuwen unde der eren
und wolte dannen keren:                                           (11,741 ff.)

As love began to affect Tristan, he at once thought of loyalty and honor
and he was determined to break away.

But love is a greater and more fundamental power:

hie mite so kertin aber an
Minne, sin erbevogetin:
der muose er aber gevolgec sin.
in muoten harte sere
sin triuwe und sin ere;
so muotin aber diu Minne me,
diu tet im wirs danne we:
si tet im me ze leide
dan Triuwe und Ere beide.                                         (11,764 ff.)

But thereupon his hereditary liege lady, Love, turned upon him again,
and he had to obey her. His loyalty and honor pressed him hard, but
love pressed him more, she caused him more than pain: she caused him
more sorrow than both loyalty and honor.

Gottfried deliberately uses a consistent image of the transfer of loyalty to another lord (*erbevogetin*), whose power is greater than that of Mark. From this point on Tristan's loyalty is not to Mark but to Love. There are no further incidents in which he serves him, for the rescue of Isolde from Gandin is only superficially for Mark's sake. Tristan is described from now on only in respect of his relationship to Isolde, not to Mark. He undertakes no work for the king and hunting is his only occupation. The court, however, continues its normal occupation—intrigue against anything which threatens to reveal its own mediocrity.

It is a commonplace of Arthurian criticism that the values of the court are those in which the hero is trained and which he must transcend in order to achieve the full development of his personality. The values of the court are represented less by King Arthur than by Gawain. There is no Gawain at the court of Mark, and the values of that court must be rejected, not transcended, by Tristan. Significantly, however, there are characters whose caliber, judged from the point of view of conventional morality, charity, courtly virtue, or any other standard, is impeccable. Equally significantly, they are not members of a court. Rual li Foitenant and his family are clearly Gottfried's representatives of true virtue unencumbered by the need to conform to a courtly convention and equally incapable of the highest type of love. For Rual there is only one guiding principle of conduct—complete and total devotion to his lord, Riwalin. For him he is prepared to make any sacrifice. When Riwalin comes home with Blanscheflur, it is Rual who urges marriage. When he is killed and Blanscheflur dies, it is Rual who risks his life in an elaborate scheme of deception to save Riwalin's child. His upbringing of Tristan is remarkable. He realizes the importance of the boy's intellectual development and encourages him in the pursuit of knowledge of foreign languages and music as well as of the usual chivalric qualifications. The portrait Gottfried draws is entirely complimentary, and one of the most touching scenes in the poem is Rual's arrival at Mark's court, weary, unkempt, travel-stained, in rags, but in spite of all noble in his bearing and happy finally to have found Tristan—who was not his own son. In Rual there is true nobility:

> er was an rehter herschaft
> aller keiser genoz.                                                   (4044 f.)

> He was the equal of any emperor in true nobility.

What is most important, however, is the self-sacrifice which Rual shows, his utter lack of any thought of himself. Gottfried uses elaborate detail to point the contrast between this humble, straightforward, and entirely loyal character and the court to which he has come, where he is indeed welcomed but which is quite incapable of similar deeds. His disclosure of Tristan's birth means that he has lost the young man of whom he says:

> "Haet ich die halben swaere
> erliten durch si [his real sons] alle dri,
> swie vremede so mir Tristan si,
> die ich durch in erliten han,
> ez waere vil und vil getan."                                    (4136 ff.)

> "If I had gone through half so much misery on account of those three as I have suffered for Tristan, stranger as he was to me, it would have been plenty."

He fully understands that the statement he has made at Mark's court will mean that there is little chance of his seeing much of Tristan in the future. His loyalty again saves Tristan when the battle against Duke Morgan is going badly. Never does he think of himself. Gottfried makes no attempt to base this extraordinary loyalty on anything but the character of Rual himself. There is no question of a courtly code. Rual and his wife, Floraete, are quite simply good people who know only one criterion of conduct. Here, if anywhere, Gottfried is unstinting in his praise of one who does good by his own lights—even if he is not a Tristan—and who, unlike all the members of Mark's court, is never envious of the younger man's success.

The conflict between envy and loyalty is also exemplified in the person of Brangaene. Other versions of the poem make her a minor figure who disappears without a trace and whose importance for either the story or the lovers is marginal. This is very far from the case in the versions of Thomas and Gottfried. She is described as inferior only to Isolde in beauty and her opinion is always sought on matters of importance. Significantly she is not mentioned in the scene in which Isolde is instructed by Tristan. It is in the struggle to frustrate the seneschal that she first appears—without introduction—and reinforces by her common sense the decision to help Tristan. She it is who provides the voice of reason when the two Isoldes discover Tristan's true identity and who urges them to accept his offer of an honorable marriage with Mark. It is because of this common sense and loyalty that she is entrusted with the love potion and from this point she decisively influences the course of action and the fate of the lovers. She can hardly be regarded as responsible for the accidental drinking of the love potion by Tristan and Isolde but her subsequent emotional reaction in throwing the remains into the sea ensures that Mark can never love Isolde as Tristan does. It is her loyalty and sense of guilt which bring her to Mark's bed on the wedding night and her loyalty alone which preserves silence when Isolde, in the grip of a morbid fear of being parted from her lover, attempts to do away with her one true friend. Brangaene's subsequent conduct—as far as Gottfried's poem goes— is apparently uninfluenced by Isolde's ungrateful and savage conduct. She devotes her attention exclusively to affording the lovers opportunities to be together. Her influence is not entirely to their advantage, since her outlook is restricted. To her, the demands of love are satisfied if the lovers can be brought into a position where the purely sexual desires can be satisfied. Experienced as she is in the ways of court, she feels able to conduct such intrigues with success and arranges frequent meetings. Unfortunately the arrangements, as Gottfried records them, are rarely successful. The light shaded by a chessboard does not prevent Marjodo from discovering the lovers together, the chips floating down the stream almost lead to a catastrophe, and it is Brangaene's weakness and hardly explicable lack of presence of mind which allows Mark to walk into the garden and catch the lovers in a situation from which there is no possibility of escape, for which there can be no clever verbalization, no other explanation but crass adultery. Brangaene's loyalty is unquestioned (although, if Gottfried continued to follow Thomas, there would have come a point at which even her patience would snap) but her understanding of the lovers' plight is very limited. Unlike Rual li Foitenant, she is unable to confine herself to those parts of the lovers' career for which her experience fits her. Rual is never called on to take part in those incidents in which Tristan is involved with Isolde. He can show his loyalty under favorable circumstances. Brangaene, on the other hand, supremely competent and self-assured in her dealings at the court of Ireland, is totally at a loss in dealing with Tristan and Isolde when they become lovers. Her sole concern is to allow them to carry on an adulterous intrigue, not because she understands it or even because she approves of such an affair but because she feels that her duty lies in protecting them from the consequences of her own carelessness. She never, in fact, understands their love. She does not participate in the scene in which Tristan instructs Isolde, nor in the scene in the lovers' cave. These areas are beyond her grasp. She reflects, in fact, the best the courtly scene has to offer—loyalty, beauty, good sense—but not understanding of love as Gottfried understands it. She is, like Mark, a figure who proves that courtliness is not all evil—but that it can never be totally good.

It will be seen that Gottfried has placed before us examples of the stock figures of the courtly scene. His seneschal is very much the same as Sir Kay, a man who professes the courtly virtues while mutilating them in his life. But he far exceeds Sir Kay in the extent of his moral turpitude. Arthur's seneschal is blundering and stupid but his mistakes derive entirely from his assumption of tasks which are beyond his capacity. He never attempts deceit nor does he aim above his station. The Irish seneschal is a perversion of all courtly values. Not only is he cowardly but he seeks to exploit the bravery of better men than himself for his own ends and he aspires to the highest position in the land on the basis of lying testimony and an account of deeds which he is quite incapable of performing. Gottfried's seneschal is not a comic figure but a sinister one who very nearly succeeds in imposing his own desires on the court of Ireland.

Minor figures of courtly romance—the giant and the dragon—are parodied by Gottfried. Their nature is not fundamentally changed. They are simply not taken seriously. The fair maiden goes to the dragon-slayer only by a very roundabout route which involves first the elimination of a verbal dragon-slayer and then the theft of the woman from the man to whom the dragon-slayer had deputed her. The giant, on the other hand, is killed to obtain a toy for Isolde. A far cry indeed from the slaying of Harpin by Yvain or the exploits of Arthur at St. Michael's Mount. The dwarf, Melot, conforms well to his model in the other romances. In Gottfried's poem his twisted nature is well reflected in his twisted body and he is a worthy companion of the dwarf who opens the action in *Erec*. It suited Gottfried's purpose very well to show Mark's court and the fate of the lovers at the mercy of such a creature.

It is the king, however, who determines the nature of a court. It is one of the presumptions of Arthurian literature—and for that matter of the ostensibly historical account of Arthur's court by Geoffrey of

Monmouth—that the values which the knights observe are those set by Arthur himself. The king who appears in the romances often seems incapable of putting such values into practice but is shown as a middle-aged man, respected rather for what he has done than for the achievements he might yet accomplish. Mark, unfortunately, falls into neither of these categories. He has no achievements, he has set no values. There is no one at the court who is willing to defend its honor, no one who shows the slightest sign of courage, of generosity, of loyalty, of breeding—except Tristan, who has been educated by Rual and Curvenal, far from Mark's court. Yet Mark's influence is there—in the court's superficiality and even more in its lack of decision. Suspicion and envy are the characteristics of the court, and Mark, instead of overcoming them, gradually falls prey to them, in spite of his own generous if feeble nature. Courtly virtue without a virtuous ruler is shown to be a travesty of morality.

There are no efficient knights in Gottfried's work. Only Kaedin is a man who actually fights with Tristan and he is very much a junior partner. Fighting, as we have seen, is an unproductive activity. It is of the essence to the action and the moral background of Chrétien's romances that the hero should come to realize the difference between fights which have no real purpose except to increase his reputation and those in which his superior powers are used to help those weaker than himself or whose situation calls for righteous force to put it right. The events in *Yvain*, *Erec*, *Perceval* are all carefully organized to this end. Lesser romances often show adventures designed to win the hero renown and more tangible rewards but in every case there is a direct correlation between the hero's prowess with sword and his success in other directions. This attitude, as we have seen, is totally rejected in Gottfried's work. None of Tristan's objectives or successes comes as a result of knightly prowess. Quite the contrary. What then does Gottfried substitute for the knight-hero? The answer appears to be—the artist.

## THE ARTIST-HERO

This judgment is, at first sight, so extreme that it requires some justification. Tristan is portrayed as an excellent knight both in the narrowest sense as a fighter on horseback and the broader sense of a man educated in all the elegances of courtly life. Yet these qualities have little bearing on the substance of the poem, the love affair between Tristan and

Isolde. We have already seen that there is no question of the so-called *Dienst-Lohn* relationship between the two. Tristan does not serve Isolde or receive a reward, in any military or chivalric sense of the term. He very rarely appears before her as the triumphant knight but often as the skilled artist.

The idea of the artist-hero was not new. Both Orpheus and Arion appear in stories which contain incidents similar to those told of Tristan. Orpheus has the power to move men and even inanimate objects without any volition on their part. He could even move the most negative of all forces, the prince of Hades himself. Arion shared Tristan's experience of being held prisoner on board ship. He escaped by divine intervention and by the miraculous appearance of dolphins whom he charmed by his music.[43] Such resemblances could be regarded as merely coincidental were it not for the frequent references to classical mythology by Gottfried—including two to Orpheus himself. All the great classical epics have a warrior as a hero, and the musical accomplishments of the great Achilles are of little significance in the epics, Greek or Latin, in which he appears. It is hard to imagine Aeneas, Ajax, or the Theban princes playing on the lyre, and Odysseus, although interested in music, achieves his successes by other means. In the classical epics the artist-musician is a minor figure but in the romances he comes into his own. The pastoral influence on these romances is strong, and their heroes usually are far removed from the sphere of military activity. Their conquests, always female, rest on physical beauty, and their adventures—and they were numerous—are brought about by the constant pressure of outside forces which work upon them, not by any willed act of the characters. The best example of the artist as hero is to be found in the *Apollonius of Tyre* romance, presumably of Greek origin and extant in Latin versions of which the earliest is that of the tenth century. Apollonius finds out that Antiochus, king of Antioch, has committed incest with his daughter and as a result of the king's wrath he has to flee. He is shipwrecked and cast up on the shores of King Archestrates, who encounters him in the public baths and brings him to his palace. Here he attends a feast and displays extraordinary skill on the lyre. The king's daughter, who hears his performance, falls in love with him and goes to great lengths to ensure that she can marry him. The king agrees and they live happily until a daughter is born and the bride of Apollonius apparently dies. There follows a series of adventures, both for the child of the marriage and for Apollonius, which can only be described as hair-raising but which culminate in reunion and happiness. Only the first part of the story concerns us here, Apollonius, the exile and artist, winning a bride from a royal family far from his home.[44]

The emphasis in the Apollonius story, as in most Greek romances, is on the triumph of true love. The hero wins the attention of his lady by his musical ability, and his ultimate triumph is due to his quick-wittedness and artistic skill rather than any military qualities he may possess. It is very likely that Gottfried knew the Apollonius romance, for by the twelfth century it had a wide circulation in Latin and the vernaculars. There were other sources for the idea of the man who succeeded by his wits, in particular the heroes of the so-called *Spielmannsepos*, and there had arisen a degree of association between skill as a performing artist and agility in finding favorable situations at court and elsewhere. No doubt there was some basis in actual twelfth-century life for the association, for minstrels, as distinct from troubadours and *Minnesänger*, had little social standing and had to rely on nimble wits for their very existence. Such men may have been creative artists, but it was chiefly as performers that they were known to the courts. They were not regarded as artists in any sense that the word has acquired since the Romantic period, nor is there any story, to my knowledge, in which a love affair is based on artistic affinity between man and woman.

It is therefore necessary to examine Gottfried's text very carefully to distinguish between his use of the conventional figure of the wandering minstrel and his depiction of the artistic and creative ability which Tristan imparts to Isolde and which is the true bond between them. The important parts of Tristan's early career occur when he is posing as a performer. In his first appearance at Mark's court, however, he is not regarded as a *Spielmann*. His clothing when he meets the huntsman is not that of a mere minstrel and in his desire to impress the master of the hunt he has to reveal knowledge of courtly ceremonial which no minstrel would ever have. When he has obtained his entrée to the court through this knowledge, Tristan quickly abandons his huntsman's office and turns his attention to playing. He has given out that he is the son of a well-to-do merchant in order to account for the numerous skills he possesses. He then proceeds to demonstrate extraordinary ability as a performer by playing on various musical instruments and singing in various languages. These are accomplishments. They show no particular artistic ability which could not be demonstrated by any well-trained minstrel. Tristan's power consists not in the fact that he can do these things but in his ability to influence the minds of men through them. His knowledge of the various stringed instruments, his ability to sing in Breton, Welsh, Latin, and French, could conceivably be found in another man. His strange power to deprive men of their rational processes could not:

> do begunde er suoze doenen
> und harpfen so ze prise
> in britunischer wise,
> daz maneger da stuont unde saz,
> der sin selbes namen vergaz:
> da begunden herze und oren
> tumben unde toren
> und uz ir rehte wanken;
> da wurden gedanken
> in maneger wise vür braht.
> da wart vil ofte gedaht:
> "a saelic si der koufman,
> der ie so höfschen sun gewan!"                               (3588 ff.)

> Then he began to play sweet notes and such excellent music on the harp in the Breton fashion that many a man who stood and sat there forgot his very name and his heart and ears began to play tricks and fool him and turn from their right path. There thoughts were expressed in various ways, and one of the most frequent was, "Happy the merchant who got such a noble son."

He has not, of course, stated that he is a *Spielmann*, a professional performer; his abilities ostensibly stem from the unusual training given to him by his merchant-father. He is careful not to describe himself as of noble birth in order to avoid the questions which must inevitably be asked if he claims its privileges. Gottfried thus describes him as "der niuwe spilman," for this is precisely what he is—a player of a new kind. He is acting a part for the court, using the skills of a minstrel without actually being a minstrel and using those skills to obtain effects which transcend the normal impact of a performer's song. He is the *homo ludens*, the man making life into a game, performing instead of participating and inevitably deceiving as he performs, since his audience understands him only through his performance, while his real nature remains hidden from them all. Thus the element of deception is there from the beginning, even though it is innocent deception, for the boy has nothing to hide. His instinct is to present only a surface, a view of life which he knows will please his audience, and since that audience at his first appearance consists of the shallow courtiers, he uses his skills to force them to like him, to accept him, and incidentally to afford them a joy which does not depend on rational comprehension. It is hard to escape the conclusion that the young Tristan is in the same position as the "normal" writer of courtly romance, except for one important consideration—Tristan is fully aware that he is the *homo ludens*, that he is not what he appears to be, and that the act he is producing is not the reality in which he moves, nor a true representation of that reality. The romance writer, on the other hand, reaches the limits of his ability in presenting his "happy-ending" story and is not aware of anything else which could be done.

Tristan's need to assume the role of minstrel ends when Rual arrives at court, but he does not altogether drop the role of player. His knighting follows and Gottfried's description of it, as we have seen, emphasizes the literary, that is, the player, aspects of that knighthood. Tristan is viewed from yet another point of view—as the character manipulated by the author, the embodiment of the author's views of knighthood, conduct, and morality. The question raised in the literary excursus, implicitly if not explicitly, is: What kind of writer best portrays the career, and particularly the career in love, of a man such as Tristan? If the conclusion is, as I believe, that no literary form has proved entirely satisfactory, then Gottfried has to use new methods to portray his player, his man who will represent to the world Gottfried's own ideas on the love problem.

The player aspects of Tristan's character are not so apparent in the episodes of combat with Duke Morgan and Morolt but they are by no means absent. The use of concealed weapons in the interview with the duke and the clever rhetoric of the speeches both to Mark's barons and to Morolt himself are out of character for a warrior but not for a player. In both instances Tristan is playing a role and is conscious of doing so.

It is at the court of Ireland, however, that his player role is most important and most significant for the interpretation of the poem. Tristan does not declare to Mark his intention of acting the part of a minstrel; it is very doubtful whether Gottfried wished to show his hero planning so far ahead. Nor does he tell Curvenal and the crew of the ship which brings him to the coast. His instructions to them are concerned entirely

with their future, not his own, and represent the one occasion on which
he appears genuinely unselfish. He is, however, ensuring by his words that
he will have a loyal body of men waiting if he does return. The first hint
of his determination to play the role of minstrel is given when he calls for
the poorest clothing in the ship. That he must play *some* role is obvious.
He would be killed at once if he appeared in Ireland as Tristan and he has
already arranged for the removal of his true self by putting out the rumor
of his death on the way to Salerno to seek a cure. The act of changing into
different clothes and entering the skiff moves him from the person of
Tristan into the person of Tantris. He is the same person although his
appearance is different. In any case he has always been just as much
Tantris the minstrel as Tristan the knight. All depends on the appearance
he presents to the world.

From now on he is Tantris but he does not, like most minstrels
announce himself as a minstrel and then proceed to prove the claim by
playing. He plays first and then lets the people draw the obvious conclusion.
The method is important. Tristan's skiff is tossing on the waves with no
means of guidance. When the Irish boats approach, they can see no one
but they can hear music. The music is so remarkably sweet that while it
lasts they listen attentively and make no effort to approach the minstrel.
He produces on them similar effects to those he had made on Mark's
courtiers. Yet this is not Tristan's real music:

> diu vröude diu was aber unlanc,
> die si von im haeten an der stete,
> wan swaz er in da spiles getete
> mit handen oder mit munde,
> dazn gie niht von grunde:
> daz herze dazn was niht dermite.
> son ist ez ouch niht spiles site,
> daz manz dekeine wile tuo,
> daz herze daz enste darzuo;
> al eine geschehe es harte vil,
> ezn heizet doch niht rehte spil,
> daz man sus uzen hin getuot
> ane herze und ane muot.                                    (7524 ff.)

But the pleasure that they had from him at that time did not last long,
for the music he made for them with his hands and voice did not come
from the depths of his being: his heart was not in it. For it is not the
way with music that one can perform it for any length of time if one's

heart is not in it. Even though it happens often enough, it cannot really be called music when it is performed superficially with neither heart nor emotion.

Tristan is a sick man and it is not surprising if he does not sing from the heart. He is acting like a minstrel, allowing only the superficial aspects of his true personality, that of the artist-musician, to appear. These superficial qualities, presented by a man almost dead, are enough for the unsophisticated audience which appears and they make it much easier for Tristan to set his role:

> "ich was ein höfscher spilman
> und kunde genuoge
> höfscheit unde vuoge:
> sprechen unde swigen,
> liren unde gigen
> harpfen unde rotten,
> schimpfen unde spotten,
> daz kunde ich allez also wol,
> als sogetan liut von rehte sol."                           (7560 ff.)

> "I was a court minstrel and was well trained in manners and skills—
> talking and keeping quiet, playing on the lyre and fiddle, the harp and
> rote, jesting and mocking, all these I could do as well as such people by
> rights should."

The description is that of the lowest kind of traveling minstrel, a man who could turn his hand to any kind of performance. The repetitious pairs of words indicate the routine nature of the performance. There is no color, no detail. Tristan embroiders the picture by returning to his earlier role of merchant, with appropriate variations. The story is convincing and Tristan's act entirely successful. In any case he is telling the truth. He was "ein höfscher spilman," but not in the way he intends the Irish to understand him. It is their kindness and pity for him—and their admiration for his fortitude and ability to play so well, although he is clearly dying— which brings him to a physician's house, where he is discovered by the priest who has tutored Isolde. His act is thus entirely successful.

The priest is well trained in music and recognizes Tristan's unusual talent. Gottfried makes the point of repeating in his description of the priest phrases he has already used of Tristan:

> wan er ouch selbe kunde
> list unde kunst genuoge,

mit handen manege vuoge
an iegelichem seitspil
und kunde ouch vremeder sprache vil.
an vuoge unde an höfscheit
haeter gewendet unde geleit
sine tage und sine sinne.                                    (7700 ff.)

For he too was proficient in all sorts of skills and arts, could perform
with dexterity on any stringed instrument, and knew many foreign
languages. He had devoted his time and his abilities to polished behavior
and the occupations of the court.

He too is a performer in the courtly sense and he has brought Isolde as far
as his talents allow. His sympathy for Tristan springs from his admiration
of a fellow performer, and his plea to the queen is thus motivated also by
Tristan's performance. Once Tristan is in the royal presence his act takes
on a different complexion. He has been brought into the queen's presence
as a man for whom there is no hope of survival and who yet produces
magnificent music. The priest sees a direct contrast between the dying
body and the living music, unaware of the act Tristan is playing—to
make his living music into a vehicle for his own rebirth. Tristan in his
turn is unaware that the physical cure which he seeks will be effected only
at the cost of a much more serious wound which can never be cured. The
words *sterben* and *generen* thus take on various significances whose whole
intent is known only to author and audience, though each character
understands them in a way different from all the others.

Tristan professes bland ignorance of the reason for his wound and
his speech to Isolde the queen is a model of humility and trust:

"... nun weiz ich mere, waz getuo,
wan daz ich mich gote muoz ergeben
und leben, die wile ich mac geleben.
swer aber genade an mir bege,
sit ez mir kumberliche ste,
dem lone got: mirst helfe not,
ich bin mit lebendem libe tot."                             (7778 ff.)

"Now I don't know what I can do except that I must trust in God and
go on living as long as I can. But may God reward anyone who has pity
on me, since I am in such a wretched state. I need help, for although my
body is alive, I am dead."

At this point he reveals his name as Tantris, receives the queen's assurance that he can be cured, and breaks into the expressions of formal panegyric which might be expected of a professional singer. He is now called upon to perform for the queen—and the reason for the request soon becomes apparent: he is to instruct her daughter Isolde when his wound is cured. Isolde herself first appears at this point in the story. She is not described except by the purely formal adjectives *junge* and *schoene*. Gottfried prefers to anticipate his story by telling us her function—it is to her that Tristan will be bound in love. The first action of which the reader is informed is her attention to Tristan's playing:

> diu schoene Isot si kam ouch dar
> und nam vil vlizechliche war,
> da Tristan harpfende saz,
> nu harpfeter ouch michel baz,
> dan er ie da vor getaete . . .                                    (7817 ff.)

The fair Isolde also came and looked carefully at Tristan as he sat there playing the harp. And he played much better than he had ever played before.

Her arrival coincides with a remarkable improvement in his playing. He no longer performs like a lifeless man but better than ever before in his life. His music has, in fact, moved to a different level. This is no longer the mere effort of a *Spielmann* but the work of an artist. Unconscious though he is at this stage of the importance of Isolde to his whole existence, he nevertheless plays in a totally different manner.

The queen now calls on him to play a different part, that of teacher of her daughter. She does not expect that her daughter will receive instruction which is fundamentally different from that which she has already had from her tutor and her mother but rather more advanced instruction of the same kind. She regards the visiting minstrel as a very accomplished performer but not a fundamentally different artist. Tristan makes the appropriate reply: he has read many books and he is expert on stringed instruments. He thus takes on the role of "meister" in the same spirit as he has assumed that of minstrel and with results far exceeding those expected by any of the parties concerned. For he is not only Isolde's "meister" in music and the arts but her master in love, a fact to which she refers ironically and with half understanding on the ship which takes her to Cornwall. Tristan, like Abélard, assumes the role of tutor but later merges it into the role of lover.

We must now look back at Tristan's own education in order to see what precisely it was that he had to impart. The first subject to be mentioned is the learning of foreign languages. The point is important, not only as evidence of Tristan's unusual ability, but because the plot hardly makes sense without such accomplishments. Gottfried clearly regards French as the language of the courts and is careful to introduce a line or two of the language at a first meeting or an important point in the dialogue. Yet Tristan is shown speaking to many men in many lands in their own tongue, and the versatility of his performance suggests the many-sidedness of the minstrel he so often pretends to be. These languages serve a higher purpose, for they are the vehicle of Tristan's music. It is of the essence of this music that it should be universal and embrace all the tongues (by medieval standards) in which songs were written. Such knowledge does not necessarily set Tristan apart from other minstrels but it does excite admiration and it is essential that Isolde too should learn so that she may move on the same level.

The second feature of Tristan's education is more general, his instruction in book learning. While it is not uncommon for training in music to be mentioned in the education of a knight, there is rarely any attention to books. The cleric, whether ultimately destined for the church or not, was the person from whom one would expect learning in the narrower sense. Gottfried appears to be turning back to an earlier view of the education of the hero, that shown in classical mythology, which in its turn reflected the views of classical Greece. For these heroes, and particularly Achilles, instruction in music is paramount but it is music in a very wide sense, a total concern with the harmony of life as expressed in the arts. The performance of music and even its theoretical aspects are but a part of such an education, indeed more a reflection of its essence than independent achievements, although to those whose own education and perceptions are of a lower order, they may appear to be so. In such a course of education as the Greeks envisaged for their heroes, the study of what would be called humane letters played an important part and in this curriculum the study of poetry in its various forms was particularly important. Plato would hardly have spoken so strongly against the poets if their work had not been influential. Such study, originally oral, had become the study of texts by classical and particularly Roman times and it was during the imperial period that there were composed such romances as that of the Seven Sages, in which the hero is a highly educated man, the favorite of Vergil, whose survival depends not on his skill at arms but on his knowledge and his wits. Here the emphasis is entirely on the boy's extraordinary ability to absorb the disciplines of the trivium and quadrivium. Gottfried avoids any such specialized description. Tristan studies books but there is no statement that he engages in religion, philosophy, or any of the recognized disciplines—except music. Nor is there any evidence in the poem that Tristan has any particular knowledge of them. Music was the queen of the arts, the one which reflected most accurately the divine harmony of the heavens and of God's own creation, and it was of all forms of expression and of all branches of learning that which was most appropriate to reflect the harmony of two people in love.

Gottfried's discussion of Tristan's introduction to written disciplines lays far more stress on the result of these studies than on their content. His studies are described as "aller slahte lere," a vague description indeed, but the results of those studies are made very clear:

> daz was sin erstiu kere
> uz siner vriheite:
> do trater in daz geleite
> betwungenlicher sorgen,
> die ime da vor verborgen
> und vor behalten waren.                                    (2068 ff.)

This was his first loss of freedom. At this point he moved into the company of painful worries which had previously been hidden and kept from him.

The obvious conclusion to be drawn from these lines is that involvement in intellectual activity brings sorrows of which those who never study are unaware. The following lines confirm this interpretation:

> in den uf blüenden jaren,
> do al sin wunne solte enstan,
> do er mit vröuden solte gan
> in sines lebenes begin,
> do was sin beste leben hin:
> do er mit vröuden blüen began,
> do viel der sorgen rife in an,
> der maneger jugent schaden tuot
> und darte im siner vröuden bluot.                          (2074 ff.)

In the flowering years, when pleasure should increase and joy be his
constant companion, at this very beginning of his life, the best part of
his life was already past. As the joys of life began to bloom, the frost
of care fell upon them, which harms many young people, and blighted
the blossoms of his gladness.

The contrast is between the flowering of youth and the sorrow which
comes from knowledge—or, more pointedly, the idea is that pleasure
can come only to those who lack knowledge. The passage recalls the
flowering Maytime of Riwalin's youth, where all the emphasis is on
the thoughtless pleasure of the young—and also Gottfried's rejection of the
"thoughtless" romance, that which describes nothing but joy and which
equates the pursuit of pleasure with the pursuit of love. Clearly Tristan's
education in books is to prepare him for a life in which sorrow will be as
prominent a feature as joy. Gottfried sums up:

> der buoche lere und ir getwanc
> was siner sorgen anevanc . . .                                    (2085 f.)

Book learning and its discipline were the beginning of his care.

In spite of this, Tristan's enthusiasm for learning is unbounded and he
learns more in a short time than any child before or since. If his knowledge
is greater, so is his sorrow. He practices his music as he learns and becomes expert. His playing and his learning are the twin peaks of his instruction. The normal activities of a noble youth, the use of weapons and
practice for war, are introduced with a perfunctory "über diz allez lernet
er" ("as well as all this he learns"), and the description of these accomplishments is a listing, without comment, of what might be expected of a
young man of Tristan's standing. Even here the stress is on horsemanship
and agility rather than on weapons (there is no mention of a sword), so
that the emphasis seems to be on skill rather than prowess.

We have seen how Tristan used this education to make his impression
in Mark's court and how his skills aided him in his quest to have his
wound cured. In his instruction of Isolde he can finally use his own knowledge to the full. Although Isolde the queen thinks of his instruction of her
daughter as merely extending the skills she has already acquired, the
reader knows that the knowledge Tristan has to impart is far beyond mere
skills and that for Isolde also it spells the end of freedom, of the carefree
flowering years. It is now Tristan's turn to devote himself to teaching. He

does not attempt for her the universality of his own learning. Gottfried
states that he set his learning before her for her to choose. Once again
there is no attempt to list the various disciplines—Gottfried refuses
explicitly to name them—but this time Isolde chooses her own. The study
of her education corresponds closely to that of Tristan. Her musical
education is described in great detail, with a statement of the foreign
languages she had mastered. Her technique in performance is already
good and Tristan improves it still further. Much more important, however,
is the *moraliteit* which Tristan imparts to her. It is introduced with a phrase
similar to that which was used of Tristan's own playing:

| | |
|---|---|
| Under disen zwein lernungen | under aller dirre lere |
| der buoche unde der zungen | gab er ir eine unmüezekeit, |
| so vertet er siner stunde vil | die heizen wir moraliteit. |
| an iegelichem seitspil: | diu kunst diu leret schoene site: |
| da kerte er spate unde vruo | da solten alle vrouwen mite |
| sin emezekeit so sere zuo, | in ir jugent unmüezic wesen. |
| biz er es wunder kunde. (2093 ff.) | (8002 ff.) |
| | |
| He devoted many hours to playing | As well as all this instruction, he |
| on all kinds of stringed instruments | taught a discipline which we call |
| as well as to these two studies, of | *moralitas*, the art which teaches |
| books and language. | fine behavior. All women should |
| | practice this in their youth. |

The structure indicates the close relation between Tristan's playing and
*moraliteit*. Gottfried places this indication of the nature of *moraliteit*—it
can hardly be called a description—between two lengthy discussions of
Isolde's music, the first of that which Isolde had already learned, the
second of the effects of Isolde's "new music."

This new music is described in great detail. The occasion is a concert
—it can be described in no other way—which Isolde gives to her father's
court. The parallel with Tristan's performance before his uncle is clear,
and the effects of the music are described in similar terms. Each is able
to sway the audience, to bend it to his or her will. But while Tristan's
performance excites admiration and a wish to emulate him, Isolde's
performance produces stronger, less rational effects. Compare these two
descriptions:

| | |
|---|---|
| den harpfeter so schone | swaz vröude si dem vater getete, |
| und gie den noten so rehte mite | daz vröutes al geliche: |
| nach rehte meisterlichem site, | arme unde riche |

daz ez den harpfaer wunder nam;
und alse ez ie ze staten kam,
so lie der tugende riche
suoze unde wunnecliche
sine schanzune vliegen in:
er sanc diu leichnotelin
britunsche und galoise,
latinsche und franzoise
so suoze mit dem munde,
daz nieman wizzen kunde,
wederez süezer waere
oder baz lobebaere,
sin harpfen oder sin singen.
sich huop von sinen dingen
und von siner vuoge
rede unde zal genuoge:
si jahen al geliche,
sin vernaemen in dem riche
an einem man die vuoge nie.
der sprach dort und dirre hie:
"a waz ist diz von kinde?
waz han wir zuo gesinde
ez ist allez umbe den wint,
elliu diu kint, diu nu sint,
wider unserm Tristande!"

(3618 ff.)

si haeten an ir beide
eine saelige ougenweide,
der oren unde des herzen lust:
uzen und innerhalp der brust
da was ir lust gemeine.
diu süeze Isot, diu reine
si sang in, si schreip und si las;
und swaz ir aller vröude was,
daz was ir banekie.
si videlt ir stampenie,
leiche und so vremediu notelin,
diu niemer vremeder kunden sin,
in franzoiser wise
von Sanze und San Dinise:
der kundes uzer maze vil.
ir liren unde ir harpfenspil
sluoc si ze beiden wenden
mit harmblanken henden
ze lobelichem prise.
in Lut noch in Thamise
gesluogen vrouwen hende nie.
seiten süezer danne hie
la duze Isot, la bele.
si sang ir pasturele,
ir rotruwange und ir rundate,
schanzune, refloit und folate
wol unde wol und alze wol:
wan von ir wart manc herze vol
mit seneclicher trahte.
von ir wart maneger slahte
gedanke und ahte vür braht.
durch si wart wunder gedaht,
als ir wol wizzet, daz geschiht,
da man ein solich wunder siht
von schoene und von gevuocheit
als an Isote was geleit.
Wem mag ich si gelichen
die schoenen, saelderichen
wan den Syrenen eine,
die mit dem agesteine
die kiele ziehent ze sich?
al zoch Isot, so dunket mich,
vil herzen unde gedanken in,
die doch vil sicher wanden sin
von senedem ungemache. (8046 ff.)

He played it so beautifully on the harp and followed the notes so exactly the way a master would that the harper was amazed. And when it was appropriate, the accomplished young man would perform his *chansons*, sweetly and with charm. He sang the notes of his lay in Breton, in Welsh, in Latin, and his voice was so sweet that no one could determine which was sweeter or more deserving of praise, his playing or his singing. As a result of his performance and his skill, there was a great deal of talk and discussion. They all agreed that they had never seen such ability in any one man in the whole kingdom. First one said and then another, "What kind of child is this? For all the children we have here at court are a mere trifle compared with our Tristan."

Any pleasure she gave to her father was a pleasure to them all. Rich and poor, they both found in her a delightful feast for the eye and a pleasure for the ear and heart. Their pleasure was the same within and without their breast. Sweet and glorious Isolde, she sang to them, she wrote, she read; and what gave them all pleasure was a delight for her. She fiddled her *estampie*, lays, and foreign notes, which could not possibly be more strange, in the French fashion of Sens and Saint Denis. She was extremely proficient in this. She struck the lyre and the harp on both sides with hands as white as ermine. Never in Lud or Thamise did a lady's hands pluck the strings more sweetly than she did here. Sweet Isolde, the fair, she sang her *pastourelle*, her *rotruange*, her *rondeau*, her *chanson*, her refrain, her *folate*, well and well and all too well; for as a result many a heart was full of yearning emotion and many thoughts and ideas flourished. Because of her, miracles were imagined, for as you know, such things happen when anyone looks at such a marvel of beauty and ability as Isolde presented. To whom shall I compare this beautiful, fortunate woman except only to the Sirens who drew ships toward them with the lodestone? Thus did Isolde, it seems to me, draw many hearts and thoughts to herself who had imagined that they were perfectly safe from disturbance by love.

The purpose of these descriptions, as is usual with Gottfried, is to represent to the reader the state of mind of those who listen. Consequently, in both passages the stress is on those features of the performances of Tristan and Isolde which are observed by the audience. For Tristan's it is his skill in languages, his versatility in performance, his mastery of his instruments as well as his glorious voice, and in particular his youth. This admiration is continued into the following passages and exemplified very neatly by his mention of the *sambjut*, an instrument as strange to his audience as his hunting vocabulary had been. The court, normally so jealous of superiority, is lost in admiration. It is knowledge that impresses its members and sheer technical skill:

> "hora!" sprach diser, "hora!" sprach der
> "elliu diu werlt diu hoere her:
> ein vierzehenjaerec kint
> kan al die liste, die nu sint!"                    (3717 ff.)

> "Listen," said this man, "listen," said that one, "everyone listen: a
> fourteen-year-old child knows every skill that exists."

There is admiration for Isolde's playing, too, but it is of a different nature. She is a woman and a beautiful one. Before she even begins to play, the audience is affected by her beauty. As they gaze and listen, they are transported into another world. What they hear is strange and new, the latest type of music from the most advanced schools in Europe at Sens and St. Denis, lyric forms which have never been performed in Ireland before—they are listed to emphasize their outlandish nature. Had Tristan sung, the court would have been impressed. But to see Isolde's pale hands move over the strings, to know or rather feel that this extraordinary music comes from a woman's mouth, produces not mere admiration but a state of irrational attraction. It is at this point that Gottfried intrudes into the description, because the listeners naturally cannot describe their own state. His metaphors are entirely concerned with attraction by irresistible forces and, furthermore, forces who cause destruction without necessarily willing it. There are several versions of the story of the Sirens, but they are usually regarded as female and commonly they perish themselves if their attraction fails. There is no record of their being associated with the magnetic mountain which drew the nails from ships and sank them, but the destructive attractive force is common to both. Like a ship without an anchor, the listeners are at the mercy of elements which they cannot control—a woman's beauty, strange and powerful music, and the love which springs from them. Gottfried's description of the effects of Isolde's playing would be almost a parody of the standard description of the impact of a lady's beauty on her lover if it were not for the fact that he is concerned much more with the music than the visual impression. The members of the audience are not her lovers but they cannot escape the subtle magnetism of the welding of beauty with exotic sound. There is a combination of the visual and the oral, of beauty of appearance and beauty of sound. The audience is impressed by the music she presents, but the real effect comes from the combination of this music and Isolde's beauty. Gottfried constantly contrasts the obvious effects of Isolde's performance with the other, less obvious, but much more effective attraction which works upon the imagination without being fully known to the audience. It is indeed magic, for it works irrationally and it is not pure joy. It is a jolt for the reader when he is suddenly reminded that this ability comes entirely from the instruction she had received from Tristan: "sus haete sich diu schoene Isot/ von Tristandes lere/ gebezzeret sere" ("Thus the fair Isolde had advanced a great deal as a result of Tristan's instruction"). Isolde's beauty has been combined with Tristan's music to produce an irresistible, attractive force.

In these two scenes, Tristan performing at the court of Mark and Isolde performing at the court of Ireland, the effect of music is disruptive. Although both courts are delighted with what they hear and have nothing but praise for the performers, they do not behave in their normal fashion. Mark's court is moved to admiration, Isolde's audience to something approaching love. This is not a normal state for either audience. They are deprived of their rational faculties. Both Tristan and Isolde demonstrate by their performances that they are capable of swaying other human beings but they are not in return moved by them. The music they play can produce harmony only between two beings on the same plane of emotion and understanding. Such harmony can come about only between the lovers themselves. It is in the *Minnegrotte*, the third scene in which music is performed, that this harmony is achieved.

### THE HARMONY OF LOVE

The milieu here is not a court. There are no persons present except the lovers themselves and there is therefore no question of producing an effect on an audience which can be moved by the music of the lovers but which cannot appreciate it fully. The grotto is a place of complete harmony. As the proportions of a Gothic church correspond to those ideal measurements which reflect the divine harmony and as the church building represents in microcosm the *Ecclesia Dei*, so the *Minnegrotte* provides the concrete setting and ideal proportions for a place in which love can be celebrated. Here within these perfectly formed walls and in this shrine dedicated to Love the music which in chivalric courts could produce only disharmony and irrationality, love and admiration on a disproportionate scale, can attain a harmony which links it with the divine order. In his discussion of *moraliteit*, Gottfried had described it as a link between the human and the divine:

> ir lere hat gemeine
> mit der werlde und mit gote.
> si leret uns in ir gebote
> got unde der werlde gevallen:
> sist edelen herzen allen
> zeiner ammen gegeben,
> daz si ir lipnar unde ir leben
> suochen in ir lere ...                                    (8010 ff.)

> Its study is in harmony with the world and with God. In its commandment it teaches us to please both God and the world. It is given to all lofty spirits as a nurse, so that they may seek for their nourishment and their life in its teaching.

This *moraliteit* is clearly an important element of life in the *Minnegrotte*, although it is not mentioned by name, since it is precisely the subject which Tristan taught to Isolde and which appears to represent the high point of his instruction. Most significant in this regard is the image of eating and nourishment. Gottfried stresses that in the cave the lovers need no food other than that which they obtain from each other's eyes. There are, of course, numerous reminiscences in this lack of desire for food. The saints in the wilderness lived without food, although some of their latter-day imitators found the process difficult. The angels needed no food; nor did the lovers, but the latter, unlike the former, showed clear evidence of their deprivation. Much more important than any of these is the recalling of the power of *moraliteit* to nurture *edele herzen*. Surely it is from this mutual power that the lovers continue to live in the cave.

Mutuality is the most important characteristic of *moraliteit*, as Gottfried's language shows—*gemeine, werlde | got; got | werlde; edelen herzen allen; lipnar | leben*—and it is the fact that Tristan and Isolde are alone in the cave that makes it possible for *moraliteit* to be exercised to the full. The lovers achieve complete harmony, one with the other, and the activities in the cave are in different ways the reflection of that harmony, as the movement of the planets producing a sound inaudible to mortal ears but nevertheless of a beauty beyond understanding is the reflection of the divine harmony of the universe. The harmony of the love of Tristan and Isolde is similarly inaccessible to ordinary mortals. Even for them it is impossible to attain such harmony at a court, and the environs of the *Minnegrotte* are carefully differentiated from the Arthurian conventionality. It is not for nothing that Gottfried calls attention to the difference:

> ir zweier geselleschaft
> diu was in zwein so herehaft,
> daz der saelige Artus
> nie in dekeinem sinem hus
> so groze hohgezit gewan . . .                                    (16,859 ff.)

Their company of two was so glorious for this pair that good king Arthur never had such a celebration in any of his houses.

The visual features of the ideal landscape, which are a background to Mark's court, are the court itself for Tristan and Isolde:

> ir staetez ingesinde
> daz was diu grüene linde,
> der schate und diu sunne . . .                                   (16,881 ff.)

Their perpetual court was the green linden tree, the shade and the sun.

The songbirds provide service—a significant point when it is recalled that the lyric poets of love regarded their songs as a service to their lady at least as worthy of recognition as deeds of chivalry and feats of arms.

> diz gesinde diende zaller zit
> ir oren unde ir sinne.
> ir hohzit was diu minne,
> ir vröuden übergulde,
> diu brahtin durch ir hulde
> des tages ze tusent stunden
> Artuses tavelrunden
> und alle ir massenie dar.                                        (16,894 ff.)

This court served their ears and senses at all times. Their high feast was
love, the peak of their joy, and through her grace she brought to them a
thousand times a day Arthur's Round Table and all its company.

The ideal landscape, used largely as a formula by the lyric poets and
writers of romances to show the ideal nature of the love they depict, has
become an integral part of the life of Tristan.

Gottfried describes the daily activities of the lovers, and they repay
careful scrutiny. Throughout, the emphasis is on shared experience, as the
imagery makes clear:

> Diu *getriuwe massenie,*
> Tristan und sin amie
> si haeten in der wilde
> ze walde und ze gevilde
> ir muoze und ir unmuoze
> besetzet harte suoze:
> si waren zallen ziten
> ein ander an der siten:                              (17,139 ff.)

The faithful company, Tristan and his love, had arranged their activities
and their leisure very pleasantly in the wilderness, in the woods, and in
the open spaces. They were always at each other's side.

Their occupation is communicating with each other. At first, as they
listen to the singing of the birds and the music of the stream, this communication is in words only:

> da giengen si her unde hin
> ir maere sagende under in . . .                     (17,153 f.)

They went about telling each other stories.

As the day progresses they move to the lime tree, love's trysting place, and
combine words and song:

> da sazen si zeinander an
> diu getriuwen senedaere
> und triben ir senemaere
> von den, die vor ir jaren
> von sene verdorben waren:
> si beredeten unde besageten,
> si betrureten unde beclageten,
> daz Villise von Traze,
> daz der armen Canaze
> in der minnen namen geschach . . .                  (17,182 ff.)

These true lovers sat there together and told sad tales of those whom
love had destroyed in the past. They talked of them and discussed them,
they grieved and sorrowed over them, over Phyllis of Thrace and poor
Canace who suffered in love's name.

Here again we have stories, closely connected with love, which bind the
lovers into a tradition. They have moved from being merely the inhabitants
of the cave ("getriuwe massenie") to being true lovers ("getriuwe sene-
daere"). In these activities they make no music. The third stage is reached
when they retire into the grotto itself:

> so slichens in ir cluse hin
> und namen aber ze handen,
> dar ans ir lust erkanden,
> und liezen danne clingen
> ir harphen unde ir singen
> seneclichen unde suoze.
> si wehselten unmuoze
> mit handen und mit zungen:
> si harpheten si sungen
> leiche unde noten der minne.
> si wandelten dar inne
> ir wunnenspil, swie si gezam:
> sweder ir die harphen genam,
> so was des anderen site,
> daz ez diu notelin dermite
> suoze unde senecliche sanc.
> ouch lutete ietweder clanc
> der harphen unde der zungen,
> sos in ein ander clungen,
> so suoze dar inne,
> als ez der süezen Minne
> wol zeiner cluse wart benant:
> la fossiure a la gent amant.                                        (17,202 ff.)

They slipped away to their retreat and took up again the delights they
knew so well. They played on the harp and sang their songs, both sad
and pleasant. They took turns both singing and playing the harp: they
played, they sang lays and melodies of love. They varied their pleasure as
they pleased. If one took the harp, the other then sang the melody with
tenderness and yearning. The sounds of harp and voice merged so well
and sweetly there inside the cave that it was properly dedicated as a
shrine of tender love: la fossiure a la gent amant.

The emphasis again is on the mutual nature but now it is on the combination of instrument and voice. There are no technical details of the singing as there were in the two previous scenes, no list of types of songs to impress the uninitiated. All we are told here is that the lovers sang and played the music of love—"leiche unde noten der minne"—and that each could assume the other's role. The music has no intoxicating effect; it is pure harmony worthy of the *Minnegrotte*, and the efforts, twofold and yet one, dedicate the cave to the harmony of true love.

Love reaches its highest expression in this harmony of words and music, not sung by one performer but by two. The role of musician and actor has moved into a higher sphere. Whereas in earlier scenes the two lovers, as individuals, had played a role, had performed, for an uninstructed audience, and by their skill and, in Isolde's case, by skill combined with beauty had swayed an audience to their purposes, in the *Minnegrotte* they cease to perform. The skills they use as performers become their real life. There is no need for the artist to differentiate himself and his abilities from those of his audience. In the *Minnegrotte* the musicians are the only possible inhabitants, for they alone can represent by their activities the harmony of love which is the only reason for their existence. Once the cave is discovered by the court, all possibility of this harmony disappears. The lovers once again must perform a role—witness Tristan's placing of the sword between him and Isolde—and the real self and the performer are once again different beings.

In stressing the harmony of the lovers in the *Minnegrotte*, we must not overlook the fact that Isolde the Fair, in performing music and singing with Tristan, is carrying out a most unusual role in medieval literature. No lady performs music in medieval lyric. It is true that there are a few poems extant which are ascribed to a Provençal poetess and that there exist certain forms (*chanson à toile, Frauenstrophen*) in which the lyric is put into the mouth of a woman, but such forms are outside the main stream of twelfth- and thirteenth-century lyric poetry. Lyrics were composed and performed by a man. Nor do we see the heroines of romances performing music. Isolde alone is an active participant in a musical performance. The role of Isolde White Hands is much more typical. Her conversation with Tristan is designed, at her brother's request, to attract him; Tristan feels attraction to her simply because she is "Isolde" and he feels intensely lonely. The original physical attraction of Tristan and Isolde the Fair, as we have seen, had come about without either's willing it. It is not too much to say that Isolde White Hands makes a deliberate play for Tristan and that he, half unwillingly, responds. The musical relationship between them reflects their attitudes:

dor an der megede gesach
ir senelichez ungemach.                                           [8097]
daz sich daz üeben began,
do leiter sinen vliz dar an,
daz er ir vröude baere:
er seitir schoeniu maere,
er sang ir, er schreib unde er las                                [8059]
und swaz ir kurzewile was,                                        [8060]
da zuo was er gedanchaft:
er leistir geselleschaft,
er kürzet ir die stunde                                           [8048]
etswenne mit dem munde                                            [7986]
und underwilen mit der hant.
Tristan er machete unde vant
an ieglichem seitspil
leiche unde guoter noten vil,
die wol geminnet sint ie sit.
                        . . .
oft unde dicke ergieng ouch daz:
so daz gesinde in ein gesaz
er unde Isot und Kaedin,
der herzog und diu herzogin,
vrouwen und barune,
so tihteter schanzune,                                            [8076 ff.]
rundate und höfschiu liedelin
und sang ie diz refloit dar in:
"Isot ma drue, Isot mamie,
en vus ma mort, en vus ma vie!"                                   (19,183 ff.)

When he saw that the girl was continually suffering from the miseries of love, he turned all his attention to entertaining her. He told her pleasant stories, he sang to her, he wrote and read and gave attention to keeping her amused. He kept her company, he whiled away the time for her, sometimes by singing, sometimes by playing. Tristan composed and invented lays and many good melodies for all kinds of stringed instruments which are well loved to this day. . . . When all the court was sitting together, he and Isolde and Kaedin, the duke and the duchess, ladies and barons, he composed *chansons*, *rondeaux*, and courtly songs and always added this refrain:

Isolde my dear, Isolde my love,
in you my death, in you my life.

The numbers in brackets indicate the lines in the description of Isolde's playing which bear a marked resemblance to lines describing Tristan's performance before Isolde White Hands. The differences in these corresponding lines are significant. "Er sang *ir*," etc., corresponds to "si sang *in* . . ." Isolde sings to the whole court, Tristan only to Isolde White Hands. What is "vröude" to the courtiers of Ireland (8056) is mere "kurzewile" for Isolde White Hands. The whole tenor of the passage is that Tristan was merely amusing Isolde White Hands. Words and expressions which Gottfried never uses of the relation between Tristan and Isolde the Fair—"kurzewile," "geselleschaft leisten," "die stunden kürzen"—occur frequently when he is talking of Tristan's performance before Isolde White Hands—for it is no more than that. There is nothing here of the magic music of the grotto or even of the earlier performances of the two lovers. The music is mere amusement, and it is followed by the shams of courtly love.

Nevertheless Tristan is confused. His music is for Isolde the Fair, although it is heard by Isolde White Hands. Gottfried says of him "er zwivelt an Isolde." He doubts not her but himself. His music is actually leading him astray, for he expects one response and receives another quite different impression. There is no harmony, merely the presentation of notes.

The musical relation between Tristan and Isolde the Fair is the perceptible reflection of the harmony of their love. The effect of music on others contrasts with and throws into relief that unusual harmony.

Love reaches its highest manifestation in the harmony of two individuals, each playing a part of which the other is equally capable. In presenting and representing this harmony Tristan and Isolde are reflecting the highest harmony of all, that of God and his universe, and their relation is thus a manifestation of all-embracing love, the same love which Dante represented in its pure and distorted forms in the *Commedia*. Gottfried was probably concerned less with the affinity between Christian love and Tristan-love than with the idea of his principal characters as participators in a universal harmony which transcended religious and social demarcations. It is for this reason that he explicitly states that his grotto, which clearly shares many features with a Christian church, is, in fact, a pagan structure deliberately created from natural rock as a place for the worship of love. Here perfect harmony can be attained and love reach its highest point.

The harmony which the lovers attain in the cave contrasts forcibly with the relations between Tristan and Isolde and the majority of the characters in the poem. These are marked by only very occasional agreement and understanding, never by harmony. Only between Rual, Floraete, Curvenal, and Tristan is the relationship always amicable, but even here there is not harmony in the sense in which we have been using it. Tristan imposes his personality on these people and they, out of affection and respect—and their essential goodness—bend to his wishes and conform to the patterns he sets. It is a fact of the poem that we always observe the impact of Tristan and Isolde on others but that the two principal characters remain virtually unaffected by anyone else except each other. There is thus inevitably a disharmony in all relations except one. Even the faithful Brangaene is rarely in touch, let alone in harmony, with her mistress, and her rapport with the lovers as a pair is rarely close, however hard she tries. This one-way effect is the result of another manifestation of the artist in the poem, the constant acting of a role.

### ROLE-PLAYING AND REALITY

Tristan is, of course, the principal actor. It is perhaps paradoxical but nevertheless true that he rarely appears in the poem as himself. He is first shown to us as a person who has learned many languages and who consequently rarely speaks his own. His education allows him to take on and put off one role after another. On the merchant ship he is a chess player, on meeting the pilgrims a young huntsman who has lost his way, a foreign expert on the ceremony of the chase to Mark's huntsmen. In all these cases he speaks presumably in a foreign language. This element of foreignness, of play acting, becomes even more obvious in the performance before Mark. It should be remembered that Tristan is consciously putting on an act, both in the sense of giving a recital of songs (in many foreign languages) and in the sense of pretending to be something he is not—a merchant's son trained as a minstrel. When he is later revealed as Mark's nephew, he has no need to sustain this role but soon assumes others. It might be questioned whether he is playing a role in seeking to resume his father's titles and in fighting Morolt, yet there is evidence that this is so. He wears armor under his civilian clothing when he strikes down Duke Morgan and it is not hard to demonstrate that his conflict with the Irish warrior began with the assumption of the role of champion for rhetorical reasons—in order to persuade the Cornish noblemen to defend their sons—which he is then obliged to put into practice. Gottfried deliberately clouds this issue by his ironic allusions to the forces which Tristan incorporates in his person as a reply to Morolt's "strength of four men."

In Ireland Tristan again reverts to his minstrel role. His playing in the harbor is designed to attract attention, his playing before the two Isoldes to win them over. He secures his object—the cure of his wound—by pretending to be someone other than who he is. The deception persists when he slays the dragon and ends only when the splinter reveals his true identity. But this identity is as the slayer of Morolt, one which almost immediately ceases to have relevance, for Tristan now takes on the role of ambassador from King Mark, a role, be it noted, which has little significance for Isolde, who knows him as the teacher whose music she and she alone has learned. The role of ambassador becomes even more of a sham after the drinking of the love potion. Now the lovers together must act a part. Their real existence is that of lovers and nothing else. Yet Isolde must play the role of queen and wife and Tristan that of the king's loyal nephew. The roles have some remarkable facets: Isolde's deliberate use of her physical charms to persuade Mark that she does not love Tristan and her murderous attempt on the life of Brangaene, Tristan's confrontation with Marjodo and Melot. The role-playing culminates, of course, in the act put on for the benefit of God, where He is invited to regard Isolde as an innocent wife and Tristan as a pilgrim. Gottfried makes it very clear that Tristan himself is confused about his identity. When he is at Kaedin's court he cannot decide which Tristan he is, the one who was the lover of Isolde in the grotto, faithful for all time in his love for her, or the minstrel Tristan, again playing his artist role before the court, producing music for effect and not as part of a greater harmony.

It should be remembered that this role of player, of representer, was assigned to the lovers by Gottfried in his prologue. They are exemplary figures and hence playing a part for all *edele herzen*. More important even than this is Gottfried's own connection with the poem. He is, of course, the artist who presents the figures of Tristan and Isolde to the world, in a very real sense their creator. This aspect of his activity is, as we have seen, treated with great care in the literary excursus.[45] The way in which the story is to be told—in other words, the artist's methods—causes Gottfried great concern, because he regards his romance not as a mere piece of entertaining fiction but as a serious study of the nature of love. Furthermore, like Tristan, he is playing a role in which he is deeply involved. When he describes the activities, the joys and sorrows, of the lovers, he cannot be completely objective, for he is one of the *edele herzen* for whom the work is written. As he makes clear in the *Minnegrotte* scene, he has himself experienced everything but the ultimate ecstasy of the love shared by Tristan and Isolde. He is thus performing a role, the artist telling the experience of a hero who is to a large degree himself.

Yet here again we must make a distinction. It would be ludicrous to claim that there is anything autobiographical in Gottfried's poem. There is not and can never be any evidence about Gottfried's own life, but the matter is hardly significant. It is the *persona* of the poet who is speaking here, just as it is in the *canzon* and the *Minnesang*. The convention of the genre was that the poet should represent himself as the lover—as he very definitely does not in the *alba* or the *pastourelle*—and thus be able to balance two functions, that of the lover whose success depends on his ability to celebrate his lady's beauty and virtue and that of the artist whose inspiration comes from his lady. If the artist ceases to function, he cannot be a lover, for his only claim to the affections of his lady is his service to her in song. Yet an artist should be rewarded, and the constant failure of his lady to do so leads him to threaten to cease his endeavors, but to do so would deny his very existence. An artist cannot cease to sing if he is to continue to be an artist any more than a lover can cease to love if his lady is unkind. The poets of the *Minnesang* therefore represent themselves as singers in love and are thus able to play off one role against the other. While the *persona* of the poet can think of no other subject but his lady and no existence without celebrating her, the real poet, detached and sometimes ironical, is able to observe the *persona* struggling with his problem. There is no reason to assume that the poet himself was in love, although he may have been. He is setting up a problem, that of the artist whose service is to celebrate a lady whose rank and qualities make it virtually impossible for her to give him the only reward he craves. This is the true meaning of *amor de lonh*, love which is distant although it may be physically nearby. The artist must continue to sing or deny his nature, and the well-known tension of the *Minnesang* is between that artist and the disappointed lover, for in the *Minnesang* and *canzon* the artist can never attain the object for which he is performing. The *persona* of the poet in these lyrics is thus a universal figure representing the artist in a special situation, not the figure of an individual poet in love.

These facts should be borne in mind in assessing Gottfried's position. The feelings of Gottfried, the man who lived in Strassburg, are irrelevant to our discussion. The *persona* of the poet is the one mentioned in the allegory of the *Minnegrotte*, the one who never, in spite of his frequent visits to the cave, had slept in the crystalline bed or been in Cornwall. This *persona* is very similar to the unsuccessful artist of the *Minnesang*. His singing has failed to bring him the happiness he sought. Yet in other respects Gottfried's *persona* is far different. Unlike the writers of *Minnesang*, he is not writing a subjective genre. His views on love are projected only to a very limited degree through a *persona* of himself. He uses rather another artist, Tristan, to express them. His principal character, therefore, functions as the successful artist-lover. Tristan's use of his artistic ability to find true love shows how the singer can attain his object but it also points out the difference between Gottfried's concept of the artist and that of the *Minnesänger*. For Tristan succeeds only because Isolde becomes an artist too. The lady in the *Minnesang* is like Isolde White Hands. She listens and admires but does not—indeed could not—participate. Gottfried has evolved a new concept of the artist in love, one who imparts to his lady the skills he possesses and in doing so makes it possible for love to be attained in the fullest sense. Yet such attainment can be achieved only at great cost, for the artist is in society but not of it. In the end he perishes as a result of his very success, for his whole concept of love is inimical to the society in which he moves. The *Minnesänger* were from the point of view of that society completely right. They stopped short of challenging its mores by showing the artist as content to celebrate without reward. Tristan is successful but his life and that of Isolde are destroyed. Gottfried's *persona*, however, is unsuccessful. He can taste of true love only through the characters he creates. He moves in the society of the *Minnesänger*, not in the world he has created for his characters, and as such he cannot experience Tristan-love. The interplay between the two artists, Tristan and "Gottfried," is the contrast between two worlds, the creation of the artists' imagination and the world of medieval culture. Gottfried succeeds in his mission as artist, although he is a self-proclaimed failure in love; Tristan succeeds in both but there can be little doubt that his success would have cost the lives of himself and Isolde.

We are faced here, as so often in medieval literature, with variations on the play concept. Play is a formalized presentation of reality conforming to its own strict but not necessarily logical rules. The so-called courtly romance had developed a set of such rules for its presentation of the relation between the knight, his court, and his lady. It is much more rewarding to regard these rules as the conventions of a game rather than a courtly code based on philosophical or moral considerations, even though these latter may have played some part in the formulation of the rules. For once we accept the courtly romance as a form of play representation it is much easier to understand Gottfried's method of dealing with it. He accepts the rules of the courtly game only for the back-ground of his story and for the characters who are either neutral or opposed to Tristan-love. His allusions to courtliness and particularly to the rules of the game are almost always disparaging. In the context of these rules he sets his principal characters, who are artists first and knightly—or courtly —characters very much second. By making these characters "game-players," minstrels by choice or instruction, he sets up a new game, a new representation of life, which appears as mere play to the courtly audience because it is outside their experience but which is, in fact, a higher form of reality. The "rules of the game" for Tristan and Isolde are close to the rules of life itself. The game they play, as Gottfried makes very clear, is as much a representation of eternal verity as the Christian religion itself.

Tristan's role as artist in Gottfried's poem thus becomes of supreme importance. Endowed with a sensitivity toward life and love which is far greater than that of his contemporaries, he is able to express that sensitivity in words and particularly in music whose appeal is universal. Everyone is made to participate in his sense of beauty, but for some, and in particular for Isolde, his artistic powers produce a new sense of understanding of the world and of love. Tristan thus becomes the master-interpreter and teacher, but, like many artists, he is not always able to follow his own teachings consistently and is by no means free of the temptation to show off, to test his powers, or to take on tasks which are beyond him. His creator, also an artist, makes him behave according to a new set of artistic rules. Gottfried, as he shows in the literary excursus, feels obliged to use the form of the courtly romance, even though he recognizes its inadequacy for representing the love story of Tristan and Isolde, but in using it he plays with its conventions and at times denies them by giving to his hero and heroine a set of rules which are far closer to reality as he sees it. Thus in the poem the portrait of the artist shifts constantly. At times it is on the lowest level, the mere anonymous performer at the court of Cornwall or Ireland. Gandin is of a higher type, but his role as minstrel comes close to parody. He is using that role exactly as the "game-rules" of courtly romance prescribe, to deceive the king into granting him Isolde as a reward. His defeat comes at the hands of a minstrel who can play the game better than he. At the very top of the minstrel scale stands Tristan, who plays in a fashion not only superior to that of all others but not comprehensible to them by rational means. He is at once the seer and the interpreter, like Orpheus, the singer and the mover. And like Orpheus he must lose his love and perish as the result of his gift.

# VI

## THE STRUCTURE OF THE POEM

THE COMPOSITION of Gottfried's *Tristan* is simple in its general features and extremely complex in detail. Like the majority of courtly romances, the structure is essentially one of large narrative blocks. Each of these is concentrated on one major incident which affects the life of Tristan directly or indirectly. Within each block the locale remains the same. There is little in Gottfried's work to remind us of the movement in such works as the *Nibelungenlied* and *Parzival*. Each narrative block is, in fact, the exploration of an incident and its significance rather than a mere step forward in the action. We have already seen that there occur in the course of the poem a number of rhyming quatrains which are clearly arranged so that the initial letters of the quatrains, had the work been completed, would have formed the names of the hero and heroine, intertwined thus: TIRSIOSL[TDAEN]. The first letters of the immediately following narrative portions perform the same function but in different order: ITSROILS[DTEAN]. The quatrains so introduced never form part of the narrative. They are invariably comments, often gnomic and even inscrutable, on the fate of lovers, on the impossibility of avoiding sorrow, on the inevitability of misery in love. The first two (41–44, 131–34) occur in Gottfried's prologue to his poem, the third (1791–94) between the narrative of Riwalin and Blanscheflur and the opening of the Tristan narrative. It is hard to see any logical reason for the position of the others. There is a comment on Rual's taking over the upbringing of Tristan (1865–68), a remark on Tristan's hatred of Duke Morgan (5099–5102), a quite trivial reference to the welcome Tristan received on his return to Parmenie (5177–80), a comment on the power of love as the ship bearing Tristan and Isolde approaches Cornwall (12,431–34), and finally a comment on the inevitability of sorrow for those in love (12,503–6) which follows Tristan's remark, full of tragic irony, that if to love Isolde is death, then it is a death he would gladly die eternally. None of the remarks contained in the quatrains is of very great significance and, except for the third, none occurs between the narrative blocks. It will be observed that six of them occur in the first 5200 lines of a poem whose extant length is 19,548 lines and that the last two are within less than 100 lines of each other, thus following a pattern of pairing evident in the earlier occurrences. Attempts have been made to extrapolate the pattern and thus predict the length of the poem. To make it approximate the shape of the version of Thomas of Britain, it would be necessary to postulate that the last extant quatrain represents a pivotal point and that those which follow would appear at closer intervals, as they had at the beginning of the poem. But this is speculation. What is quite certain is that the quatrains have no function as dividers of narrative blocks, and the only reason which can be advanced to explain their position in the text is the subjective argument that they occur at points of emotional crisis.

There are other quatrains which do not fit into the Tristan-Isolde pattern. The first occurs at lines 233–36, a very significant quatrain which is the strongest of all the comparisons made between the significance of the poem for lovers and that of the Eucharist:

Deist aller edelen herzen brot
hie mite so lebet ir beider tot
wir lesen ir leben, wir lesen ir tot
und ist uns daz süeze alse brot                                  (233 ff.)

This is bread to all lofty spirits. Through it their death lives on. We read of their life, we read of their death, and for us it is as sweet as bread.

The second occurs after the death of Blanscheflur (1751 ff.)—one sorrow is followed by a deeper sorrow. A similar theme is expressed in the third (5069–72), which occurs after Tristan's knighting ceremony and before his encounter with Duke Morgan, and in the quatrain (11,870–73) which follows the drinking of the potion. The last follows shortly afterwards (12,183–86) when the goddess Minne has secured her triumph over Tristan and Isolde. These quatrains, which exhibit no really convincing pattern of initial letters (although "Godeidees" has been suggested), seem to have more relevance to the narrative text in which they occur but they still have no structural significance. They merely call the reader's attention to the conclusions he should draw and, more important, to the fact that Gottfried is telling the story to make a particular point, the inescapability of sorrow in the pursuit of love.

## THE NARRATIVE BLOCKS

The narrative blocks are these:

I     Tristan's Parents
II    Education of the Hero
III   Tristan's Establishment at Mark's Court
IV    Revenge on Duke Morgan
V     The Defeat of Morolt
VI    First Journey to Ireland and the Education of Isolde
VII   Second Journey to Ireland and the Union of the Lovers
VIII  The Abuse of Brangaene
IX    The Outwitting of Gandin
X     The Tricking of Mark
XI    The Ordeal by Hot Iron
XII   Petitcreiu
XIII  The Grotto of Love
XIV   Parting and Isolde White Hands

It is, of course, possible to subdivide these incidents and to isolate other subjects within them. For example, Tristan's establishment at Mark's court consists of his kidnaping by the merchants, his meeting with the pilgrims, his instruction of the huntsmen, his arrival at the court of Cornwall, his prowess as minstrel, his acceptance of a position as Mark's closest friend, the revelation of his true identity by Rual li Foitenant, and his "knighting." Each of these is a perfectly legitimate subdivision but equally clearly each is only a part of a narrative block. The "Education of the Hero" block is clearly separated from what follows by a passage summing up what had been achieved:

> . . . daz in den ziten unde do
> in allem dem riche
> nie kint so tugentliche
> gelebete alse Tristan.

al diu werlt diu truogin an
vriundes ouge und holden muot,
als man dem billiche tuot,
des muot niwan ze tugende stat,
der alle untugende unmaere hat.                                   (2140 ff.)

. . . that at that time and in all that kingdom no young man ever showed
such qualities as Tristan. Everyone looked on him with a friendly eye
and kindly feelings, as is right for a person whose thoughts are turned
entirely to excellence and who abhorred all baseness.

The new block begins with a clearly resumptive expression:

In den ziten unde do
kam ez von aventiure also . . .                                  (2149 f.)

At that time it so happened that . . .

Each of the incidents within it is related to Tristan's acquisition of power
at court. Even the arrival of Rual li Foitenant is carefully linked to this
narrative. The literary excursus has already been discussed. It is obviously
an interjection by the author, even though it is formally tied to the narrative. It is sharply separated from the next block, "Revenge on Duke
Morgan," by the following lines:

Truoc ieman lebender staete leit
bi staeteclicher saelekeit,
so truoc Tristan ie staete leit
bi staeteclicher saelekeit
Als ich ez iu bescheiden wil:
im was ein endeclichez zil
gegeben der zweier dinge,
leides unde linge . . .                                          (5069 ff.)

If ever there was a man who, for all his life, endured sorrow and constant
happiness together, then it was Tristan who endured lasting sorrow and
constant happiness together—as I intend to tell you. The ultimate end set
to his life had two parts, sorrow and success.

Here the quatrain is used as a divider, but Gottfried also makes it clear
that Tristan's life is entering a new phase. He has reached an apparent
peak of happiness, but sorrow lurks behind it. And the narrative moves to
Tristan's highly dubious attack on Morgan. It ends, as usual, with a
summing up by Gottfried and a statement of the sorrow of Rual's family

at Tristan's departure. Nor is there any change in the pattern of introduction for the new narrative block "The Defeat of Morolt." The personal
remark by Gottfried "waz lenge ich nu me hier an?" ("But why do I
linger on this subject") is followed by the indication that a new subject is
being opened:

> der lantlose Tristan,
> do der ze Curnewale kam,
> ein maere er al zehant vernam . . .                                    (5868 ff.)

When Tristan the landless came to Cornwall, he at once heard a story . . .

The story is that of the arrival of Morolt to enforce payment of the tribute
whose origin Gottfried now describes. The narrative proceeds smoothly
and without interruption until Morolt is dead and his body brought back
to Ireland. There are no subsidiary incidents or digressions except Gottfried's own interspersed comments on the relative strength of Tristan
and Morolt and the justice of Tristan's cause. Clear indication is given that
the narrative block is at an end:

> Nu herre Morolt der ist tot:
> tribe ich nu michel maere
> von ir aller swaere
> und von ir clage, waz hülfe daz?                                    (7196 ff.)

Now my lord Morolt is dead. If I were to make a long story of all their
wretchedness and all their lamentation, what use would that be?

Gurmun and his family lament, and many innocent people die as a result
of Gurmun's decree that any person from Cornwall caught on Irish soil
shall suffer the extreme penalty, but

> . . . was daz allez ane not,
> wan Morolt lac billiche tot:
> der was niwan an siner craft
> und niht an gote gemuothaft
> und vuorte zallen ziten
> ze allen sinen striten
> gewalt unde hochvart,
> in den er ouch gevellet wart.                                    (7223 ff.)

That was all without cause, for Morolt died justly. He put his trust in
his own strength, not in God, and at all times, in all battles, he practiced
violence and pride and in these he was struck down.

No time is shown to elapse between the conclusion of the "Morolt"
block and the beginning of that which tells of Tristan's first visit to Ireland,
but the division is clear enough:

> Nu grife wider, da ichz liez.                                                                 (7231)

> Now I shall begin again where I left off.

and:

> und enbeit ouch do niemere,
> er vuor von dannen zEngelant,
> von Engelanden al zehant
> ze Curnewale wider heim.                                                                      (8222 ff.)

> And stayed there no longer but departed for England and then from
> England at once back home to Cornwall.

Both in this block and in that which follows it there are numerous subdivisions which make the structure much more complicated than any
we have examined up till now. These will be discussed later. The divisions
between "The Union of the Lovers," "The Abuse of Brangaene," and
"The Outwitting of Gandin" are perfectly clearly designated by Gottfried.
It is perhaps less obvious why the incidents involving Marjodo and Melot
should be brought together as one block, "The Tricking of Mark." The
opening and closing lines reflect the complete nature of the incident:

> Tristandes lob und ere
> diu bluoten aber do mere
> ze hove und in dem lande.
> si lobeten an Tristande
> sine vuoge und sine sinne.
> er und diu küniginne
> si waren aber vro unde vruot,
> si gaben beide ein ander muot,
> sos iemer beste kunden.                                                                        (13,451 ff.)

> Tristan und sine vrouwe Isot
> diu lebeten aber liebe unde wol:
> ir beider wunne diu was vol.
> sus was in aber ein wunschleben
> nach ir ungemüete geben,
> swie kurz ez wernde waere,
> an' iteniuwe swaere.                                                                           (15,040 ff.)

> Tristan's fame and reputation continued to flourish more and more, both at court and throughout the land. People praised his ability and good sense. But he and the queen were happy and gay. They cheered each other whenever they possibly could.

> Tristan and his lady Isolde, however, lived happily and pleasantly. Their delight in each other was complete. Thus they were given an ideal existence after their troubles, short though it might be, before new misery came.

The narrative block begins and ends at a peaceful lull in the existence of the lovers when they are for a brief period unsuspected and able to enjoy each other's company. The incidents which take place within it, although separate, are similar in form and purpose. A rendezvous is arranged by Tristan and Isolde with the assistance of Brangaene, which is discovered by a member of the court other than Mark. The incident leads to suspicion on the part of the king but not to certain proof of the lovers' guilt. The evil disposition of those who seek to trap the lovers is one of the reasons for failure but it should be noticed that in this block—and this alone— they are behaving like courtly intriguers. Their subsequent meetings are of a different kind.

Gottfried begins his next block, "The Ordeal by Hot Iron," with a general moral observation by the poet on the evil nature of false friends, and deception is the theme of the block, deception of people and of God. Here there is no mere lovers' tryst but a cold-blooded attempt to trap the lovers by Melot and Mark, a trap which still produces no absolute certainty, followed by an attempt to produce that certainty by an appeal to the divine power. That appeal again comes to nothing because of Isolde's cunning.

There can be little dispute about the homogeneous nature of the remaining completed narrative blocks. Each is a clearly defined incident with a definite single theme—the winning of Petitcreiu for Isolde and her rejection of the dog because the happiness it brought could not be shared by Tristan, and the lovers' life in the grotto. The episode with Isolde White Hands is incomplete and no decision about its nature can be made.

The narrative blocks fall into two categories, those which are homogeneous, confined to one incident without substantial digression and with little intrusion on the part of the poet, and those which are compounded of one main theme with digressions and subsidiary incidents. Although the first type contributes considerably to our knowledge of the lovers and of Tristan-love, the purely narrative element in this type is strong. Of these homogeneous blocks only the incident in the *Minnegrotte* is more concerned with analysis than action. The other ("compound") blocks mark important crises in the lives of the lovers and they contain important incidents, for example, the killing of the dragon, but action in them is relatively unimportant. They are concerned with emotional and intellectual development.

The arrangement of the blocks is as follows:

> Homogeneous:   I, IV, V, VIII, IX, XII, XIII
> Compound:       II, III, VI, VII, X, XI

The block which deals with Tristan's parents stands alone; the others alternate in pairs. It is very likely that the Isolde White Hands narrative block would have been compound and that it would have been followed by another compound block containing the episode of the Hall of Statues and the proof given to Kaedin. The attempted revenge of Brangaene and the incident of the poisoned spear could have been homogeneous blocks and the work would then conclude with the treachery of Isolde White Hands and the death of the lovers, a compound incident balancing the one homogeneous block at the beginning of the work. The whole structure would thus be carefully balanced.

In general it may be said that the homogeneous blocks of Gottfried's work are less interesting than the compound ones and that they display less of the features which are characteristic of Gottfried as a poet. The Morgan and Morolt episodes are designed primarily to provide essential links in the story, for without the defeat of Morgan there could have been no renunciation of the lands of Parmenie and hence no permanent return to the court of Mark. The Morolt episode provides the reason for the voyage to Ireland. Gottfried inherited these episodes and their function from his predecessors. His original contribution consists in their application to the assessment of Tristan's character and of courtly culture. Both contain fights, both are utterly unchivalrous in tone, both show Tristan's opponents as persons more efficient in combat than Tristan—or reputed to be so—who are defeated by his superior cunning even though they have a great deal of legality—as opposed to justice—on their side. In both cases it is shown that combat and law settle very little. Tristan obtains the right to his lands by a deed which comes close to murder; Morolt almost kills his opponent by a poisoned sword, an utterly unchivalrous act, and in any case his "defense" leads to Ireland's passing to the crown of Cornwall—by a marriage which is no marriage! In these blocks the narrative element is dominant; in second place is the presentation of *one* aspect of the society—the futility of decision by combat—and one aspect of Tristan's character, his refusal to fight in conventional chivalric single combat. Episodes VIII and IX, Brangaene's sacrifice and the trickery of Gandin, are also essentially narrative, but less so than the two already discussed. The deception of Mark is necessary so that Isolde may continue to live at court but there is no narrative reason in the poem as we have it for the attempted murder. The Gandin incident could undoubtedly be eliminated without loss to the story as a whole. Its *raison d'être* is exactly the same as that for the Brangaene episode—the exposure of Mark's unworthiness to be Isolde's husband. In the former incident he is unable to distinguish between Isolde and Brangaene, since, as we have seen, love for him is purely sensual; in the latter he shows himself incapable, of preserving her. He is tricked by a minstrel and is not man enough to refuse the impudent request or to resort to force of arms to recover her. In terms of the complete narrative he has abdicated every claim to Isolde except the legal one. The emphasis on legality appears here as it did in the Duke Morgan and Morolt episodes.

The last two homogeneous blocks are of a different kind. The winning of Petitcreiu is again a self-contained narrative incident. Like the abuse of Brangaene and the tricking of Gandin, it could be omitted without serious effect on the total narrative. Like them, it is of great importance as a mark of progress in Tristan-love. The incident shows that Isolde has moved to the point at which she cannot experience true happiness without sharing it with Tristan. Her attitude is one of positive refusal. When perfect music is offered for her enjoyment, she rejects it, since her delight in harmony cannot exist without her lover. Tristan's dilemma is expressed in different terms in the episode with Isolde White Hands, where he offers music which she can neither understand nor share. Between these two episodes comes the last of the homogeneous narrative blocks, "The Grotto of Love," where, for the first and last time in the poem, perfect harmony can be realized, untroubled by external considerations. Here, of course, the narrative element is of minimal significance.

Although every version of the Tristan story has some reference to the exile in the forest, none except that of Thomas treats it as a major incident and even Thomas does not make it the key scene of his work. Its homogeneous nature derives less from the unity of its narrative (although it is the simplest and most unified of all the incidents in the work) than from the unity of feeling and style. It is a culmination of narrative, for it represents the climax before the descending action, and a culmination of experience, for never again do the lovers achieve such harmony.

The narrative blocks which we have called "compound" present very different features, of which the most obvious is that they lack one central narrative theme. The episode of Tristan's childhood and education break down into his rescue by Rual, his early nurture by Floraete, the details of his "education," and an explanation of its reasons and results. The establishment at Mark's court is extremely complex. There are at least six subdivisions—the abduction by merchants, the meeting with pilgrims, the hunting ceremonial, the young minstrel, the revelation by Rual, and the investiture. The only narrative movement needed is the actual journey from Parmenie to Mark's court and the revelation of Tristan's parentage. Yet these occupy very little of the narrative block. Most of it is taken up by careful exploration of Tristan's effect on others—on the merchants, on the pilgrims, on the huntsmen, on the minstrel, and most particularly on Mark. We are very little concerned here or in the "education" block with narrative progression but with the establishment of the bases on which Tristan-love is to be built. Hence these compound blocks contain a high proportion of descriptive and discursive matter. A detailed examination of two of them will serve as an example of the structure of a compound block. The subdivisions are as follows:

| II | III |
|---|---|
| 1789 Quatrain | 2147 Arrival of merchants |
| 1793 Observations on loyalty by Gottfried | 2214 The game of chess |
| | 2254 Tristan's accomplishments |
| 1816 Burial of Blanscheflur. Lamentation. Observations by Gottfried on sorrow | 2316 Abduction and despair |
| | 2450 Decision to land Tristan |
| 1867 Submission of Riwalin's men to Morgan | 2480 Tristan's experience and sorrow |
| | 2531 Description of Tristan's |

1892 Pretended delivery of
Floraete
1953 Baptism of Tristan.
Comment by Gottfried
on his Christianity and
name
2041 Tristan's education—
languages, books,
physical exercise
2129 The results of this
education

appearance
2618 Sighting of pilgrims
2651 Tristan joins the pilgrims
2757 The hunting ceremonial
3079 Tristan's story and arrival
at Mark's court
3754 Rual's travels and
reception at court
4119 Rual's revelation of
Tristan's origin. Gottfried's
comment
4545–5066 Tristan's investiture and
the literary excursus

The second of these narrative blocks is almost eight times as long as the former, and although it is possible to see some arithmetical features—the description of Tristan's baptism, with Gottfried's comments, is exactly as long as the description of his education—it would be straining credulity to find "number symbolism" or arithmetic-architecture in any of these blocks. It is more instructive to observe the proportion of narrative, dialogue, and personal comment by Gottfried.

THE USE OF DIALOGUE

An examination of Gottfried's use of dialogue reveals that it appears unevenly in the work. There are long stretches of the poem where there is no dialogue whatsoever. Good examples are the description of Riwalin's arrival at Mark's court, Tristan's investiture, the early description of the encounter with Morolt, the descriptions of the effects of the love potion, the scene-setting for the various deceptions of Mark, and above all the *Minnegrotte* scene. It will be observed that in many of these scenes Gottfried is either speaking in his own person (the literary excursus) or providing information as the omniscient author (the history of the tribute to Ireland, the characters of Marjodo and Melot). The *Minnegrotte* scene is described by an author who not only knows what is in the hearts of Tristan and Isolde but who speaks from personal involvement in their problems. On the other hand, there are parts of the poem where dialogue is frequent and highly concentrated, such as the whole passage in which Tristan is kidnaped, meets the pilgrims, instructs the hunter, and performs at Mark's court. Here third-person narration is kept to a minimum and dialogue provides the narrative movement. Tristan's arrival in Ireland for the first time follows the same pattern: he leaves his followers with a speech of farewell which makes dispositions for his possible failure to return and from then on conducts a series of dialogues with the different persons he encounters before the decisive meeting with the queen and Isolde. There is a similar concentration when he returns to Cornwall and again after the conflict with the dragon when he is brought back to the palace. As might be expected, the scene on shipboard produces a great deal of conversation before the drinking of the potion but little afterwards. The various attempts to deceive Mark produce many speeches, very few of them addressed by the lovers to each other. Only when they are about to part for the last time in the poem do they once again speak to each other at length.

The distribution of dialogue in the poem is not an accident. There is no reason, for example, why Tristan and Isolde should not be shown speaking to one another in the *Minnegrotte*—they undoubtedly did not preserve total silence during their stay. They are not described as speaking because in their situation speech was not important and, more significantly, they have nothing to hide or dissemble. For an examination of Gottfried's use of dialogue soon reveals that it is used as a means of hiding rather than expressing thought. Speeches, particularly long speeches, are either "policy statements" or deliberate role-playing, the putting on of an actor's mask. Inevitably it is Tristan who makes the most frequent use of speech to deceive or to induce a result which he desires. His first words in the poem are those which begin the chess game with the merchants and are spoken in their language. His role-playing has begun. It continues with his performance as a local noble to the pilgrims, as an expert on hunting to Mark's huntsmen, as the well-taught son of a merchant with skills in music and languages before the court of Mark. Gottfried's frequent use of direct speech in these scenes is designed to show that Tristan is playing a role. He determines the part he will play in a given situation and speaks the words which are appropriate to that part. The result, of course, is that the speeches put into his mouth make him a dreadful liar. He uses speech as a means to an end, to produce a given effect, not as a means to express his true thoughts. There must inevitably be a strong suspicion that Tristan *never* says what he really thinks but what he feels his role of the moment calls for. Some of these roles are obvious and are needed for the story—the role of Tantris on the first visit to Ireland is a case in point—and Tristan must rely on the skillful use of speech to establish his assumed personality, but there are examples of speech in role-playing which are not so obvious: Tristan's pose as the indignant observer at the supine way in which the Cornish nobles accept the inevitability of a Morolt victory; the air of injured rectitude in the confrontation with Duke Morgan; the role of rival minstrel in the conflict with Gandin; the role of ambassador when his true identity has been revealed at the Irish court. In all of these encounters Tristan wishes to present a particular image to make a particular impression and in the majority of cases his role-playing is a success. There are exceptions. He totally fails to impress Morgan and has to resort to the crudest violence to obtain his ends; he also fails to impress the courtiers at Mark's court and has to make good his offer to fight with Morolt himself. Here the dialogue fails.

Only rarely is there dialogue between Tristan and Isolde. During the important period of her instruction, Gottfried uses no dialogue—there is no role to be played. The first real exchange of speech between them takes place when Tristan is in his bath. The situation can be called, without irony, somewhat odd. In all his previous dealings with Isolde, Tristan has been playing the role of Tantris. His only direct speech in her presence as recorded by Gottfried has been made rather to her mother than to her. Now, at a moment when she was inclined to feel at least pity and possibly love for him, she finds out that everything he has pretended to be is false. The course of Tristan's speech now has to be determined by completely new criteria. He must rapidly take on a new role, that of helpless guest protected by the laws of hospitality, and later, more quietly, that of indispensable witness to the steward's perfidy.

More important than Tristan's role-playing here is the first instance of it by Isolde. Her role, as proclaimed by her speech, is that of the injured niece of Morolt, the avenger of her uncle's death. Her act is unconvincing. While proclaiming her fury at the deceit practiced by Tantris-Tristan, she is totally unable to use the sword in her hands and is only too glad to accept the advice of her mother and Brangaene to spare their guest. Her words do not reflect her true sentiments; she is merely playing a part. Her subsequent speeches continue this tradition. In talking with Tristan on the ship which bears them both to Cornwall, she addresses him with scorn, blames him for all her misery. Yet the narrative makes clear that she is afraid more of herself than of him. After the drinking of the potion there is no more of such dialogue, indeed no dialogue at all, for the true state of their love is revealed through the mediation of Brangaene and we are told by Gottfried, not by the lovers themselves, of the fulfillment of their love.

Isolde's role-playing does, however, continue. It must not be forgotten that every speech she makes to Mark is a manifestation of her acting ability. She has chosen to play the role of a virgin brought to the king's bed and after that the role of a faithful wife. This decision leads inevitably to a tissue of lies and to the deliberate assumption of roles which serve the purposes of the moment. Such is the speech to the men ordered to murder Brangaene—and indeed the speech to Brangaene herself—and more significantly the speeches made to Mark by which she hopes to convince him that she has no interest in Tristan. There is interesting byplay here, for both Isolde and Mark are expressing not their thoughts but views which they hope will produce a specific reaction. Mark hopes that his speeches will either make Isolde implicate herself as Tristan's paramour or clear her of the charge. Isolde is trying to gauge his intentions and make the reply that will convince him. She is not always successful, for her eagerness to keep Tristan with her leads her to break through her role and express her real desires. She must then hastily revert to her act, beg Mark to send Tristan from court, and say that she loathes him. Isolde reinforces her words by the adriot and cynical use of her physical charms. Every speech which Isolde utters, every gesture she makes to everyone but Tristan, are parts of a play, culminating, as we have already seen, with her speech before seizing the hot iron.

This view of Isolde's speeches raises an interesting question about the last dialogue between her and Tristan. There is a sharp contrast here between the almost abject determination of Tristan to escape while he still has his life and the words of Isolde, which emphasize eternal loyalty. This is the first long set speech which is recorded from Isolde to Tristan— except those in which we know they are playing a role. Are we to take Isolde's speech as her true thought as she sees Tristan go? It seems likely that we should, for the sentiments are sincere and appropriate to the occasion. Yet Gottfried does not usually allow Tristan and Isolde to express their true feelings for one another in speeches. Even the crucial revelation after the drinking of the potion is expressed with extraordinary brevity by Tristan, and by Isolde quite simply with "herre, als sit ir mir" ("Sir, so you are to me"). In the scene in the *Minnegrotte* there is even less conversation. This parting, however, produces a long speech from Isolde, and it is difficult to escape the conclusion that Isolde is saying what she thinks is appropriate to the occasion—remember that we are inseparably united: never look at another woman: do not forget me. The sentiments are conventional enough, but in view of Tristan's behavior with Isolde White Hands her speech is full of tragic irony. It is impossible to determine precisely what Gottfried's purpose was in putting this speech into Isolde's mouth. Clearly there is no role-playing in the sense of insincerity: Isolde means what she says. If she is to be regarded as playing a role, it must be that of the lady parting from her lover, a commonplace of courtly romance and hence foreign to Gottfried's normal approach but a role which here coincides with Isolde's true position. It seems most likely that Gottfried uses this speech structurally, to anticipate the doubts of Tristan at Kaedin's court.

We may note here the obvious parallel between the departure of Tristan and that of Aeneas. Dido is left lamenting the perfidy of her lover, his ruthlessness in abandoning her for a cause she does not understand; Isolde laments for a lover who has no option but to leave. Each woman is separated from her lover, so far as she knows forever, but while Dido feels and is abandoned, Isolde is sure that her heart can never again be separated from Tristan's.

> sin leben half ir, daz si genas;
> sin mohte leben noch sterben,
> ane in niht erwerben.
>
>    .   .
>
> iht mere muget ir ane mich
> iemer geleben keinen tac,
> dan ich ane iuch geleben mac.
>
>    .   .
>
> wir zwei wir tragen under uns zwein
> tot unde leben ein ander an;
> wan unser enwederez enkan
> ze rehte sterben noch geleben,
> ezn müeze ime daz ander geben.
>
>    .   .
>
> Isote lip, Isote leben

diu sint bevolhen unde ergeben
den segeln unde den winden.
wa mag ich mich nu vinden?
wa mag ich mich nu suochen, wa?
nu bin ich hie und bin ouch da
und enbin doch weder da noch hie,
wer wart ouch sus verirret ie?
wer wart ie sus zerteilet me?
ich sihe mich dort uf jenem se
und bin hie an dem lande.
ich var dort mit Tristande
und sitze hie bi Marke.                                    (18,474 ff.)

His living helped her to stay alive; she had no power to live or die
without him. . . . "You can no more live a single day without me than I
can without you . . . . We too bear death and life, each for the other, for
neither of us can really die or live unless the other grant it . . . ." "Isolde's
person, Isolde's life, have been committed and handed over to sails and
winds. Where can I find myself now, where can I seek myself, where?
Sometimes I am here, sometimes there, and yet I am neither here nor
there. Who was ever so distracted, who was ever so divided? I see myself
out there at sea and am here on land. I sail away with Tristan and sit
here with Mark."

Unlike Dido, who sees the ship's departure as a final severance, Isolde
feels that she too is departing in spirit. There is clear reference here to the
lyric commonplace of physical separation which still fails to divide the
lover's heart from his mistress, a convention which forms the basis of
numerous crusading songs. This is the *amor de lonh* with which Isolde
must be satisfied. Until now she and Tristan had been in just the opposite
situation. They had been separated neither physically nor emotionally
but only, at times, by social convention. Unlike the lovers of the *canzon*
and *Minnesang*, each had assurance of love from the other. Their problem
was thus only a part, and that the smaller part, of the lyric poets'—the
avoiding of discovery by the *jaloux*, whether they be husband, rival, or
spy. Isolde's speech to Tristan and the monologue which is later put in
her mouth both suggest to the reader the new plight of the lovers—and
particularly of Isolde—and turn the reader's attention to the aspect of
love which will dominate the poem from now on—the preservation of
love in absence. In Gottfried's poem Isolde does not appear again.

The speeches of Tristan and Isolde are the most obvious examples of

Gottfried's use of direct discourse to show his characters consciously acting a role, using speech to produce a particular effect and not necessarily to express their true thoughts. The technique is used for other characters but with a difference. Some, like Melot and Marjodo, are by nature treacherous, and the only speeches they ever make are deceptive and cunning, designed to entrap the lovers. The Irish seneschal also uses speech entirely in this lying fashion, but his words have only one end, the promotion of his attempts to win Isolde and gain the kingdom. His speeches differ from those of Marjodo and Melot by their bluster. The audience—and later Tristan, the queen, Isolde, and Brangaene—know the true facts of the case and can compare them with the speeches the seneschal utters in public. He is playing the role of the chivalric dragon-slayer, and Gottfried takes care to make him play it in King Cambyses vein. There are elements of this braggadocio in the speeches of Gandin, but Gottfried is better disposed toward unsuccessful minstrels than toward boasting knights.

The two most interesting users of direct speech are Mark and Brangaene. Both in their different ways are representatives of the courtly ethic, and their conduct is determined by its conventions. An examination of Brangaene's speeches shows that they are entirely concerned with her duties, not with her feelings. She appears in the role of adviser when the unconscious Tristan is found after the battle with the dragon, she persuades the two Isoldes to listen to his proposal when his true identity is revealed, and it is her speech and pledge of silence which breaks down the barrier between the lovers on shipboard *before* she tells them of the love potion. We are not told of the words she used in discussing and finally accepting Isolde's plea that she substitute for her on the wedding night, but we are given the speech in which she sets forth her reason for doing so—her failure properly to safeguard the love potion. Her next recorded utterances again refer to her duty—first to save her mistress from pain and then to explain to her potential murderers, in a thinly veiled figure of speech, the service she had done for Isolde. Although in her rare monologues Brangaene gives vent to her misery, her speeches to others are always concerned with her duties as confidante and, after the marriage, organizer of meetings between the lovers. All these speeches indicate that she has no existence apart from her function as Isolde's—and even more Tristan's—helper in their love affair. Her role-playing is confined to this one thing; it is not acting in the sense that we use the word of Tristan, for Brangaene is not taking on and shedding roles to produce different effects. She has completely subordinated her person to the role. Whether she would have continued to do so in the scenes in which Thomas describes her as offered to Kaedin for his night's amusement is a matter for speculation. Her complete devotion to her duty makes her a highly sympathetic person, a characteristic she shares with Rual li Foitenant, whose speeches are also concerned with one thing only—his duty to Tristan as the son of his liege lord.

Mark is a more complex problem. He appears in two roles, that of king of Cornwall and uncle of Tristan and that of Tristan's rival in love. In view of the importance of his character in the poem, remarkably few long speeches are attributed to him. In the whole of the episode of Riwalin and Blanscheflur only a few words of welcome are put in his mouth. Everything else we know about him appears indirectly. In the early scenes with his nephew he expresses his interest, his delight in Tristan's accomplishments, and his determination to keep him as a friend. After Rual has told him Tristan's history, he makes a formal pronouncement that Tristan will be his heir. None of these speeches is long and none goes beyond the immediate needs of the narrative. The first speech of any length is at Tristan's investiture. It is a typical string of moralistic platitudes and when Tristan later complains of the attitude of the barons and states his well-justified belief that his life may be in danger if he stays at the court, he receives more of the same:

> "hazzen unde niden
> daz muoz der biderbe liden:
> der man der werdet al die vrist,
> die wile und er geniten ist.
> wirde unde nit diu zwei diu sint
> reht alse ein muoter unde ir kint."                    (8395 ff.)

> "Hatred and envy are what a worthy man must put up with. A man like that grows in worth even when he is being envied. Worth and envy are a pair, just like a mother and child."

This speech is meaningless, and Mark does not affect the subsequent events in the least. Tristan does go in search of Isolde, which is what the barons demand, and it is Tristan's skill which involves them in the expedition against their will, not Mark's authority as king. The fact is that Mark's speeches are all sham. He is sincere in his love for Tristan before the involvement with Isolde and he is, in his own way, in love with Isolde himself, but all this is expressed not in his speeches but in Gottfried's narrative. Mark's speeches are the utterances of a king of shreds and patches—his feeble remarks to Gandin when he is about to lose Isolde, his feeble attempts to trap Isolde into an admission of love for Tristan, his failure to make use of his opportunities at the ordeal. Only once does he make a speech worthy of the dignity of a king. His banishment of the lovers from his court on the grounds that he can no longer bear to see their obvious affection for each other before his very eyes is a noble gesture, nobly expressed. It is the one occasion on which Mark rises to the true dignity of a king and even more of a man. Yet he cannot sustain it. When he sees the body of Isolde below him in the *Minnegrotte*, all his noble intentions disappear, and he is once again the slave of appetite.

Mark's speeches serve a rather different purpose from those of Tristan and Isolde. They are few in number and, with the one exception noted, they reveal his bankruptcy as a ruler. He is, indeed, playing the part of a king, not because he is consciously acting but because acting the part is as close as he can attain to kingship. He is pleasant and kind, he can carry out the ceremonial functions of his office, he can encourage the young Tristan and honor Rual li Foitenant. But he has no idea how to handle Morolt or Gandin—or Tristan himself when he ceases to be the young musician and becomes the rival. He has no more than clichés at his disposal, and his speeches reveal this.

Direct speech in Gottfried's work is thus not a measure of a person's true character. It is used to show what image he is trying to project or what he considers to be his role. Tristan makes the most brilliant and varied use of speech to impose his personality, ideas, and aims upon others. For him speech is an instrument of policy. The same is true, to a more limited degree, of Isolde. Gottfried puts direct speech into their mouths only when he wishes to show them playing a role or hiding their true purpose. Other characters, whose role in the poem is less complex, are given speeches to show them functioning in this role, sometimes simply and honestly like Rual, sometimes unconsciously revealing their limitations, like Mark.

### THE MONOLOGUE

Gottfried's use of monologue differs considerably from his use of direct speech. The internal monologue, the turning-over of a problem, is found in classical epics—Dido's agonized thoughts at the departure of Aeneas would be the best-known example to medieval writers—but the writers of courtly romance were excessively fond of it because it gave them an opportunity to allow their characters to set forth their feelings and the symptoms of love in a lively and effective way. The French *Roman d'Enéas* is the work which sets the style in this respect, but the works of Chrétien also provide many examples, notably the long monologue of Yvain trapped in the castle and seeing Laudine for the first time. Although monologues are sometimes used to express thoughts and emotions other than those connected with sexual attraction, their principal purpose is for love analysis. It might be thought, therefore, that Gottfried would make great use of them, since analysis of the love phenomenon is the principal theme of his poem. In fact, quite the opposite is the case. Gottfried makes relatively little use of monologue and at the point in the narrative where we would expect to see it, after the drinking of the love potion, there is virtually none. Tristan's only thoughts directly revealed concern his loyalty, not his love; no internal monologue is attributed to Isolde at all. Gottfried's failure to use internal monologue at a crisis of his poem is surely deliberate, and a clue is given to his reasoning by the fact that he does use such monologue, in a highly conventional way, in describing the love symptoms of Riwalin and Blanscheflur. Riwalin's feelings are described in a short piece of dialogue with Blanscheflur but principally by Gottfried himself. Blanscheflur's thoughts when she falls in love are remarkably like those of Lavine in the *Roman d'Enéas* and, when she finds that Riwalin is preparing to leave, like those of Dido. They are expressed in internal monologues. As we have seen, Gottfried makes the love affair of Tristan's parents much more like those in normal romances than the love of Tristan and Isolde. His use of internal monologue for Blanscheflur and his omission of it for Isolde sharply point up the contrast.

Nevertheless there are important monologues attributed to Isolde, and it is clear from their position in the narrative that Gottfried considers these musings to be important indications of the true emotional state of his heroine. The first occurs when she becomes aware of Tristan as a person, as he recovers from the fight with the dragon. The monologue never mentions love. It does show a woman very much aware of a man as a person and subconsciously weighing the circumstances which separate him from her, particularly the fact that, as far as she knows at this time, he is not of noble birth. Her subsequent, almost fearful pairing of the names Tantris-Tristan indicates her hope and fear that he may indeed be noble—and still barred to her. These internal monologues are far from conventional. They are subtle presentations of a mind in turmoil and as such a far more effective indicator of the beginnings of love than the monologues of the earlier romances.

During the period when Tristan and Isolde are together, the only monologue recorded of Isolde is a very brief thought while Brangaene is taking her place with Mark. Only when Isolde is parted from her lover, when he sends her the little dog Petitcreiu, does she contrast her state with his and point out that she has no right to pleasure when they are apart. Her last monologue springs from the same cause. She sees Tristan depart and tells herself that, even though they are physically separated, there can be no separation of their lives or their love. It is the ultimate statement of the immutability and eternity of Tristan-love and it is the exact opposite of the love monologues of the other romances. These are marked by doubt of reciprocation and hatred of separation. Isolde knows that Tristan loves her and that separation does not exist. The internal monologues attributed to Isolde, few as they are, are the most important indicators of her emotional state.

Gottfried gives more monologues to Tristan and their artistic purpose is more varied. Yet they still occur almost entirely when the lovers are separated, at crises in which Tristan is at a loss as to the course of action he should take. Abducted by the merchants and alone in a strange land, he very naturally turns his thoughts to prayer and a hope that he may yet be preserved by divine providence. These early monologues are expressions of fear and uncertainty and so, in a different way, are those attributed to Tristan after his meeting with Isolde. The brief passage of direct speech which tells us of his thoughts after drinking the love potion emphasizes not his love but the struggle between love and loyalty. A very different kind of loyalty is involved in the welling confusion which is recorded in his thoughts when he meets Isolde White Hands. Now his loyalty is to Isolde the Fair, and everything logical in him says that Isolde White Hands is far inferior to her in every way. Yet there is sensual attraction and the totally illogical feeling that, because she is *an* Isolde, she must partake to some degree of the virtues of *the* Isolde. Whatever his spiritual attachment to the absent Isolde, he cannot escape altogether from physical desire. The confusion of names recalls, as Gottfried undoubtedly intended, the puzzlement of Isolde as she tried to work out the connection between Tantris, the minstrel whom she pitied and admired, and Tristan, her uncle's killer, whom she had never consciously met but whom she was supposed to hate and, if possible, destroy. There one person had been two. Tristan has two people who persist in coalescing behind one name. Monologue is thus used of Tristan at moments of crisis which are *not* concerned with any questions of love for Isolde. He never is shown as wondering whether Isolde loves him but only as involved in conflicts between love and loyalty, love and uncertainty, and simple fear.

Mark is never given any significant monologues. We hear his public utterances and we are told what his thoughts are, but he is never allowed to show us his thoughts. There must be a strong suspicion that he does not have any thoughts or even doubts worth recording. This may sound a harsh judgment, especially as it is an *argumentum ex silentio*, but all indications point to the probability that Gottfried wished to show Mark as a man who might be driven by a few primitive emotions and be torn between them but who lacked any subtle perceptions. Brangaene also has few lines of monologue, for she, too, does not doubt, although she may despair. Her thoughts, which are almost always recorded in the third person by Gottfried, are concerned entirely with any lapses from her own high standards of service to her mistress. The same is true of Rual li Foitenant, the other personification of perfect loyalty. Since neither of these is faced with a crisis of decision, neither need show the torture of indecision in internal monologue.

THE AUTHOR AND HIS NARRATIVE

Gottfried clearly makes less use of internal monologue than Chrétien de Troyes or most of the courtly writers and he sharply restricts its artistic purpose to the exposition of crises of decision for Tristan and Isolde, as he restricts the use of long passages of direct speech to the playing of a role or an attempt by one character to influence another in a specific direction. For his highly detailed exposition of the emotions and motivations of his characters, Gottfried relies on third-person narration. He prefers to tell his audience what his characters feel and what their intentions are rather than let them speak for themselves or indicate by their actions what their purposes are. The narrative passages fall into two clearly differentiated types. In the first, simple language moves the story rapidly and without intervention by the author. The very speed with which such passages move indicates Gottfried's lack of interest. In the other, much larger category, fall those sections of the poem where the plot moves little or not at all but where the reader is acquainted with the forces which provoke action and, more important, decide the lives of the protagonists. The contrast in styles can easily be seen by comparing the following passages:

|  |  |
|---|---|
| Nu Markes hohgezit ergie | Nu Tristan was uf sine vart |
| und sich diu herschaft gar zerlie, | und schiffete allez hinewart, |
| do kamen Marke maere, | er unde sine geselleschaft; |
| daz ein sin vient waere, | der was ein teil vil sorchaft: |
| ein künec, geriten in sin lant | ich meine die barune, |
| mit also creftiger hant, | die zweinzic companjune, |
| der in niht schiere taete wider, | den rat von Curnewale: |
| er braeche im allez daz dernider, | die haeten zuo dem male |
| daz er beriten kunde. | vil michel angest unde not; |
| zehant und an der stunde | si wanden alle wesen tot: |
| besande Marke ein michel her | sie vluocheten der stunde |
| und kam in an mit starker wer. | mit herzen und mit munde, |
| er vaht mit ime und sigete im an | daz der reise unde der vart. |
| und sluog und vienc so manegen | zIrlande ie gedaht wart. |
|   man, | sine kunden umbe ir eigen leben |
| daz ez von grozen saelden was, | in selben keinen rat gegeben: |
| der dannen kam oder da genas. | si rieten her, si rieten hin |
| da ward der werde Riwalin | und enkunden nie niht under in |
| mit eime sper zer siten in | geraten, daz in töhte |
| gestochen und so sere wunt, | und daz rat heizen möhte. |
| daz in die sine sa zestunt | und enwas ouch daz kein wunder |
| vür einen halptoten man | hier umbe noch hier under |
| mit manegem jamer vuorten dan | was rates niht wan zweier ein, |
| hin heim ze Tintajele wider. | in müeze einez under zwein |
|           (1119 ff.) | bringen umbe ir leben vrist, |
|  | aventiure oder list. |
|  | der list was aber da tiure; |
|  | so was ouch aventiure |
|  | ir keinem in wane: |
|  | si waren beider ane.    (8629 ff.) |

|  |  |
|---|---|
| Mark's celebration was over and the nobles dispersed. The news reached Mark that a king, an enemy of his, had invaded his land with | Now Tristan was on his way, and he and the whole company sailed away. Some of them were very worried, the barons I |

such powerful forces that he would
destroy everything he overran
unless he were quickly thrust back.
At once Mark summoned a large
army and opposed him in great
strength. He fought and defeated
him and killed and captured so
many men that those who escaped
or survived were very fortunate.
There the noble Riwalin was pierced
in the side with a spear and wounded,
so severely that his men at once
brought him back home to Tintagel
like a man half dead, amid great
lamentation.

mean, the company of twenty,
the planners from Cornwall.
They were full of fear and misery
on this occasion; they thought
they were all as good as dead.
In their hearts and with their lips
they cursed the hour that the
thought of an expedition and
voyage to Ireland had entered
their heads. They could not
think of any plan of saving their
own lives. They planned here,
they planned there and could
not evolve any plan between
them that did any good or was
worth calling a plan. And that
was not remarkable. For on this
subject and among them there
could be only one of two plans.
It had to be one of two methods
which saved their heads, either
skill or trusting to luck. But there
was a scarcity of skill there, and
trusting to luck never occurred to
them. They had none of either.

Both these passages have a strong narrative element but their purpose
and style are markedly different. The first passage does nothing but
provide facts: it tells of an invasion, a mobilization, a victory, and a
near-fatal wound for Riwalin, all in the space of twenty-three lines. There
are very few adjectives (9), and those of little significance, but many verbs
(21). Little attempt is made at vivid description, for Gottfried, as usual,
is not interested in the fight as such but only in providing the reason for
the condition of Riwalin which leads to the conception of Tristan. The
second passage is also an important narrative link for it shows Tristan
going back to Ireland. Gottfried could have dealt with this very briefly
(he brings Tristan back from his first visit in four lines), but his purpose
here is not merely the provision of a narrative link but an illustration of
one of the basic premises of his poem, the treacherous nature of those
who make their life at court. He pauses during the ocean voyage to let us
see the cowardice and baseness of a group which had hoped to trap

Tristan and now found themselves hoist with their own petard. We are no longer provided with mere narrative incident but with observations which show the author's knowledge of the inner thoughts of his characters and of their motivations and with ironical remarks which show the author's own sympathies: the courtiers are Tristan's "companjune"; although they have made a hideous miscalculation, they are described as "den rat von Kurnewale." Forms of the word *rat* appear no less than seven times in a passage whose purpose is to show how conspicuously any form of wisdom was lacking in these men. The only qualities which could save them were skill and daring, two things which Tristan had and they did not. It will be noted that Gottfried is making judgments here, even though he does not speak in the first person. He is contrasting his hero with the normal inhabitants of the court, much to the latter's disadvantage. The proportion of verbs, adjectives, and nouns remains about the same in both passages, but the use of them differs: the verbs in the second passage are little more than copulatives and show no real action. The power of the description springs from its nouns and adjectives and from the juxtaposing and repetition of the compounds of *rat*, already mentioned, *list*, and *aventiure*.

These two passages are in the narrative but Gottfried makes even more significant use of his authorial privileges in his descriptions and analysis of emotional states. Here action is nonexistent and concentration is entirely on analysis:

> Alsam geschach Isote:
> si versuochtez ouch genote,
> ir was diz leben ouch ande
> do si den lim erkande
> der gespenstegen minne
> und sach wol, daz ir sinne
> dar in versenket waren,
> si begunde stades varen,
> si wolte uz unde dan:
> so clebet ir ie der lim an;
> der zoch si wider unde nider
> diu schoene strebete allez wider
> und stuont an ieglichem trite.
> si volgete ungerne mite;
> si versuochtez manegen enden:
> mit vüezen und mit henden

nam si vil manege kere
und versancte ie mere
ir hende und ir vüeze
in die blinden süeze
des mannes unde der minne.
ir gelimeten sinne
dien kunden niender hin gewegen
noch gebrucken noch gestegen
halben vuoz noch halben trite,
Minne diun waere ie da mite.
Isot, swar si gedahte,
swaz gedanke si vür brahte,
sone was ie diz noch daz dar an
wan minne unde Tristan:
und was daz allez tougen.
ir herze unde ir ougen
diu missehullen under in:
diu schame diu jagete ir ougen hin,
diu minne zoch ir herze dar.
diu widerwertige schar,
maget unde man, minne unde scham,
diu was an ir sere irresam:
diu maget diu wolte den man
und warf ir ougen der van;
diu schame diu wolte minnen
und brahtez nieman innen.                                (11,789 ff.)

And so it fared with Isolde. She kept trying hard enough, and this life
was wretched for her. When she recognized the birdlime of sinister love
and saw clearly that her senses were sunk deep in it, she began to make
for firm ground, she was determined to get out and away. But the lime
kept sticking to her, it pulled her back and down. The beautiful girl
fought back each time and she stood firm at every step she took. She
yielded reluctantly, she tried every way out. She made many a twist and
turn with hand and feet and plunged her hands and feet ever deeper into
the unseeing sweetness of the man and love. Her limed senses could not
move anywhere, over neither bridge nor path, not even a half foot or a
half step, without love accompanying her. Wherever Isolde's thoughts
turned, whatever thoughts she produced, there was absolutely nothing in
them but love and Tristan. All this she kept secret. Her heart and her
eyes did not agree. Modesty drove her eyes away, love drew her heart
along. The dissident factions, maid and man, love and modesty, brought
her great confusion. The maid wanted the man—and turned her eyes
away. Modesty wanted to love—but let no one know.

Gottfried's technique here is typical and worth close examination. The early part of the passage is at first sight full of action; line after line has a verb at or near its beginning and the verbs express repeated and continuous action: *erkande, sach, begunde-varen, wolte uz, clebet, zoch, strebete, stuont, volgete, versuochte,* etc. In fact, of course, none of these actions is taking place except in Isolde's mind. The verbs are part of an elaborate extended metaphor by means of which Gottfried expresses the power of love. He can see into Isolde's heart and represents the hopeless struggle going on there by the figure of a bird fighting against the insuperable power of birdlime. Only an occasional word reminds us that this is a metaphor, that we cannot see the struggle except through the author's eyes ("versancte ie mere/ ir hende... *in die blinden süeze...*"). The passage continues by a different method. Gottfried now describes symptoms which would be visible to an acute observer (Isolde's eyes dwelling on Tristan), but the fact is far less important than the interpretation. Gottfried is concerned not with the physical act but with its cause and with the contradictory nature of Isolde's emotions, her desire for love and her sense of modesty. This contradiction he expresses directly ("diu widerwertige schar," etc.) and indirectly by juxtaposing opposites ("diu schame diu wolte minnen"). The emotional state in which Isolde finds herself is expressed by stylistic devices rather than described, but nevertheless it is clearly Gottfried who tells us of Isolde's feelings. She is not allowed direct thoughts or internal monologue. In other words, Gottfried believes that it is more effective for an author to select those emotions he wants to convey and use various stylistic devices to convey them rather than put words into the mouths of his characters and allow his audience to interpret them.

His use of extended metaphor (love as doctor, love as feudal mistress) is one way of doing this, and it is a method he particularly likes in his analysis of the emotions of his two lovers. But he can be much more direct. The description of the situation which leads to the banishment of the lovers to the *Minnegrotte* illustrates admirably Gottfried's technique. He begins with a statement of the position of Tristan and Isolde after the Petitcreiu episode: they are happy and the court is full of their praises:

> der hof was aber ir eren vol:
> ir beider lobes enwart nieme.                                    (16,406 ff.)

The court was full of their renown, their fame was never greater.

But the court is as shallow and deceptive as ever. Their reputation depends on their ability to conceal their love, for everywhere there is suspicion. Gottfried, speaking in his own person, points out that when there is no opportunity to make love, then the intention must be taken for the deed. The lovers realize this and try hard to achieve such a state, but the intensity of their passion gives them away. Once again Gottfried moves to an extended metaphor. Instead of referring to the individual suspicions of such courtiers as Marjodo and Melot, he shows us suspicion as an abstraction, growing, feeding, entwining, and becoming ever more powerful. For his audience there would be immediate reminiscences of the figure of Rumor in the fourth book of the *Aeneid* and, in a very different context, of the grain of mustard seed. Tristan and Isolde had no control over this rapid growth of suspicion:

> Nust aber der minnen arcwan
> und sin same also vertan:
> swa so er hin geworfen wirt,
> daz er diu wurzelin gebirt,
> da ist er also vrühtic,
> so biric und so zühtic,
> die wile er keine viuhte hat,
> daz er da kume zegat
> und joch niemer mac zergan:
> der unmüezege arcwan
> der begunde aber genote
> an Tristande unde Isote
> sinen wuocher bern und spil.                              (16,455 ff.)

> But suspicion in love and its seeds are so constituted that, wherever they are scattered, they strike root. It is so fruitful, so productive, so hardy, that it comes close to dying but can never die entirely. Active suspicion began to flourish and play close about Tristan and Isolde.

The whole emphasis of the metaphor is on unrestrained and unrestrainable growth. Gottfried's vision moves to another figure, the search of the eye for the heart, which in a lover is equally uncontrollable. Thus there are two forces at work. Gottfried has not shown us these by any speeches or monologues of his principal characters but by a highly figurative description of the forces at work among the courtiers and between the lovers, and his knowledge of these powers and their effects is far greater than the awareness of them among the characters in the poem, so that the reader is able to pity the lovers and scorn the courtiers while realizing that for the

conduct of both parties the blame should be placed on the conventions
of the society in which they live. The conduct of the lovers, involving
concealment and deceit, is reprehensible by any standards unless one
condemns the system which causes it.

All these emotions now come together in Gottfried's portrait of
Mark's reaction. The lovers cannot conceal from him the fact that their
eyes were always on one another, and he cannot remove his eyes from
them:

> Dur daz nam er ir allez war.
> sin ouge daz stuont allez dar:
> er sach vil dicke tougen
> die warheit in ir ougen
> und anders aber an nihte
> niwan an ir gesihte:
> daz was so rehte minneclich,
> so süeze und also senerich,
> daz ez im an sin herze gie
> und solhen zorn da von gevie,
> solhen nit und solhen haz,
> daz er diz unde daz,
> zwivel unde arcwan
> allez zeiner hant lie gan:
> im haete leit unde zorn
> sinne unde maze verlorn.
> ez was siner sinne ein tot,
> daz sin herzeliep Isot
> ieman solte meinen
> mit triuwen wan in einen;
> wan ime was ie genote
> niht dinges vor Isote
> und was ie dar an staete.
> swaz zornes er haete,
> so was im ie sin liebez wip
> liep unde lieber dan sin lip.
> swie liep sim aber waere,
> doch brahtin disiu swaere
> und diz vil tobeliche leit
> in also groze tobeheit,
> daz er sich ez gar bewac
> und niwan an sime zorne lac:
> ern haete niht gegeben ein har,
> waer ez gelogen oder war.                         (16,501 ff.)

Because of this he watched them, his eye was always on them. He secretly observed the truth in their eyes over and over again—and in nothing else but their gaze. It was so truly loving, so sweet, so full of yearning that it went to his heart and caused him so much rage, so much envy and hatred, that he was at once rid of doubt and suspicion. His misery and rage had lost all sense and proportion. It was death to his reason that his heart's love, Isolde, should feel bound to any man but himself. For to him there was nothing as valuable as Isolde and in that he never wavered. However angry he was, his dear wife was still dear to him— dearer than life itself. But however dear she was to him, this misery, this raging pain brought him to such a pitch of rage that he shook himself free of love and was aware of nothing but anger. It was a matter of complete indifference to him whether he was hearing lies or not.

Again Gottfried is observing from his superior position but with due regard to the figures he has already used. Mark's eyes never leave the lovers, as theirs never leave each other. He, too, is motivated by deep love for Isolde, even though it is desire for possession rather than true love, but his observation of Tristan is motivated by the same suspicion as that which motivates the jealous courtiers around him. He is thus torn between the conflicting emotions of the court and the lovers, embodying in his own person the tensions which afflict his court. The passage which describes him is a subtle observation of progressive emotional involvement. It begins with the physical fact of observation, followed by realization of the significance of what he saw (*diu warheit*—the deep feeling they had for each other). It strikes him to the heart and produces anger, envy, hatred, doubt, and suspicion; in other words, all the products of jealousy. Gottfried takes us from the observation to its results. Mark was not necessarily aware of the sequence of feelings within him, nor of the fact that he was concentrating in himself the feelings of his court. He *is* aware of his deep love of Isolde—but it is his *senses* which are affected. Again we know more about him than he does himself, and his struggle with anger is due to this very love; otherwise he would have yielded to his rage and taken drastic action. No man can long remain sane under this conflict of forces, and the result is "tobeheit"—blind, unthinking rage. He simply cannot bear to reason any more, to weigh probabilities and assess evidence. Gottfried, like Wolfram, delights in showing the progression of mood in his characters and, like most medieval authors, he thinks of it in terms of the appearance of abstract qualities. The subtlety of the portrait, however, lies in the fact that Mark, the head of the court, is manifesting the suspicion, envy, and hatred characteristic of his basest courtiers as a result of love for the same person for whom Tristan suffers. We should not forget that Tristan never expresses jealousy of Mark because of his possession of Isolde's body, because he knows that her heart remains with himself. Thus Gottfried indulges in his favorite amusement of contrasting passions apparently similar but really very different.

The amount of narrative in this passage is very small. The lines are laying the groundwork for future action and, more importantly, showing the audience the direction in which Mark's feelings were moving. As a result it is essentially nominal and adjectival, not verbal, in texture. There are half as many nouns again as verbs, even if modals and forms of *wesen* are included. The whole sense of progression can be traced from the nouns even if the verbs are ignored: *ouge—tougen—warheit—ougen— gesihte—herze—zorn—nit—haz—zwivel—arcwan—leit—zorn—sinne—maze (verlorn)—sinne—tot—Isot—triuwen—Isot—staete—zorn (liebes)—wip—lip —swaere—leit—tobeheit—zorn.* The word *zorn* runs like a red thread through the list of nouns and Gottfried achieves neat ironic effects by the juxtaposition of words which should be closely akin but which in this context are jarring (*tot—Isot—triuwen—Isot—staete—zorn*) and culminates his analysis of Mark's state by a summary of its causes: (*wip— lip—swaere* produce *leit—tobeheit—zorn.*

Having told his audience of the conflict in Mark's mind and made that conflict graphic by the tightly intertwined abstract nouns, Gottfried now tells us of the surprising result. Mark makes a formal speech of considerable length in front of the whole court. It should be remembered that Mark had brought the "case" to the public eye before but had never made a pronouncement on the subject in his own person. Now he does so. The decision is a surprising one. Mark might be expected to demand a trial, even to condemn the lovers outright. He explicitly refuses to do any of these things. Instead, he gives them leave to go—an abdication of his rights both as king and as husband—on the grounds that he can no longer bear to see the love between his nephew and his wife. We have already pointed out that Gottfried rarely lets his characters express their true selves in set speeches. They present a picture which they wish to be accepted, they play a role. Mark is no exception. Even though he *is* furious with the lovers and *does* suffer pain when he sees them, he cannot wash his hands of the whole affair. In banishing them he has given them virtual permission to do what he most detests; in yielding to his anger, he has lost his love. Is Gottfried intending us to understand that Mark's speech is a grand gesture which he does not really mean? Banishment from court was not a thing to be taken lightly. Almost all authors of Tristan poems regard it as a severe punishment. Doubtless Mark thought of it in these terms. There are indications that other characters did not regard the offer of freedom as serious: Brangaene is left behind

> daz si die suone von in zwein
> wider Marken aber trüege in ein.                          (16,677 f.)
>
> ... so that she could effect a reconciliation between the two of them and Mark.

Surely such a reconciliation would be pointless if Mark were really sincere in letting them go. Nor would there be any point in putting about the story that they had returned to Ireland in order for Isolde

> ir unschulde offenbaeren
> wider liut und wider lant.                                (16,780 f.)
>
> ... to make clear her innocence before the land and its people.

Mark has expressed his belief in their guilt, they have acquiesced in the finding. Why should they now attempt to assert their innocence? The matter becomes clear at the end of the *Minnegrotte* scene, when Mark finds them and is only too ready to accept the flimsy "evidence" of their innocence. Gottfried is using his normal technique. Mark does not mean what he says. The lovers are granted their highest fulfillment as a result of a temporary yielding on his part to very human emotions, emotions which Gottfried analyzes but which he does not allow Mark to express.

DESCRIPTION AND ITS PURPOSE

Gottfried's descriptions, unlike those in most courtly writers, are far from being mere ornament.[46] There are some types of description which are conspicuously absent in his work, notably the portrait of the individual. At no time does he describe any of his major characters in the accepted terms of the books of rhetoric. Mark's external appearance is never described, and we have only the vaguest idea of his age and appearance. Brangaene is seen only as a foil to Isolde, beautiful but not quite so beautiful as her mistress, Rual is seen only as a figure of loyalty. Tristan and Isolde are described but under very specific circumstances. Tristan first appears not as a person but through the education he received (2060 ff.). The only mention of this person is very general:

> ouch was er an dem libe,
> daz jungelinc von wibe
> nie saeleclicher wart geborn.
> sin dinc was allez uz erkorn
> beid an dem muote und an den siten.                    (2123 ff.)

His person was such that no boy born of woman was more fortunate. Everything about him was outstanding, both in mind and in manners.

The description, of course, concentrates on what is significant both for Rual and for the audience, namely, his education. This pattern of emphasizing the significant is continued. The merchants see in him a collection of desirable—and salable—qualities. The pilgrims in Cornwall observe only Tristan's exterior, his fine clothes and polished manners, and these are noted, as they are when he joins the huntsmen. It is the obviously high standard of his breeding and appearance which makes it possible for him to impress these groups. When Tristan appears before Mark's court, Gottfried again pays attention to the skills which attract the attention of the courtiers. In none of these instances does Gottfried pretend to give a formal description. He merely mentions a few characteristics which excite the attention of the group before which Tristan is appearing at the time, each of which is only one facet of Tristan's personality. The first elaborate description of Tristan, except for the allegorical figures in the investiture section, is that which refers to his armor as he prepares himself for the battle with Morolt. The arming is, of course, significant for Morolt in the same way that the singing is for Mark's court. This kind of "oriented" description can be found throughout the work. Let us observe it as it occurs between the two lovers in the early part of their acquaintance. Significantly, there is no description of the external appearance of either of them. Tantris makes his impression through music, and Isolde, after instruction by Tristan, is shown (as we have already seen) as the personification of the irrational power of beauty and music. The first full-length picture of Tristan and Isolde is presented at the beginning of the confrontation with the seneschal. This is a tableau before the full court of Ireland

and each character is presented as that court saw him. By using powerful graphic description Gottfried can show how his principal characters appeared to a court uninfluenced by music:

> . . . die liehten maget Isote;
> diu sleich ir morgenrote
> lise und staeteliche mite
> in einem spor, in einem trite,
> suoze gebildet über al,
> lanc, uf gewollen unde smal,
> gestellet in der waete,
> als si diu Minne draete
> ir selber zeinem vederspil,
> dem Wunsche zeinem endezil,
> da vür er niemer komen kan.
> si truoc von brunem samit an
> roc unde mantel, in dem snite
> von Franze, und was der roc da mite
> da engegene, da die siten
> sinkent uf ir liten,
> gefranzet unde genget,
> nahe an ir lip getwenget
> mit einem borten, der lac wol,
> da der borte ligen sol.
> der roc der was ir heinlich,
> er tet sich nahen zuo der lich:
> ern truoc an keiner stat hin dan,
> er suohte allenthalben an
> al von obene hin ze tal;
> er nam den valt unde den val
> under den vüezen alse vil,
> als iuwer iegelicher wil.
> der mantel was ze vlize
> mit herminer wize
> innen al uz gezieret,
> bi zilen geflottieret;
> ern was ze kurz noch ze lanc:
> er swebete, da er nider sanc,
> weder ze erden noch enbor.
> da stuont ein höfscher zobel vor
> der maze, als in diu Maze sneit,
> weder ze smal noch ze breit,
> gesprenget, swarz unde gra:
> swarz unde gra diu waren da

also gemischet under ein,
daz ir dewederez da schein.
der nam ouch sine crumbe
reht an der wize al umbe,
da der zobel diu vuoge nimet,
da diz bi dem so wol gezimet.
diu tassel, da diu solten sin,
da was ein cleinez snuorlin
von wizen berlin in getragen.
da haete diu schoene in geslagen
ir dumen von ir linken hant.
die rehten haete si gewant
hin nider baz, ir wizzet wol,
da man den mantel sliezen sol,
und sloz in höfschliche in ein
mit ir vingere zwein:
vürbaz da viel er selbe wider
und nam den valt al zende nider,
daz man diz unde daz da sach,
ich meine vederen unde dach:
man sach ez innen und uzen
und innerthalben luzen
daz bilde, daz diu Minne
an libe und an dem sinne
so schone haete gedraet:
diu zwei, gedraet unde genaet,
diun vollebrahten nie baz
ein lebende bilde danne daz.
gevedere schachblicke
die vlugen da snedicke
schachende dar unde dan:
ich waene, Isot vil manegen man
sin selbes da beroubete.                                        (10,889 ff.)

... the fair Isolde glided along with her dawn, gently and even-paced,
step for step, stride for stride, beautifully formed in every part, tall, well
shaped, and slim, fitting her clothes as if Love herself had designed them
for her falcon, the very ultimate of perfection which can never be
surpassed. She wore a robe and mantle of richly colored samite, cut in
the French fashion, and so in the places where the sides meet the hips it
was fringed and gathered in, drawn close to the body by a girdle, which
was naturally worn where a girdle usually is worn. The robe was
intimately close to her, it kept close to her body, never loose at any point
but clinging close from top to bottom. It lifted as much of the folds and

pleats above her feet as each of you cares to imagine. The mantle was
beautifully trimmed with white ermine inside in a pattern of diagonal spots.
It was neither too short nor too long: as it hung down it neither swept the
floor nor hung too high. In front there was fine sable trimming cut
neither too narrow nor too broad for the proportions set by good taste,
speckled black and gray. The black and gray were so intermingled that
neither appeared separately. It curved closely all round the white, where
sable and ermine were laid edge to edge and where they match so well.
The clasp that was supposed to be there was made of a little string of
white pearls let in. And there fair Isolde had slipped in her left thumb and
had brought her right hand down to where, as you know, the mantle is
kept closed. She held it together properly with two fingers. There it fell of
its own accord in one last fold, revealing this and that, I mean fur and
cover. The inside and the outside could be seen and inside there lay in
hiding the image which love had fashioned so beautifully in body and
spirit. These two, shaped and sewn together, never created a better living
image. Greedy feathered glances flew like snow, hunting in every corner. I
believe that Isolde robbed many a man of his very self.

The description continues with an account of the beauty of Isolde's circlet
and the jewels it contains.

This description of Isolde is entirely unconventional. It begins with a
movement, not mere walking but gliding, smooth, slow, and sensuous.
There follows a general impression of her person—no details of the head
and face, as is usual in medieval portraits, and none of the normal "top-to-
toe" order. Instead we are given an unusully full account of Isolde's
outer garment. Every small detail of her dress is dwelt on lovingly—its
material, its ornaments, its pattern, and in particular its cut and fit.
The description inevitably leads the eye to the shape of Isolde's body, and
the mention of the holding-together of the mantle, with, as Gottfried
hints, the possibility of revealing more than should be shown, emphasizes
the concentration of greedy, devouring eyes which are turned upon her by
the members of the court. They are interested in her as an object of sensual
love, in precisely the same way in which Mark shows his interest when he
observes her lying in the *Minnegrotte*, and Gottfried's description is
carefully designed to show only what appears to the eye of the court,
obsessed as it is with the visual-sensual aspects of love which alone it
understands. Isolde's superb dress indicates her nobility and high rank,
her pride and unattainability, just as at the ordeal she shows her humility
by her thin garments, her short sleeves, and her exposed ankles. Gottfried

shows us the emotions of the beholders through the things they see and the
way in which they see them. He has no use for the description that is a
mere indication of the conventional excellence of a character.

The description of Tristan follows. He has not been present when
Isolde entered, and none of the impressions made by her can be attributed
to him. He is brought in by Brangaene:

>ouch gieng ir ir geverte bi
>in stolzlicher wise;
>des dinc was ouch ze prise
>und ze wunder uf geleit
>an iegelicher saelekeit,
>diu den ritter schepfen sol:
>ez stuont allez an im wol,
>daz ze ritters lobe stat.
>sin geschepfede und sin wat
>die gehullen wunnecliche in ein:
>si bildeten under in zwein
>einen ritterlichen man.
>er truoc cyclades cleider an,
>diu waren uzer maze rich,
>vremede unde lobelich.
>sine waren niht von hove geben:
>daz golt das was dar in geweben
>niht in der hovemaze:
>die sidenen straze
>die kos man kumeliche da:
>si waren wa unde wa
>so mit dem golde ertrenket
>und in daz gold versenket,
>daz man das werc da kume sach.
>ein netze das was uf daz dach
>von cleinen berlin getragen:
>die maschen also wit geslagen,
>als ein hant an der breite hat.
>dar durch so bran der cyclat
>reht als ein glüejender kol.
>er was von timit innen vol,
>vil bruner danne ein violate,
>reht ebenbrun der gloien blate.
>der selbe pfelle der tet sich
>an den valt und an den strich
>alse nahe und alse wol,

als ein pfelle beste sol;
er stuont dem lobelichen man
wol unde lobelichen an
und alle wis nach siner ger.
uf sinem houbete truoc er
von spaehem werke spaehen schin,
ein wunneclich schapelekin,
daz rehte alsam ein kerze bran:
da luhten alse sterne van
topazen und sardine,
crisoliten und rubine.
ez was lieht unde clar,
ez haete im houbet unde har
clarlichen umbevangen.
sus kam er in gegangen
rich unde hohe gemuot.
sin gebar was herlich unde guot.
al sin geverte daz was rich:
er was selbe rilich
an allen sinen sachen.
si begunden ime rum machen.
da er zem palas in gie.                    (11,090 ff.)

Her companion too went with her in stately fashion; he too was endowed with wondrous excellence with every grace that should go to make a knight. He had everything that goes with knightly distinction. His person and clothes suited one another remarkably and between them portrayed a man of chivalry. He wore clothes of ciclatoun, rich beyond measure, unusual and distinguished. They were not the kind given away at court! The amount of gold worked into them was not what you would get by the court's standards. You could scarcely follow the line of the silk, so heavily was it buried in gold and everywhere so sunk in gold that the material was hardly visible. There was a net of small pearls over the surface, the meshes a handbreadth apart. Through them the ciclatoun shone like glowing coals. It was heavily lined with dimity, more purple than a violet and as dark-colored as an iris petal. This same cloth of gold clung in fold and grain as close and as well as any clothing of gold should. It suited a superb man superbly and was entirely to his taste. On his head he wore the glittering glory of fine workmanship, a beautiful chaplet that gleamed like a candle and from it there shone like stars topazes and sardonyx, chrysolites and rubies. It was bright and clear and encircled his head in glory. Thus he came walking in, magnificent and of high spirit. His bearing was lordly and fine, all his attire splendid. He was superb in every detail. They kept clearing the way for him as he went into the palace.

The resemblances between this description and that of Isolde are striking. Each opens with a mention of the movement of the principal character into the view of the courtly audience. The concentration is once again on the total impression and in particular on clothing. The unusual material (ciclatoun), the cunning interwoven gold thread in massive quantity, the oversewn pearls, the purple silk dimity lining—all these convey an impression of richness, of nobility. There is, however, little stress on the fit. The audience is interested in Tristan as a knightly figure, not as a shapely body inviting love. Gottfried describes the circlet on Tristan's head in terms very similar to those he had used of Isolde:

si truoc uf ir houbete
einen cirkel von golde
smal, alse er wesen solde,
geworht mit spaehem sinne.
(10,962 ff.)

uf sinem houbete truoc er
von spaehem werke spaehen schin,
ein wunneclich schapelekin . . .
(11,130 ff.)

She wore on her head a
circlet of gold, narrow as it
should be and wrought with
fine feeling . . .

On his head he wore a glittering
glory of fine workmanship, a
beautiful chaplet . . .

In each case a list of the precious stones follows—emerald, jacinth, sapphire, and chalcedony for Isolde, topaz, sardonyx, chrysolite, and ruby for Tristan. Gottfried has shown, without once saying so explicitly, that in this great court scene Tristan and Isolde make very similar impressions —of great nobility, splendor, and beauty—and that these impressions are based entirely on visual evidence. The impressions ignore the true nature of the lovers, in particular the great part which music plays. The court sees only the beauty of their persons. Neither here nor anywhere else do we learn what Tristan and Isolde really look like, only what they appear to be to one kind of audience.

There is another type of description which is of great importance in Gottfried's poem—that of natural phenomena. The question of descriptions of ideal landscape, its origin and detail, has been well explored. Less attention has been paid to its structural function. The ideal-landscape description was a set piece, a *topos* form used in the schools of rhetoric and following very specific rules. Inevitably, therefore, conformity with the norm was to be expected, while departure from it would alert the reader to something unusual. To cite one obvious example, Chaucer's character descriptions in the Prologue to the *Canterbury Tales* are effective very largely because of their variations from standard descriptions. The ideal landscape *topos* is not merely an ornament, or perhaps we should say it is not merely an ornament when it is properly used. It can become a mechanical opening to a poem with no relevance to what follows, but in the best works, particularly lyrics, it performs the function of removing the setting from that of the world of sense, that known and experienced by the audience, to a milieu beyond time and space where the bonds of the ordinary world are loosed and material life transcended. So it is in the *Odyssey*, in the *Metamorphoses*, and in the *Roman de la Rose*. When an author uses the ideal landscape *topos*, he must reckon with at least a part of his audience which is aware of its function. Gottfried is aware of this necessity. He is also aware of the connection in the minds of his audience between the ideal landscape *topos* and courtly poetry. Ideal love blossomed in this ideal landscape. When Riwalin and Blanscheflur meet, it is in such an ideal landscape, a place of singing birds and flowering meadows. All the elements of the ideal landscape *topos* are there and Gottfried pointedly calls attention to the fact that this *is* such a landscape by such remarks as:

> so der vil süeze meie in gat
>
> .   .   .
>
> diu haete ir süeze unmüezekeit
> mit süezem vlize an si geleit;
>
> .   .   .
>
> und swaz dem ouge sanfte tuot
> und edele herze ervröuwen sol
> des was diu sumerouwe vol:
> man vant da, swaz man wolte.                                  (539 ff.)

When charming May comes in . . .
She had devoted her sweet energies to it with such care . . .
Whatever is pleasing to the eye, whatever may delight noble hearts, was to be found in full measure in the summer meadow. There you could have whatever you wished.

Nature and the human condition mirror each other in this unthinking world of love and the passage ends:

> . . . daz da manc edele herze van
> vröud' unde hohen muot gewan.                                 (585 f.)

. . . so that many a noble heart found joy and exaltation in it.

Gottfried has quite deliberately identified his courtly audience with the spring landscape, emphasizing in both the smiling joy of spring.

The description of an ideal landscape occurs again under very different circumstances—when Tristan and Isolde are expelled from the court and seek refuge in nature. It should be remembered that in earlier versions of the poem this expulsion was a real hardship, a *Waldleben*, which the lovers hated and from which they were glad to be released. Gottfried's description, therefore, is written with an awareness of two connections, the primitive isolation and the courtly landscape. He makes sure that the audience also will be aware of the similarities and contrasts.

His description begins with figures of remoteness—the two-day journey through woods and moors to a savage mountain, an impressive contrast to the accessibility of the ideal landscape from the court of Cornwall. The next step is to describe the cave. It is separated from the outside world by a bronze door which, as we are told later, can be opened only by true lovers. The resemblance to the "Open Sesame" motif is very clear, and it is not remarkable that the ideal landscape is found on the other side of the door, that is, separated from the normal world not only by the distance and rough country already described, which would be obstacles any determined person could overcome, but by a barrier impenetrable to all except true lovers. It will be observed that Gottfried nowhere defines these true lovers but he indicates in several places that they are different from those at court. The most important of these indications is the constant stress on separation, not only by the use of the figure of the door but in Gottfried's explanation of his own allegory in which he points out that love is a shy being:

> ouch hat ez guote meine,
> daz diu fossiure als eine
> in dirre wüesten wilde lac;
> daz man dem wol gelichen mac,
> daz minne und ir gelegenheit
> niht uf die straze sint geleit
> noch an dekein gevilde;
> si loschet in der wilde,
> zir cluse ist daz geverte
> arbeitsam und herte . . .                                   (17,071 ff.)

It is also significant that the grotto lay in such a remote and deserted place. Thus it may well be compared with love, whose affairs do not lie

around on any street or in any open field. She steals away to the
wilderness. The way to her retreat is toilsome and hard.

The way is hard and the goal uncertain. But once inside the door the
separation from normal life is complete. Even normal food is no longer
necessary. To use Gottfried's own term, this is a *wunschleben*, an ideal
existence, one which, as he pointedly remarks, is superior to any that
Arthur's court could provide.

Since Gottfried takes such pains to point out the differences between
the *Minnegrotte* and the normal milieu of courtly love, it is surprising to
find that he reverts again and again to the features of the conventional
ideal-landscape description (16,735–64; 16,885–99; 17,143–85). All of
these passages contain the normal features of the *topos* and many of the
lines either correspond exactly to those in the description which appears
when Riwalin is at Cornwall or differ only in minor details. This recalling
of the earlier passage to the reader is doubtless deliberate. Tristan-love
has much in common with the love of Riwalin and Blanscheflur but it
transcends it as surely as Gottfried felt that his work excelled that of
Hartmann von Aue and his other contemporaries. There are differences
as well as resemblances when we read of the landscape in which Tristan
and Isolde spend their time. There are three lime trees and three only
which stand near the cave, the symbols of love. These are the very center
of this miniature landscape. The birds are described in far more detail
than in the earlier passage, as befits a milieu in which music is more important than visual pleasure. And always there is the contrast with the
grim world outside.

Gottfried has described here a setting of eternal spring and glorious
beauty in which love can flourish. In doing so he has used and intensified
the features of the ideal-landscape description but he has carefully differentiated it from the courtly *paysage idéal* into which it is so easy for courtly
figures, even Riwalin and Blanscheflur, to move. This small retreat of
perfect beauty is inaccessible to all but Tristan-lovers and it is just the
setting for a spot even holier for all those who believe in true love.

The grotto is to a large degree the product of Gottfried's imagination.
Whatever the details of the description of the cave given by Thomas of
Britain may have been, we may accept it as certain that Gottfried molded
this most important section of his poem according to his own lights. The
grotto is love's most important shrine and as such partakes of the nature

of many sacred places. Since Ranke's brilliant study, it has been assumed
by all critics that for lovers the *Minnegrotte* is a counterpart to the church
for Christians, and this has led further to a great stress on those aspects of
Tristan-love which can be explained or elucidated by reference to Christian
mysticism. There is no doubt a great deal of truth in these explanations,
but it is not the whole truth. We should note that the *Minnegrotte* is not
a building. It is a natural phenomenon which has been "improved." It
has some features which would be found in a church. The vaulting recalls
characteristics of late twelfth-century style:

> das gewelbe daz was obene
> geslozzen wol ze lobene;
> oben uf dem sloze ein crone,
> diu was vil harte schone
> mit gesmide gezieret,
> mit gimmen wol gewieret . . .                                    (16,707 ff.)

The vault above was finely keyed and there above on the keystone there
was a crown which was beautifully ornamented with goldsmith's work
and studded with gems.

But most of the characteristics mentioned could be those of any well-
proportioned building. (It must be admitted, of course, that a church
would be the only type of large public building with which Gottfried was
acquainted. Otherwise a domed late-classical temple would come to mind.)
The importance of Gottfried's description lies not so much in the details of
the cave he describes as in his method of describing it. He begins with a
description which confines itself to the proportions, the keystone, and the
crystalline bed. He then moves, as we have seen, to the natural phenomena.
After a brief digression in which Curvenal is dismissed, Gottfried, in his
own person, explains the ability of the lovers to exist without food. He
then returns, in greater detail, to the ideal landscape. There follows a
long section in which Gottfried carefully explains the meaning of the
various parts of his description of the cave and tells how he himself has
visited it. Finally he describes how the lovers spent their time.

THE INTERVENTION OF THE AUTHOR

It will be observed that the incident of the cave begins on the level of
narrative, simply telling the reader what the lovers themselves did and
saw. Gottfried then moves to the explanatory, informing the reader of

things which the lovers could not know. Finally we turn to allegory, to the hidden meaning, explained by Gottfried, not left to the reader's own power of interpretation. The culmination is the portrait of the lovers as examples of perfect harmony. On the surface we have here a standard procedure—the story *ad litteram* and the explanation *per allegoriam*— but actually the original story is composed not of historical events but of fiction. The force of the allegory lies not in the fact that Gottfried produces abstractions for the concrete features of the cave but in the fact that he is applying to his cave, which he explicitly states to be pagan, the technique used by the Church to demonstrate the validity of the Faith and the relation of the temporal building to the eternal *Ecclesia Dei*. In other words, it is an allegory of an allegory and depends for its effects on the consciousness in the mind of the reader of the existence of the Christian allegories. Gottfried makes the point even clearer by following the technique of the Fathers in giving first the story, then the interpretation. Had he stopped at this point, we would have accepted his technique as merely the application to a secular work of something already well developed in theology. But he does not stop here. He intrudes the person of the author into the poem, not, as is usually done, as an omniscient interpreter, but as an interpreter who knows because he has participated. This is a new kind of allegorical technique, quite different from that used in the interpretations of the Fathers, in such works as the *Psychomachia*, or in the poems of the twelfth-century Chartrians. It anticipates the technique of Guillaume de Lorris in the first part of the *Roman de la Rose* in making the author a lover, but Guillaume is crude by comparison. He is the only character in the poem with whom Love is really concerned. All others are ancillary, mere adjuncts and ornaments to the main theme. Tristan and Isolde never cease to be the center of interest in Gottfried's poem. The author allegorizes, but his personal intrusion into the narrative shows that he is inferior to the characters he has created as an exemplar of love. Although, as an author, he knows more about love and its effects than they do (an author is omniscient), as a human being he is their inferior. The line between the narrative and real life is deliberately blurred. Obviously Gottfried could not really visit the *Minnegrotte*. It did not exist except in the story which he himself had created but by an act of the same imagination which created the story he could project himself into the love situation of Tristan and demonstrate how difficult it was to achieve true love. Thus he makes clear the universal application of his story, the fact that his narrative is what he had promised it would be, at once an example and a solace to those who love. Between fiction and reality there is no sharp division.

There is no passage in the poem in which the intrusion of the author is more significant or its aspects more varied but such intrusion is frequent. There is little point in attaching too much importance to those occasions on which Gottfried makes such statements as "Now let us return to the story." We are concerned much more with those where he interposes, often at critical points in the narrative, discussions of some aspect of life and love, often of considerable length. These digressions or interpolations are usually lengthy disquisitions on one abstract quality or term and their effect is to criticize both the actions of characters in the poem and commonly received ideas. These are the more important of them:

| | |
|---|---|
| 4506–46 | The different desires of youth and age |
| 6870–96 | The powers of Morolt and Tristan |
| 7939–65 | Apology for not giving details of Queen Isolde's medical skill |
| 12,187–361 | A discussion of the nature of real love |
| 13,037–77 | Anger never absent from love |
| 13,781–846 | A discussion of doubt and suspicion |
| 16,927–17,142 | The allegorization of the *Minnegrotte* |
| 17,774–18,118 | The nature of the female and the vanity of surveillance |

A glance at these passages immediately makes several points clear. The major interpolations by Gottfried occur after the drinking of the potion. Those before it are relatively short and are little more than comments on an occurrence in the narrative. The first concerns the remarkable ability of Tristan and Rual to understand each other's point of view in spite of a difference of age which would normally lead to fundamental disagreements. The second intervention is a half-playful discussion of the "helpers" of Tristan against Morolt, a play with abstract forces to counter the traditional superpowers attributed to Morolt in earlier stories. This intervention is like that in which Gottfried denies the motif of the yellow hair as a force in sending Tristan to woo Isolde. Similarly the brief refusal to detail the medical abilities of the elder Isolde is a rejection of material which Gottfried regards as unsuitable not only for his poem but for any romance. Thus these earlier interpolations and many briefer ones are little more than marginal comment. Those which follow the drinking of the potion are quite different. They might be described as major statements of policy.

Each of them is provoked by an event in the narrative, but none has any function in that narrative. The story is made to stand still while Gottfried draws from the material of his poem what might be called a text for a sermon. The occasion is a crisis in the poem and in the lives of the lovers. Love personified and described by the significant epithets "arzatinne" (physician) and "strickaerinne" (binder, spinner of webs) has led Tristan to Isolde. Love heals them but in doing so ties them in a web so tangled that there can be no escape. Gottfried is continuing in another form his metaphor of the bird entangled in lime. His lovers are consummating what, to all *edele herzen*, must be the greatest of all loves. Now is the time for Gottfried to explain what he means by love and he introduces a quatrain of some significance:

> Ein langiu rede von minnen
> diu swaeret höfschen sinnen:
> kurz rede von guoten minnen
> diu guotet guoten sinnen. (12,183 ff.)

> A long discussion of love bores a well-trained mind. A short discussion of true love is good for good minds.

As usual in the quatrains, Gottfried is playing with words. The people mentioned in the first couplet may be "polite society"—a positive evaluation—or "courtly minds"—a negative one. Neither group can apparently tolerate a long speech. The next couplet seems to differentiate "good love" from that mentioned in the first line; presumably this is Tristan-love, for it makes "good minds" even better. Once again there is an echo of the intentions proclaimed in the quatrains of the prologue. In fact, the discourse on love which Gottfried now gives is not particularly short (171 lines) and a great deal of it is not about love at all but about an aspect of the courtly-love scene which the lyric poets discuss constantly, namely *huote*, the watch kept over the lady by her husband, father, brother, or any other person who has an interest in preventing her from meeting her lover. With such a speech against "surveillance" all the poets of courtly love would heartily agree—in theory. In fact, however, surveillance was part of the game. It prevented the poet-lover from fulfilling his desire and thus kept him in the ambivalent but artistically satisfying role of forever lauding the unattainable. So perhaps a long speech about love would not bore courtly minds?

Gottfried's irony is clear. Although he is talking about *huote*, he does not treat it in the conventional courtly way. Tristan and Isolde are genuinely glad to be free of it, as they are here on board ship and will be again in the *Minnegrotte*. There will be no other occasion. Here love can blossom as it should, and Gottfried's own heart exults at the prospect. Unfortunately love such as this is rare. Most of the "sermon" proves to be about false love, love which involves deceit and guile, love which is love only in name. The first part of the speech is an extended metaphor on the theme "as ye sow, so shall ye reap" and is full of biblical imagery. It is hard to escape the conclusion that Gottfried is here alluding to the standard clichés of the love game, where love by definition must be deceitful, since the beloved is constantly watched. This leads him to a surprising new line of argument. Love is debased by the deceit and treachery practiced in her name but she is not to blame. It is the system that demands surveillance that is the cause of the low repute in which love is held. The practice of deceit to obtain love in spite of this surveillance is dishonorable but it would not be necessary if one quality were fully recognized—*triuwe* (loyalty, constancy, sincerity), which is the only true companion of love. Gottfried hopes by the story he will tell to show true lovers how true love can be achieved.

Any reader will note at once that for much of the remainder of the poem Tristan and Isolde will be obliged to practice deceit to keep their love. Not only that, they will be prepared to sacrifice Brangaene to do so. Gottfried is clearly apologizing for them in advance by blaming the society in which they have to live. It is noteworthy, for example, that he condemns in this digression many qualities which he specifically points to as absent:

| | |
|---|---|
| wir buwen die minne | diu sinewelle binnen |
| mit gegelletem sinne, | daz ist einvalte an minnen: |
| mit valsche und mit akust | einvalte zimet der minne wol, |
| und suochen danne an ir die lust | diu ane winkel wesen sol; |
| des libes unde des herzen . . . | der winkel, der an minnen ist, |
| (12,237 ff.) | daz ist akust unde list.    (16,931 ff.) |
| | |
| We cultivate love with deceit and | The smooth curve within indicates |
| hypocrisy and minds that are | love's simplicity. Simplicity is right |

poisoned and then seek in it the
pleasures of the body and the
heart.

for love, since it should have no
angles. Any angle connected with
love is cunning and sharp practice.

The whole story from the landing of Isolde in Cornwall until the final parting of the lovers—and beyond if we took to Thomas' poem—is an account of deceit. It is a contest of *huote* (surveillance) against love, which leads to deceit not only of Mark, in the sense that he is a cuckold, but of Mark by Gandin, Mark by Brangaene, Gandin by Tristan, Marjodo and Melot by Tristan, and a host of attempted deceits by Mark and his courtiers. In some versions of the story the deceiving of Mark is a principal and comic element. Gottfried's intervention is to show that he believes that the courtly system of surveillance and its manifestations in literature are themselves evil and that they are not a subject for comedy. We are thus given an important indication of the structural reason for his interpolations. They are meant to ensure that the reader interprets the events of the story correctly. These events are not in themselves fundamentally different from those in other versions of the story. Gottfried has already told us that Thomas alone told the story rightly. He is now making sure that this "right" story is correctly understood.

Gottfried's next personal interpolation is minor and almost playful. He is commenting on the fact that Tristan and Isolde were occasionally angry with each other. He is at some pains to point out that this was the passing anger of people brought to a high emotional pitch by their love and consequently hypersensitive to any real or imagined slight, particularly when one partner seems to pay too much attention to a third person. The purpose of the passage is to show that the effect of such passing anger is to renew love. It is consistent with Gottfried's thesis that sorrow is a part of love and cannot be separated from it.

Mark makes a desperate attempt to trick Isolde into betraying herself and almost succeeds. As a result of her far too obvious desire to have Tristan appointed as her guardian during Mark's projected absence, the king falls into doubt and suspicion, a state which Gottfried describes carefully as it applies to Mark personally and then as a general phenomenon. The comment by Gottfried may be summarized as follows: Doubt and suspicion are the enemies of love. They lead to constant confusion, and as fast as a man thinks he is free of them, something occurs to bring them back. But what is far worse is when a person becomes certain that his suspicions are justified. Then he wishes he could return to mere doubt and suspicion. Love is like that. It cannot exist without suspicion, so much so that when there are no grounds for doubt, love will seek them and even gain pleasure from the pursuit.

This is a strange series of comments which amounts to a statement that anyone in love will be in a state of uncertainty and suspicion. Yet it is quite clear that Gottfried despises the attitude of Mark and his courtiers and he has already explicitly condemned the constant watch that leads to suspicion. We must note the context in which the observations occur. The person about whom Gottfried has been talking is Mark and no one else. Furthermore, throughout this passage the word used for "love" is always *liebe*, never *minne*. The distinction between the two words is not so precise as some critics have tried to show,[47] but in this passage there can be no doubt that Gottfried's intention is to speak of the kind of sensual attraction he ascribes to Mark and Gandin. Such people think of love in terms of physical enjoyment and possession. They lack any sense of mutual love and are perpetually fearful that their partner will be unfaithful. Since they live in this fear, they feel lost when it is not there. Although he does not say so explicitly, Gottfried is contrasting the *zorn ane haz* which exists between Tristan and Isolde, as it does between all true lovers, and which can be banished by the *triuwe* they have toward each other, with the nagging persistent distrust felt by Mark and his kind. This mistrust causes the desperate attempts at surveillance which he castigated in his earlier interpolation. It brings nothing but misery to those who watch and those who are subject to surveillance. It will be seen that Gottfried's interpolations have a constant theme—the problem of mistrust in love, by those who love, by those who think they do, and by those whose one desire is to frustrate true love in all its forms. His first mention of the theme shows how deceit springs from attempts at surveillance; his second, how true love may experience momentary anger at some supposed slight but needs only its own sincerity to banish such emotion. Love of a lesser kind lives in a state of perpetual doubt.

Gottfried's last personal intervention is his longest and most comprehensive. It may even be regarded as a summary of his views on the position of women in society and on the way in which they should be treated. Again it derives directly from a critical incident in the story, the fact that Mark had brought the lovers back to court, having persuaded himself to ignore their obvious love for each other, so that he could enjoy Isolde as a woman, whether she loved him or not. Very shortly he is to find Tristan and Isolde in bed together, so that even he cannot blind himself to the facts. At this moment of concord, suspended between the banishment to the *Minnegrotte* and the final departure of Tristan, Gottfried discusses in his own person the central theme of his poem—the clash between love and society in its principal manifestation, the attempt of the male to obtain love by securing a woman for himself and ensuring by constant watchfulness that she has no opportunity to love another. In such an arrangement the feelings of the woman have little significance, whatever lip service may be paid to her, and there can be no question of love in any real sense. Gottfried's argument takes up several of the principal antifeminist arguments and turns them to his own advantage. He asks the simple question of who was to blame for Mark's situation, and answers that it was Mark himself. Isolde was not guilty of deceit because he was perfectly well aware of what she was doing and that she had no affection for him. Affection cannot be forced, and a man who knows that his wife loves another and still insists on remaining with her is not deceived but blinded by lust. The lovers, especially Isolde, could not bear separation. The constant surveillance brought misery but it did not prevent their love. Surveillance is useless, for a virtuous woman does not need it, while a truly vicious woman will find some means to circumvent it. It will rather make a good woman resentful. A wise man realizes that only tenderness will be effective in dealing with women, for love cannot be extorted. Surveillance is likely to force a woman to revert to her nature and make her seek what is forbidden. Eve was forbidden to eat of the fruit of the fig tree, and the prohibition may have been the very thing which caused her to eat it. The woman who can resist the pressure of the nature with which she has been endowed is as upright as a man. Any woman who can resist the urges of her body is worthy of the highest praise, but she should not neglect it merely for her reputation any more than she should do the reverse. The highest ideal for a woman is the golden mean. If she behaves badly she cannot demand respect, for promiscuity is woman's worst enemy. Any woman who truly respects her womanhood is worthy of the greatest respect, and the man upon whom she bestows her love is in paradise.

This passage is remarkable in many ways. It denies one of the basic beliefs of medieval society, that a woman was an inferior being who must be treated like a child to prevent her falling into the sin to which her body and nature predisposed her. Not only does Gottfried advocate the total removal of any surveillance and put the matter of her morals and behavior entirely in the hands of the woman herself but he, by implication, blames the Creator (a man!) for His error in forbidding Eve the fruit. It is true that he also assumes that a woman's nature is contrary, that she does not like being told what to do and that her body will dispose her to sin. But he has already shown that males are just as liable to be blinded by their lust. A woman's body (in other words, the enjoyment of sexual pleasure) is not to be scorned and rejected out of hand. A woman has no more right to reject her body to gain "honor"—respect and reputation—than she has to indulge her body at the expense of her reputation. This is a startling remark for a medieval writer to make. Christian doctrine made no doubt of the matter. The body should be suppressed, and sex existed only for procreation. Virginity was the highest state. Courtly romances did not, of course, accept this doctrine, for there a man pursues a woman for her beauty. Yet even here it is the man who pursues, not the woman who entices. Her beauty may attract the knight, even drive him to despair. She may, as in the *Roman d'Enéas*, be very conscious of her own bodily desires, but nowhere does a courtly writer explicitly take up the conflict between the nature of woman as Eve had bequeathed it to her and the responsibility to preserve her reputation. Gottfried does. It is for the woman to decide to whom she will give her love, it is for her to decide on the true proportion of restraint and sexuality there will be in her life. She is as capable of making a correct decision as a male and she should be left to make it. Love consists of sex freely given but always under the control of a sense of decency and never in any sense promiscuously.

The whole stress here is on equality between the sexes. No medieval author would have disputed that it is impossible to extort love from a woman. The writer of romance would have regarded such an attempt as unchivalrous, a religious man as pointless. For both, love was an extraneous matter which had little to do with society as constituted. Both sides would have agreed that a woman was unable to decide important matters for herself and that she needed the assistance of a man. Gottfried's originality—almost a heresy—lies in his statement that it is not only useless but positively harmful to attempt to force views on a woman. She must, in effect, be treated as an equal. This is what he means when he says that she is "a man" when she can control her body. It will be observed that he does not reject the idea that a woman's body may be the source of sin but declares that the decision is in the hands of the woman herself. Even more powerful is his statement that her body should not be sacrificed or repressed.

There is no mention of *marriage* here. The question is one of love. Only a woman can decide whom she can love, and the fact that she is married to someone else does not alter this principle. In that case the husband will attempt to safeguard his property, she will attempt to circumvent his attempts, and the result will be deceit on both sides and a breakup of moral values. Gottfried thus appears to agree with the lyric poets that love should not be prevented by marriage to a third person, but in fact he goes much further. He does not feel that there should be marriage between persons not in love, because if there is, deceit will result. He disapproves of the deceits of courtly love, of "tougen minne," as strongly as he does of surveillance and the blindness of married lust.

Gottfried's interpolations thus follow a definite sequence. Those which occur before the drinking of the potion are usually short and are concerned with a variety of subjects. (The longest by far is Gottfried's discussion of the literary forms of his day and his attempt to determine what would be the best literary vehicle for his own purposes.) The digressions after the love-potion episode are all of considerable length and are all, in one way or another, concerned with the problem of mistrust and suspicion. One is lighthearted and talks of lovers' tiffs, their anger which soon passes and their jealousy, but the others are very serious. They show that love can never flourish in an atmosphere of suspicion and watchfulness and that society has totally failed to understand what is meant by true love. The prevailing view of women is characterized by constant mistrust. The most important personal interpolation of all, that in the *Minnegrotte* scene, makes it very clear that there can be no understanding of true love in the courtly world. Only by withdrawing from it can the lovers free themselves from surveillance and even there chance may very well bring it back. We have already said that Gottfried's personal remarks are very much like sermons. Their nature and position in the structure strengthens this impression. Like all good sermons they direct the reader to the correct understanding of events which might be interpreted in many different ways. More clearly than any other writer of courtly romance, he indicates the interpretation of his work.

The general structure of Gottfried's poem its thus clear. There are large narrative blocks clearly set apart by time gaps and resumptive phrases. Within these we may distinguish several types of writing. The least common is plain narrative of events, quick, unadorned narration. It provides the bare bones of the story, is largely dependent on verbs for its effects, and is used for those parts of the story which are of least interest to Gottfried. The great bulk of the material consists of a much more leisurely type of narration in which the person of the narrator is felt to be present. The actual progress of the story is slight. The interest lies in the characterization of persons and motivations, the establishment of their effects one upon another, and the illustration of the fabric of the society in which the characters live. The third-person narration is varied by short passages of direct speech and by descriptions. Such descriptions are not mere ornament but are designed to show the perceptions and emotions of the characters. We see and feel things through their senses. The long speeches are almost invariably attempts by the characters themselves to play a role other than their normal one, in other words, to give an impression to the hearer different from that which he might expect. The events narrated in all these different ways are directed to the correct interpretation by Gottfried's own observations made in his own character.

# VII

## THE TEXTURE OF THE LANGUAGE

THE STYLE used by Gottfried varies markedly in the various types of writing. In the narrative passages it is almost naïvely simple, in the descriptions and interpolations almost incredibly complex. We should note certain general principles at once. Gottfried's style is not designed merely to tell or describe nor can it be judged by the normal rules of rhetoric. It is, of course, perfectly simple to find examples in *Tristan* of the accepted rhetorical figures, but their existence is not a criterion of what Gottfried regarded as significant in his style. His work, in fact, is not rhetorical in the sense that it followed the rules of the medieval *artes poeticae*, although it sometimes plays with their conventions. In the highly stylized parts of his poem, Gottfried develops a technique of his own which relies heavily on the patterning and juxtaposition of similar words and on word play. The best way to discuss these techniques is to analyze passages which illustrate them.

Plain narrative occurs most frequently at the beginning and end of narrative blocks and narrative incidents. Before the episode of the fight with Morolt, Gottfried feels that it is necessary to explain the historical background of the need for Cornwall to pay tribute to Ireland:

Umb den zins was ez so gewant:
der do zIrlanden künic was,
als ichz an der istorje las
und als daz rehte maere seit,
der hiez Gurmun Gemuotheit
und was geborn von Affrica,
und was sin vater künic da.
do der verschiet, do viel daz lant

an in und sines bruoder hant,
der als wol erbe was als er.
Gurmun was aber so richer ger
und alse hohe gemuot,
daz er dekein gemeine guot
mit niemanne wolte han.
sin herze enwolte in niht erlan,
ein müese selbe ein herre wesen.

. . .

er vuor mit eime starken her
über lant und über mer,
bis daz er zIrlande kam
und an dem lande sige genam
und si mit strite des betwanc,
daz sin ze herren ane ir danc
und ze künege namen
und sit her dar an kamen,
daz sime zallen ziten
mit stürmen und mit striten
diu bilant hulfen twingen.
in disen selben dingen
betwanc er ouch ze siner hant
Curnewal und Engelant.                  (5878 ff.)

The situation about the tribute was this: the man who was king of
Ireland at that time, as I have read in history and as the true story
relates, was Gurmun Gaylord, born of a family in Africa, where his
father was king. When he died, the territory passed into the hands of
Gurmun and his brother as co-heirs. But Gurmun was so ambitious
and high-spirited that he had no desire to share with anyone. His heart
desired only that he should rule alone . . . . He set out with a powerful
army over land and sea until he came to Ireland, where he was victorious
and compelled the people by force to accept him as ruler and king,
whether they wanted to or not. Then they came around to helping him
subdue their neighbors in assault and battle at all times. In the course of
all this he brought Cornwall and England under his dominion.

The passage begins with a formal introduction and a series of events
follows in chronological order. Usually each line contains one event and
in consequence one verb. No attempt is made to indicate that one event
is more important than another, and consequently there are few adjectives
and adverbs to add color to verbs which are neutral or commonplace (*was,
was, las, seit, hiez, was geborn, was, verschiet, viel, was, was, wolte han,*

*enwolte erlan, müese wesen . . . vuor, kam, genam, betwanc, namen, kamen, hulfen twingen, betwang).* The verbs show clearly that the passage begins with an account of Gurmun's origins and ends with his conquest of Ireland and Cornwall. There are no details. Five descriptive adjectives appear—*rehte (maere), hohe (gemuot), gemeine (guot), richer (ger), starken (her)*—and none of them conveys anything but a routine impression. There are two repetitive pairs of the kind which will be discussed frequently in the following pages—"über lant and über mer"; "mit stürmen und mit striten"—of the type we shall call "conventional," since they are simply reinforced expressions common in normal speech. The syntax is loosely paratactical, with one clause strung to another so that punctuation is difficult to determine. Such a style would be monotonous in the extreme if it were not confined to a few passages of a purely factual and historical nature.

This plain style can be made much more effective by the use of significant detail. The fight with Morolt has reached a critical point:

Morolt der listege man
den schilt ze rucke er kerte
als in sin witze lerte.
mit der hant so greif er nider,
den helm den nam er aber wider.
er haete in siner wisheit
also gedaht und uf geleit
so er wider zorse kaeme,
daz er den helm uf naeme
und rite aber Tristanden an.
nu er den helm ze sich gewan
und hin zem orse gahete
und dem also genahete,
daz er die hant zem britel liez
und den linken vuoz gestiez
wol vaste in den stegereif
und mit der hant den satel ergreif,
nu haetin ouch Tristan erzogen:
er sluoc im uf dem satelbogen
daz swert und ouch die zeswen hant,
daz si beidiu vielen uf den sant
mit ringen mit alle;
und under disem valle
gab er im aber einen slac

reht obene, da diu kuppe lac,
und truoc ouch der so sere nider,
do er daz wafen zucte wider
daz von dem selben zucke
des swertes ein stucke
in siner hirneschal beleip
daz ouch Tristanden sider treip
ze sorgen und ze grozer not:
er haetin nach braht uf den tot.

Morolt, daz trostelose her,
dor ane craft und ane wer
so sere türmelende gie
und sich an den val verlie . . .                                    (7028 ff.)

But Morolt was clever. He pushed his shield back, as his experience
taught him. He groped down and picked up the helmet again. His skill
made him calculate that when he had remounted he would put on his
helmet again and ride Tristan down. Now that he had picked up the
helmet and got to the horse and was near enough to take hold of the
bridle, he put his left foot firmly in the stirrup and grabbed the saddle
with one hand. But now Tristan had caught up with him. He slashed
down on his sword and right hand as they lay there on the pommel of
the saddle, so that they both fell to the sand, ring mail and all. As
Morolt fell, Tristan struck him again on the very top of his head, where
the coif was, and he struck so deep that, as he wrenched the blade out,
the jerk left a piece of the sword in his skull. This later brought Tristan
great sorrow and misery. It came close to causing his death. Morolt,
now a company in despair, now bereft of strength and defense, staggered
back and forth, lost control, and fell.

The similarities of style in this passage to those of that just discussed are
obvious. There is the same chronological style, the same parataxis, the
same lack of descriptive adjectives, the same lack of pause for reflection
or comment. Yet the effects are very different. Gottfried is here describing
a battle in a courtly romance, a *topos* for which numerous examples were
available. Such battles were usually described in very general terms with
descriptions of broken spears, flying sparks, and armor hacked in shreds.
Gottfried, while appearing to use a plain narrative style, is actually
doing something bold and new. He is describing the fight as if it were real.
Every single movement is detailed—the picking up of the helmets, the
seizing of the charger's rein, the left foot into the stirrup, the right hand on
the saddle. The movements are familiar to anyone who has ever ridden a

horse. But just when Morolt is in this highly vulnerable position, Tristan slashes off his right hand with his sword, and then delivers a tremendous blow on his helmet. What could have been plain narrative becomes a vivid realistic picture. The succession of verbs, many of them at the end of a line, admirably portrays the rapid action, and the lack of any but the most necessary adjectives (*linken zuoz, zeswen hant, grozer not*) prevents the reader from dwelling on any point. On the other hand, there is frequent and effective use of adverbs which intensify the feeling of movement: *ze rucke, nider, wider, wider, uf (naeme), an (rite), nu, hin, also, wol, vaste, nu-ouch, mit (ringen) mit alle, aber* (again), *reht obene, nider, wider, sider, nach.* It will be seen that these adverbs, with numerous adverbial phrases, are in themselves enough to ensure the effect of constant motion, of the rapidly changing pattern of the fight. The nouns are almost all concrete objects used in battle.

It will be noted that there is little evidence of either approval or disapproval of this highly unchivalric episode, yet some words and expressions should be noted. Gottfried is using a technique which he frequently employs in describing Morolt as "der listege man." This does not mean that Morolt was by nature clever, still less cunning. It indicates that at this point he thought he was and may be so described. Gottfried is very fond of what may be called the adjective of transitory description and in the whole episode he has described Tristan as "der wise," "der hövesche," "der unversuochte," "der lobebaere, der genaeme kindesche man," "der gemuote," each in accordance with the action he is about to take at different points in the episode. Morolt is never so described. Instead we are told categorically:

> so was ouch Morolt alse starc,
> als unerbermic unde als arc,
> daz wider in lützel kein man,
> sach er in under ougen an,
> getorste wagen den lip . . .                    (5973 ff.)

Morolt, however, was so strong, so pitiless, and so harsh that hardly any man who looked him in the face would dare to risk his life against him.

These are permanent characteristics, for Morolt represents only one thing —brute force. The significance of the one occasion on which Gottfried uses the "transitory" adjective is thus clear. Morolt moves out of character. He tries to be "listig" and in that department he has no chance against

Tristan. As he crashes to the ground he becomes "daz trostelose her," an ironical reference to his much-vaunted strength of four. The irony has already been prepared by Gottfried's statement about his motivations— "als in sin witze lerte"; "er haete in siner wisheit/ also gedaht . . ."—for wisdom was not an area in which Morolt excelled.

Gottfried thus plays brilliant variations on his plain narrative style. He deliberately uses it to obtain realistic effects where the reader would expect a *topos* description and provides just sufficient stylistic guidance to allow us to appreciate his irony.

Gottfried's narrative style can be very different. Shortly after the death of Morolt he describes Tristan's return to his men:

> Sus kerte er wider zuo der habe,
> da er Moroldes schif da vant;
> da saz er in und vuor zehant
> gein dem stade und gein dem her.
> alda gehorter bi dem mer
> groze vröude und groze clage,
> vröude unde clage, als ich iu sage:
> der saelde an sinem sige lac,
> den was ein saeleclicher tac
> und michel vröude erstanden:
> si slageten mit handen,
> si lobeten got mit munde,
> si sungen an der stunde.
> ze himele michel sigeliet.
> so was aber der vremeden diet,
> den leiden gesten von Irlant,
> die da waren gesant,
> ze michelem leide ertaget:
> von den wart alse vil geclaget,
> als von disen gesungen.
> si wunden unde twungen
> ir jamer under ir henden.                                      (7086 ff.)

And so he returned to the landing, where he found Morolt's boat; he went aboard and at once went back to the beach and the army. There by the sea he heard both great joy and great lamentation, joy and lamentation, as I shall tell you; for those whose joy depended on his victory, a happy day and much joy had arisen. They clapped their hands, they praised God with their lips, they sang then and there hymns of victory to Heaven. But for the foreign crew, the wretched strangers from

Ireland, a day of great sorrow had dawned. They lamented as much as
the others had sung. They wrung their hands and so expressed their grief.

There is no question here of events succeeding one another. The only
occurrences are the return of Tristan to his men and the reception of the
news. This reception is what Gottfried wishes to describe—the contrast
between the victors and the vanquished. There is, of course, nothing
particularly significant about the events, but the descriptive method
employed in this relatively unimportant passage is worth noting. The tone
is determined by the fact that there are two sides, Tristan's winners and
Morolt's losers. Tristan returns in Morolt's boat—a source of confusion
and ambiguity to those who watch—and this difference between the two
sides is reflected in a number of different ways, of which the most obvious
is the use of pairs. We have already noted that in his plain narrative passages Gottfried uses one verb in each line. In the third line of the quotation
there are two ("saz" / "vuor"). The next line has a pair ("stade" / "her")
unnecessary for the narrative but effective to show the difference between
mere landing and returning to the land of men. After this come contrasting
pairs in various forms—"vröude" / "clage" first, to express simply the
immediate reaction, repeated for emphasis and rhymed internally as well
as finally with "sage." Then follows the joyful side—"saelde" in one line,
"saeleclich" in the next, alliterating with "sage" and "sinem sige" and
followed again by "vröude." The resemblance to a religious "Gloria" is
heightened by the parallel lines, each with its verb in the same position
("slageten," "lobeten," "sungen") and its adverbial modifier. The effect
is that of a joyful chorus. There is no such parallelism in the contrasted
description of the Irish but rather long-drawn descriptions of misery—
"vremeden diet," "leiden gesten"—but there are deliberate contrasts with
figures used in the description of rejoicing—"michel vröude" contrasts
with "michelem leide," "saeleclicher tac" with "leide ertaget." Further,
the religious figure is continued in "si wunden unde twungen ir jamer
under ir henden," with its reminiscence of the biblical weeping and
wailing and gnashing of teeth.

The reasons for the contrasts here are clearly determined by the
nature of the incident. In others Gottfried employs a standard technique
of setting a mood by the employment of a recognizable stylistic device
which is to be interpreted in the same way wherever it appears.

The characteristic of a courtly atmosphere (which Gottfried despised)

is indicated very frequently by the repetition of "conventional pairs,"
groupings which add nothing to the meaning or mood of a passage but
simply say the same thing in a different way. This stylistic technique is
used throughout the poem. Mark speaks to Tristan:

> "bedarft du ritterschefte me,
> die nim, als dir ze muote ste:
> nim ros, nim silber unde golt
> und swestu du bedürfen solt,
> als dus bedürfen wellest;
> und swen du dir gesellest,
> dem biutez so mit guote,
> mit gesellechlichem muote,
> daz er din dienest gerne si
> und dir mit triuwen wese bi.
> vil lieber neve, wirb unde lebe,
> als dir diu vater lere gebe,
> der getriuwe Rual, der hie stat,
> der michel triuwe und ere hat
> mit dir begangen unze her;
> und si daz dich des got gewer,
> daz du dich da verrihtest
> und din dinc beslihtest
> nach vrumen und nach eren,
> so soltu wider keren:
> kere wider her ze mir."                                  (5131 ff.)

"If you need any more knights, take as many as you want, take horses,
take silver and gold and whatever else you require, as the need arises.
And to whomever goes with you, give so generously and with such good
fellowship that he likes your service and stands by you loyally. My dear
nephew, act and live as your father taught you, the loyal Rual who
stands here and who all this time has treated you with such loyalty and
honor. And if—and may God so arrange it—you settle your affairs and
order everything to your advantage and honor, then come back here,
come back to me."

The speech is kindly and well meant but its Polonius-like quality is obvious.
Mark can never use one word where two will do, and this speech could be
reduced to a quarter of its length without loss of content. The length is
brought about by several means. Conventional pairs abound—"silber
unde golt," "wirb unde lebe," "triuwe und ere," "nach vrumen und nach
eren"—but Mark has other ways to expand his utterances. He repeats

verbs ("nim"—"nim"—"nim"), he says the same thing in two different ways ("daz er din dienest . . . und dir mit triuwen . . .," "so soltu wider keren: kere wider . . ."), but most of all he loves the unnecessary descriptive clause or phrase ("der getriuwe Rual, der hie stat"), which is either cliché or repetition of well-known information.

There is no doubt that Mark is characterized by this repetition and that Gottfried intends us to recognize his insensitivity to words through this stylistic device. But Mark is the head of a court. He is the only head of a court who is significant in the poem, and it is natural that the style he uses should be an exaggeration of that which Gottfried uses to characterize courts in general. Even Tristan can be part of such a context when he is winding up affairs at the court of Parmenie. There he is "Tristan der tugendriche" with "Curvenal der hoveliche." Pairs come thick and fast— "sine mage und sine man"; "von sinnen oder von jaren"; and many others. He can adjust to the courtly scene at the Irish court when he appears as Tantris:

> "ich was ein höfscher spilman
> und kunde genuoge
> höfscheit unde vuoge:
> sprechen unde swigen,
> liren unde gigen,
> harphen unde rotten,
> schimpfen unde spotten . . ."                                     (7560 ff.)

"I was a musician at court and knew courtly behavior and accomplishments well enough—when to talk and when to keep silent, to play the lyre and fiddle, the harp and rote, to jest and mock."

Thus he sums up the very essence of being courtly in a neat group of pairs.[48]

By establishing the conventional pair as a characteristic of the courtly milieu, Gottfried can impart to a passage a secondary meaning more significant than that conveyed by the words he uses. For example, after Brangaene has substituted for Isolde on Mark's wedding night and Isolde has then gone to Mark, his affection for her is described like this:

> Isot diu was so starke
> von ir herren Marke
> geminnet unde geheret
> gepriset unde geret

von liute und von lande.
wan man so maneger hande
vuoge unde saelde an ir gesach.
ir lop unde ir ere sprach,
swaz lop gesprechen kunde.                                          (12,675 ff.)

Isolde was loved and worshipped intensely by her lord Mark, prized and
honored by the people and country. People saw in her such a variety of
gifts and talent. Anyone who was capable of uttering praise told of her
fame and honor.

The language is what we would expect whenever Mark is involved,
but the whole court is involved too. No doubt they do praise her, but we
know better. By their standards she is not worthy of the praise they give
and very soon they will be seeking to destroy her. We have here the usual
courtly convention and superficiality. After the vicious struggle between
Marjodo and Melot on the one side and the lovers on the other, which
culminates in Isolde's ordeal, apparent harmony is restored:

... und wart aber do starke
von ir herren Marke
geminnet unde geret
gepriset unde geheret
von liute unde von lande
swaz so der künec erkande
dar an ir herze was gewant,
daz was sin wille zehant:
er bot ir ere unde guot.
al sin herze und al sin muot
die waren niwan an si geleit
ane aller slahte valscheit.
sin zwivel unde sin arcwan
diu waren aber do hin getan.                                        (15,751 ff.)

... and she was loved and honored so intensely by her lord Mark, so
prized and worshipped by the people and the country. Whenever the
king saw something that her heart desired, it immediately became his
determination to obtain it. He offered her honor and material goods. His
heart and emotions had no focus but her without any trace of deceit.
His doubts and suspicions were totally gone.

The virtual repetition of five lines makes it clear that Gottfried wishes to
show that the relationship between Mark and Isolde has returned to what
it was at the very beginning, which, ironically, was itself totally unstable

and differed from that after the ordeal in only one respect—that Mark was not suspicious then whereas now he has overcome his suspicions. We are told they are "hin getan." Everything Gottfried says is superficially correct but we soon find out that doubt and suspicion are still there. The calm is as deceptive as ever, and the conventional pairs show it.

We may state with virtual certainty that Gottfried uses the conventional pair as a mark of courtliness and hence of superficiality. It is tempting to think of these pairs as evidence of double-dealing, but pairs are not confined to courtly situations. They occur in many situations where there is emotional tension and it is necessary to attempt a distinction between the conventional pairs we have been discussing and the pairs set up by Gottfried to intensify emotions. Such pairs have not usually the cliché, redundant character of the conventional pairs and, more important, they rarely appear only once in any given passage. Much more frequently they are repeated and varied and often the pairs which are found first in one line ("in-line pairs") are varied by being set in successive lines ("column pairs"). Gottfried has different stylistic uses for the two types, as may be seen from the following passage, which is closely connected with the two we have just examined:

Hier under was ie Marke
bekumbert harte starke
mit zweier hande leide:
in leideten beide
der zwivel unde der arcwan,
den er haete und muose han:
er arcwande genote
sin herzeliep Isote;
er zwivelt an Tristande,
an dem er niht erkande,
daz valsche gebaere
und wider den triuwen waere.
sin vriunt Tristan, sin vröude Isot
diu zwei waren sin meistiu not:
si twungen ime herze unde sin.
er arcwande si und in
und zwiveltes ouch beide.
dem gebeidetem leide
dem gienger rehte nach dem site
und nach dem billiche mite,
wan alse er an Isolde

der liebe dienen wolde,
so wantes in der arcwan.
dem wolter danne ie nach gan
und volgen uf die warheit;
als ime diu danne wart verseit,
so tet im aber der zwivel we,
so was ez aber rehte als e.                              (13,749 ff.)

Meanwhile, Mark was grievously burdened by sorrow of two kinds:
both doubt and suspicion tormented him, which he had and could not
help having. He was deeply suspicious of Isolde, his heart's love. He was
dubious about Tristan, in whom he did not perceive a deceptive attitude
or disloyalty. His friend Tristan, his wife Isolde, these two were his
greatest misery. They wrung his heart and feelings. He was suspicious of
her and him and was dubious about them both. He put up with his
double pain in the usual way and according to common procedure, for
when he wished to make love to Isolde, his thoughts turned to suspicion.
He wanted to go along with it and follow it to get to the truth. When
this was denied him, the doubt caused him pain and everything was as
before.

Mark is the victim of doubt and suspicion, and Gottfried wishes us to
judge his state of mind not only from his own "omniscient author"
description but from the stylistic devices used. The "in-line" pair used here
is "zwivel unde arcwan." This is not a conventional pair but one which
Gottfried has put together for the express purpose of describing Mark's
attitude. He prepares the reader by his references to "misery of two kinds"
and the assonance of "Marke / harte / starke," followed by "zweier /
leide / leideten / beide." Mark is torn by two emotions. "Zwivel" means not
simply doubt about the truth or falsehood of the accusations made against
Tristan and Isolde but doubts about his own status, his own power of
judgment (he had believed totally in Tristan's loyalty), a sense of the
collapse of his values. Such doubt destroys a man's soul. "Arcwan," on
the other hand, is a more positive, hostile attitude, a suspicion that
demands action against the person who has betrayed him. Yet neither
word (and particularly not the verbs which are based on them) can be
translated in the same way each time. Gottfried deliberately forces the
reader to ask himself which of several possible meanings is the right one
in a particular context. The two words have associated meanings but they
can be set off against each other, differentiated and contrasted.

Courtly persons think in pairs, as we have seen, and Mark is forced to do so here. The problem is put bluntly before him: "der zwivel unde der arcwan." This is the only time that the pair appear in the same line in this passage, for a pair in the same line indicates some degree of connection, of consistency and harmony. Now Mark's thoughts begin to wander in disharmony and confusion. The accompanying schema shows how Gottfried has represented these thoughts.

|  |  |  |  |
|---|---|---|---|
|  | Marke |  |  |
|  | bekumbert |  |  |
|  | zweier | leide |  |
|  | leideten | beide |  |
| zwivel |  |  | arcwan |
| haete |  |  | han |
|  | arcwande |  |  |
|  | Isote |  |  |
| zwivelt |  |  | Tristande |
|  | niht erkande |  |  |
|  | valsche gebaere |  |  |
|  | wider den triuwen |  |  |
| vriunt Tristan |  |  | vröude Isot |
|  | zwei |  |  |
| herze |  |  | sin |
| arcwande |  |  | si und in |
| zwiveltes |  |  | beide |
|  | gebeidetem |  |  |
|  | nach dem site |  |  |
|  | nach dem billiche |  |  |
|  | Isolde |  |  |
|  | liebe |  |  |
| wantes |  |  | arcwan |
| wolter |  |  | nach gan |
| volgen |  |  | warheit |
|  | verseit |  |  |
| tet (we) |  |  | zwivel |
| was |  |  | rehte |

The passage is twenty-eight lines long. Line 14 ("diu zwei waren sin meistiu not") is the pivot. Before this line zwivel applies to Tristan only, arcwan to Isolde only. After it, they are linked together. Mark's problem is stated in the first four lines. The second pair stresses the double nature of his torture by the cross pattern of the key words. It will be noted that they can be read in any direction to produce the same effect. The next two lines state the nature of that problem by two juxtaposed pairs in line, an apparently clear-cut division. But confusion follows. "Arcwande" is in a different line from its object, "Isote," while "zwivelt" and "Tristande" are in the same line, for, as explained in the next two lines, Mark was not aware of his deceit. His straightforward belief in Tristan is shown by the "in-line harmony," but the truth (disharmony) by the "column pair" which follows. "Sin vriunt Tristan" / "sin vröude Isot" are an obvious "in-line" pair and in harmony, but for themselves, not for Mark. His attitude is expressed by two words in the next line: "zwei"—the double attitude of doubt—and the rhyming word with "Isot," "not." This pattern of apparent in-line harmony disrupted by column repetition and hence disharmony continues for the rest of the passage. The cross pattern mentioned in regard to lines 3 and 4 is repeated over and over again. At line 23 we return to "arcwan" but in a different context. It has now been shown to apply to both lovers and what Mark now desires is the truth. But that he cannot find, for there is no truth in the sense he means. So he is back to doubt, but in another sense. He just does not know what is happening. Everything, says Gottfried, is exactly as it was before. Mark's thoughts have gone full circle, as the style showed with its movement from apparent separation of emotions in regard to Tristan and Isolde, to linking them and then confusing them. His thoughts turn and twist and the style is as intertwined as they are.

Some other pairings are worth noting: "wante" and "wolte," the irrational-rational contrast, and particularly the connections within the cruciform pattern about the center of the passage:

```
sin vriunt Tristan, sin vröude Isot
                zwei
herze                          sin
```

There is sharp irony in the juxtaposition of "vriunt" (in two meanings) with "vröude" (who was so in name only, but was Tristan's "vröude" in a widely accepted sense). The repetition of "sin" points up the irony.

Gottfried's use of pairs and of significant juxtaposition is characteristic of what might be called the reflective sections of his work, where he is representing rather than describing the workings of emotions under stress. The technique reaches a high point in the scene of stormy and conflicting emotions which marks the revelation of love between Tristan and Isolde.

It should be remembered that Gottfried has gone to considerable pains to show the conflict in the minds of Tristan and Isolde between the attraction they feel and loyalty on the one hand and maidenly shame on the other. As the ships push on into the wild and unpredictable element, the sea, the struggle grows more intense and more confused. Gottfried actually uses the expression "turn off course" for the effect of love on their emotions:

> ... daz Minne
> zwei herze dar inne
> von ir straze haete braht                    (11,877 ff.)

... that love had turned two hearts away from their course ...

The tone is set by the following series of figures:

> daz honegende gellet,
> daz süezende siuret,
> daz touwende viuret,
> daz senftende smerzet
> daz elliu herze entherzet
> und al die welt verkeret.                    (11,884 ff.)

... that turns honey to gall, what is sour into what is sweet, sets moisture on fire, turns pleasure into pain, makes hearts into non-hearts, and turns the world upside down.

The last line sums up everything—the world turned upside down. Every one of these lines is an apparent impossibility, indeed most of them are proverbial for that which cannot be done, and Gottfried has deliberately used an active verb in each line with a generalized abstraction. The lines are composed of words which are not only contrasted but mutually contradictory and against nature. Yet they are in line, not in column, and hence must be regarded as in harmony. So indeed they are, for love reconciles the incompatible and performs the impossible. Words which would normally be regarded as harmonious are arranged in column, for love is "diu verwerraerinne," the disturber, the bringer of confusion. This confusion is graphically portrayed:

> *Minne* die *verwerraerinne*
> dien *duhtes niht* da mite *genuoc*,
> daz mans in *edelen herzen* truoc
> *verholne* und *tougen*,
> *sin wolte* under ougen
> ouch *offenbaeren* ir gewalt;

der was an in *zwein manicvalt*:
unlange *in ein* ir *varwe schein*.
ir *varwe schein* unlange *in ein*:
si *wehselten* genote
*bleich* wider *rote;*
si wurden *rot* unde *bleich*,
als ez diu *Minne* in *understreich*.
hie mite erkande *ietwederez* wol,
als *man* an solhen dingen sol,
daz *eteswaz* von minnen
in *ietwederes* sinnen
*zem anderen* was gewant . . .                                    (11,908 ff.)

Love the disturber did not regard it as enough that she should be kept
in noble hearts, secret and concealed; she wanted to make clear her
power to everyone. There were many manifestations of it in the two
lovers. For a very brief time the color stayed the same. Their color
stayed the same for a very brief time. They frequently changed white for
red; they became red and white, as love painted them. And thereby each
recognized, as one should in such cases, that anything to do with love
in the senses of either of them was turned toward the other.

The principal figure here is the contrast between what is seen and what is
not, and here too there is confusion of the normal rules. "Minne" and
"verwerraerinne" would normally be a contrasting pair, but here they are
identical and in harmony. A series of column contrasts follows—"dien
duhtes" / "sin wolte"; "verholne" / "offenbaeren"—but here they are
not really contrasted because they are part of Love's design. In the same
way "verholne" and "tougen," which one would normally regard as a
conventional pair, particularly in view of their associations with the clichés
of courtly love, are here contrasted, since the lovers are trying to keep the
evidence of love from each other and themselves and not from society in
general. Their attempt is foiled by the blushes which appear on their
faces. Gottfried shows this mutual change of color by using virtually the
same words in lines 8 and 9 of this passage but in different order. The
colors change and they change on different people. "In ein" (the same)
rhymes with "schein" in column and line and with "varwe schein" (shows
up) and "schein" (appears) in the two lines. The graphic delineation
continues with the cruciform "bleich" / "rot" contrast, and "Minne" is
described as "painting," "making-up" the faces of the two lovers. Now
this is precisely what Love in Gottfried's sense is not supposed to do,

since she should be honest and straightforward. Yet her painting here is not to conceal the truth but to reveal it. There follows a series of indefinite pronouns which are of importance because they show the alternation of relationship, ill-defined yet significant, between the two lovers.

The passage which follows this contains a large number of conventional pairs and for a good reason. It recounts how Tristan and Isolde conducted long conversations with each other which, on the surface, were innocent enough, since they were merely reminiscences of the events in which both had taken part. There are very few lines in which an innocuous pair of words does not appear. The underlying tension is, however, allowed to surface:

> "waz wirret iu? waz wizzet ir?"
> "swaz ich weiz, daz wirret mir;
> swaz ich sihe, daz tuot mir we:
> mich müejet himel unde se;
> lip unde leben, daz swaeret mich"                    (11,965 ff.)

> "What is disturbing you? What do you know?" "It is what I know that disturbs me, what I see causes me sorrow: the sky and the sea weary me; my person, my existence annoy me."

There is a cruciform contrast here between "wirret" (disturb) and "wizzet" (know), repeated by each lover. The statement that what she sees annoys her is true, but not in the sense she means it. Throughout these lines there are in-line pairs whose components clash in column, as do the words "wirret," "tuot we," "müejet," and "swaeret." What is said is not the truth, but that truth can be obtained from the structure. The truth begins to be apparent in physical terms in line 11,979, where Isolde's emotions express themselves. The confusion culminates and is resolved in the passage which follows:

> Der Minnen vederspil Isot,
> "lameir" sprach si "daz ist min not,
> lameir daz swaeret mir den muot
> lameir ist, daz mir leide tuot."
> do si lameir so dicke sprach,
> er bedahte unde besach
> anclichen unde cleine
> des selben wortes meine.
> sus begunder sich versinnen,
> lameir daz waere minnen,

lameir bitter, la meir mer:
der meine der duht in ein her.
er übersach der drier ein
unde vragete von den zwein:
er verzweic die minne,
ir beider vogetinne,
ir beider trost, ir beider ger,
mer unde sur beredet er:
"ich waene" sprach er "schoene Isot,
mer und sur sint iuwer not
iu smecket mer unde wint;
ich waene iu diu zwei bitter sint?"
"nein, herre, nein! waz saget ir?
der dewederez wirret mir,
mirn smecket weder luft noch se:
lameir al eine tuot mir we."                                    (11,985 ff.)

Love's falcon, Isolde, said: "Lameir is my misery, lameir is weighing
on my spirit, lameir is what is paining me." When she said "lameir" so
many times, he thought over and contemplated carefully and in detail
the meanings of the word. Then he began to recall that "lameir" could
mean "love," or "bitter," or "sea." There seemed to be a whole host of
meanings. He ignored one of them and considered the other two. He
ignored "love," the mistress of them both, their consolation and desire,
and discussed only "sea" and "bitter." He said: "I think, fair Isolde,
that the sea and bitterness are your wretchedness. The sea and the wind
don't appeal to you. I think both are bitter to you." "No, no, sir. What
are you saying? It is neither of these that is bothering me; neither air nor
sea disturbs me. It is only *lameir* that pains me."

The whole passage is not only a play on the various meanings of "lameir"
but an exercise in mental confusion. Tristan, of course, wants to believe
that "lameir" means love but he feels that he should exhaust every other
meaning first. It is a brilliant portrait of a man who dare not believe the
truth, just as Isolde's reminiscences are those of a girl exploring every
memory she has of Tristan to see if any of them gives any indication of
his attitude toward her. So the word appears in column, repeated to show
the disharmony of his thoughts, the shying away from the truth. But at the
same time a fundamental truth is being shown in the in-line pairs at the
beginning of the passage. For whatever "lameir" means, it is misery, and
most of all when it means "love." The in-line pairs continue throughout
the passage to indicate the logical truth of Tristan's thoughts ("anclichen

unde cleine"—in great detail) but the column contrasts of confusion continue also. Not only is "lameir" repeated in this fashion but words of thinking are so contrasted—"duht" / "übersach" / "vragete" / "verzweic"—and so are numerals: "ein her" / "drier ein" / "zwein" / "beider" / "beider . . . beider," and most important the in-line pair "bitter" / "mer," alternated with "mer" / "sur." The effect is to put the reader into Tristan's state of confusion; neither is any longer aware of the exact meaning of what he is thinking. Constantly Tristan's mind is torn two ways, until Isolde finally crystallizes his thoughts with the cry:

> "lameir al eine tuot mir we."

Now the significant word here is not the "lameir" which Tristan has been debating but the "eine." It is this which suddenly jerks his attention to the truth and resolves the constant opposition and pairing. The passage which follows (12015–32) has many in-line, harmony pairs, but the column contrasts are lacking:

> "lameir und ir, ir sit min not.
> herzevrouwe, liebe Isot,
> ir eine und iuwer minne
> ir habet mir mine sinne
> gar verkeret unde benomen . . ."                    (12,015 ff.)

> Love and you, you are my misery. My heart's lady, Isolde, you alone
> and your love have distorted my senses and taken them from me.

It is not until the entrance of Brangaene that confusion begins again.

> Brangaene diu wise,
> diu blicte dicke lise
> und vil tougenliche dar
> und nam ir tougenheite war
> und dahte dicke wider sich:
> "ouwe, nu verstan ich mich,
> diu minne hebet mit disen an."
> vil schiere wart, daz si began
> den ernest an in beiden sehen
> und uzen an ir libe spehen
> den inneren smerzen
> ir muotes unde ir herzen
> si muote ir beider ungemach,
> wan si si zallen ziten sach
> ameiren und amuren,

siuften unde truren,
trahten und pansieren,
ir varwe wandelieren.                                    (12,051 ff.)

The wise Brangaene looked at them quietly and surreptitiously and
observed their secrecy. She often thought to herself: "Alas, now I see
that these two are falling in love." Soon she began to perceive how
serious the matter was with them and to see from their behavior the pain
in their hearts. She was hurt by their misery, for she saw them constantly
in *ameir* and *amur*, sighing and sorrowing, in reveries and in dreams, and
ever changing color.

There are a few in-line pairs here but they are largely conventional.
Brangaene is always "diu wise" and appears here in her courtly function.
"Ir muotes unde ir herzen," an in-line pair, exists for the contradiction
which follows. Only in the last four lines of the passage quoted do we see a
series of in-line courtly pairs, and they express Brangaene's view of the
situation. She never understands the love of Tristan and Isolde as anything more than a courtly intrigue brought about by her own remissness
in leaving the potion unattended. She is prepared to go to any length to
help her mistress and Tristan but she sees the affair through courtly eyes.
The clash with courtliness and her understanding of love is indicated by
the column repetitions ("tougenliche" / "tougenheite"; "dahte" / "ver-
stan"; "hebet . . . an" / "began"; "beiden" / "uzen" / "inneren"; "muotes"
/ "muote"). The verbs in the last four lines are, of course, arranged in the
cruciform pattern of similarities with which we are familiar.

Harmony and disharmony are at the very foundation of Gottfried's
style. The apparent superficial harmony of courtly existence is shown by its
repetitive conventional pairs, the true harmony of the lovers in the pairing
and repetition of words not so commonly associated, while disharmony,
whether of thought or action, actual or potential, is expressed in column
pairs. It might be expected that the scene in the *Minnegrotte*, where the
harmony of the lovers reaches its fullest expression, would show this
technique at its best, and this is indeed the case. There is not only repetition
of words but a careful and consistent echoing of sounds which gives the
impression of total harmony. It is impossible to quote all the relevant
passages but those which follow illustrate the technique:

das gewelbe daz was obene
geslozzen wol ze lobene;
oben uf dem sloze ein crone

diu was vil harte schone
mit gesmide gezieret,
mit gimmen wol gewieret
und unden was der esterich
glat und luter unde rich,
von grüenem marmel alse gras . . .                              (16,707 ff.)

The vault above was finely keyed and there above on the keystone there
was a crown which was beautifully ornamented with goldsmith's work
and studded with gems. Below there was a pavement, smooth, gleaming,
rich, made of marble green as glass.

In a passage like this there is little evidence of pairs in the sense in which
the term has been used up to now. It is sound repetition which occurs:
"obene" / "lobene" / "oben"; "geslozzen" / "sloze"; "gesmide" /
"gezieret" / "gimmen" / "gewieret." The sounds are interwoven and the
effect is even more pronounced:

ouch vant man da ze siner zit
daz schoene vogelgedoene.
daz gedoene was so schoene
und schoener da dan anderswa
ouge und ore haeten da
weide unde wunne beide:
daz ouge sine weide,
daz ore sine wunne
da was schate und sunne,
der luft und die winde
senfte unde linde.                                             (16,750 ff.)

And at the proper time birdsong was to be found there. The song was so
beautiful, more beautiful than anywhere else. Eye and ear had both
their delight and joy, the eye its delight, the ear its joy. There was shade
and sunshine, air and breezes, soft and gentle.

The theme of "oe" assonance dominates the early lines, followed by
"da" and the "w" alliteration. Such lines as these are not mere repetition
but the conscious building up of sound harmony.

In passages such as these, which are descriptive rather than reflective,
Gottfried achieves his effects by sound, and such passages convey their
full impression only when they are read aloud, as medieval works normally
were. The "in-line" and "column" repetitions, however, are better perceived by a reader than a hearer. If the work were read or declaimed to a
listening audience, some of the effect would be lost. It is reasonable to

suppose that Gottfried was more accustomed to visual reading than listening and hence he would think in terms of the line on the page, as a poet would do when he wrote *carmina figurata*. Once again we meet the familiar division in Gottfried between the oral and the visual.

Gottfried's style is largely based on oppositions. Just as his theme is the opposition between love and society, so his portrayal of the nature of love is effected by the opposition between Tristan-love, represented in this poem by its highest manifestation in the love of Tristan and Isolde, and various other episodes in which love of a lower nature appears—Mark for Isolde, Gandin for Isolde, Tristan for Isolde White Hands, and even such low manifestations as the seneschal's desire for Isolde and the jealousy of Marjodo. When Gottfried sets a narrative block about Gandin within the account of Tristan's love for Isolde, he is able to point up the difference between one type of singer and another, between Mark's idea of responsibility in love and Tristan's, and particularly between love at court and Tristan-love. But the theme of incompatability between courtly society and the kind of love it favors is integrated into the whole stylistic fabric in several ways. One is the use of significant variations on such standard *topoi* of the courtly romance as the ideal landscape, another the use of conventional pairs as stylistic indicators of courtliness, in-line pairs to show harmony, column pairs to show disharmony, actual or potential. The principle is one of constant invitation to the reader to think of earlier works, of the so-called courtly code, of courtly ideas of love, of the language of love in romance, and of earlier passages in Gottfried's own poem. Such a technique goes far beyond double meaning, although play on words is an important constituent of his style. It is a constant reflection of the ambiguity of almost every situation and particularly of the ambiguities of thought and emotion, which rarely lend themselves to clear-cut description.

It is probably because of his desire to convey the difference between thought and action, emotion and deed, that he evolves a plain narrative style, rich in simple verbs, for those parts of his poem which he regards as least important, the epidodes of action, and a far more elaborate style, in which adjectives and nouns bear the burden of significance, for conveying emotion and for the analysis of motive. The intention here is to implicate the reader by stylistic means in the feelings of the characters. The method used moves on several levels. Gottfried will sometimes describe in his own words the emotional situation in which his characters find themselves, pointing up his description by key epithets, but more frequently he is content to allow the characters to give their own account of themselves— from their own point of view—or to indicate their feelings by allowing the reader to see into their minds. At the highest level their motivations become generalized into allegory, that is, into representation of human emotions and not merely those of two lovers.

Gottfried's style is an integral part of his narrative. There can be no question for him merely of using the recognized rules and methods of rhetoric to convey his meaning. He seeks and has found a way by which the unique story of Tristan and Isolde may convey to the *edele herzen* who are his chosen audience the true meaning of love as Gottfried understands it.

# CONCLUSION

GOTTFRIED intended his poem to be an experience of love for the *edele herzen* to whom he addressed himself. He knew that there was no literary form which would allow him to communicate that experience in its fullest measure, for neither lyric poetry nor the romance could convey the perfect harmony which was achieved when such love reached its pinnacle, nor could they express the wretchedness of separation and frustration to which life at court exposed Tristan and Isolde. He therefore determined to use the romance form but to incorporate in it every device available to him which would illuminate that love both positively, in describing it and letting it appear in allusion and imagery, and negatively, in contrasting it with those forms of love, whether serious or merely conventional, which had been widely accepted in the literature of his day.

His poem is less a narrative than a constantly shifting series of impressions, each of which, while effective in itself, attains its full meaning only when considered in the light of other impressions and within the totality of the poem. Words, phrases, descriptions, incidents, characters, even the characters of the lovers themselves shift meaning according to context and reaction, and as words are set against each other to contrast and reinforce, to confirm and deny, so scenes and *topoi* and personalities intertwine, dissolve, and come together.

Gottfried's poem is the true anatomy of love, for while dissecting and articulating to make clear love's nature, it also constitutes that love in its fullest and most perfect totality.

# NOTES

1. See, for example, the references in Steven Runciman, *The History of the Crusades*, 3 vols. (Cambridge, England: University Press, 1951–54), especially II, 103, 144, 191.

2. Jesus in Matthew, 19.10–12; St. Paul, 1 Cor. 7.25–31; Tertullian, *De virginibus velandis*; Cyprian, *De habitu virginum*; Ambrose, *De virginibus, De virginitate, De institutione virginis, Exhortatio virginitatis*; Jerome, *Adversus Helvidium de Marie virginitate perpetua*; Augustine, *De sancta virginitate*; Bernard of Clairvaux, *Sermones super Cantica Canticorum*.

3. Hennig Brinkmann, *Die Geschichte der lateinischen Liebesdichtung* (Halle: Niemeyer, 1925).

4. Heinrich Ostler, *Die Psychologie des Hugo von Sankt Viktor*, Beiträge zur Geschichte der Philosophie des Mittelalters, Vol. VI (Münster, 1909) and the references there cited.

5. Andreas Capellanus, *De amore libri tres*, ed. E. Trojel, 2d ed. (Munich: Eidos, 1964).

6. See Arthur K. Moore, *Studies in Medieval Prejudice: Antifeminism* (Nashville: University Libraries, 1943). The works of, for example, Serlo of Wilton, Caesarius of Heisterbach, and Peter Damian, as well as the collections of *exempla*, abound with stories against women.

7. Dares Phrygius, *De excidio Troiae*, ed. Ferdinand Meisten (Leipzig: Teubner, 1873); Dictys Cretensis, *Ephemeridos belli Troiani libri sex*, ed. Ferdinand Meisten (Leipzig: Teubner, 1872).

8. Bernardus Silvestris, *De mundi universitate libri duo*, ed. Carl S. Barach and Johann Wrobel (Frankfurt: Minerva, 1964), repr. from edition of 1876; Alanus de Insulis, *Anticlaudianus*, ed. with intro. R. Bossuat (Paris: Vrin, 1955); *idem, Opera omnia*, Patrologiae Latinae cursus completus, ed. Migne, Vol. CCX (1955).

9. Denis de Rougemont, *L'Amour et l'occident*, 2d ed. (Paris: Plon, 1956); Arno Borst, *Die Katharer* (Stuttgart: Hiersemann, 1953). There is excellent bibliographical information of this question and the whole subject of the love phenomenon in the lyric in Rudolf Baehr, ed., *Der provenzalische Minnesang* (Darmstadt: Wissenschaftliche Buchgesellschaft, 1967), pp. 20–114, 513 ff.

10. Reto Bezzola, *Les Origines et la formation de la littérature courtoise en occident* (*500–1200*), 3 parts (Paris: Champion, 1944, 1960, 1963).

11. Notable examples are: Eleanor of Aquitaine, the grandaughter of William IX of Aquitaine and wife of Henry II of England; her daughter, Marie, Countess of Champagne, mentioned by Chrétien de Troyes as his patroness and by Andreas Capellanus as an arbiter in love questions; Ermengarde of Narbonne; Azalais, Countess of Béziers; Eudoxie of Montpellier.

12. The *chansons de geste* have several notable women—Berthe au grand pied and particularly Guibourg, the Saracen lady originally called Orable, whom Guillaume d'Orange takes as his wife. The women of the *Nibelungenlied* are notoriously strong in body and spirit. The Cid's womenfolk, although less grim, are an important motivating force in the epic. Yet the stress is on domestic affection, not love.

13. Geoffrey of Monmouth, *Historia regum Britanniae*, ed. Acton Griscom (London, New York: Longmans, Green, 1929), IX, 13.

14. Stefan Hofer, *Chrétien de Troyes: Leben und Werke des altfranzösischen Epikers* (Graz: Böhlau, 1954).

15. Herbert Kolb, *Der Begriff der Minne und das Entstehen der höfischen Lyrik* (Tübingen: Niemeyer, 1958).

16. Peter Haidu, *Aesthetic Distance in Chrétien de Troyes: Irony and Comedy in "Cligès" and "Perceval"* (Geneva: Droz, 1968). Useful list of editions and recent works on Chrétien.

17. Sister Amelia Klenke and Urban T. Holmes, *Chrétien, Troyes, and the Grail* (Chapel Hill: University of North Carolina Press, 1959); David C. Fowler, *Prowess and Charity in the "Perceval" of Chrétien de Troyes* (Seattle: University of Washington Press, 1959).

18. For the evidence that the early manuscripts were written in Strassburg, see Gottfried Weber and Werner Hoffman, *Gottfrieds Tristan*, Sammlung Metzler No. M.15, 3d ed. (Stuttgart: Metzler, 1968), p. 13.

19. The references to Sens (Sanze) and Saint Denis (San Dinise) are almost certainly to the schools of music there, which were in the forefront of the innovations of the second half of the twelfth century. Gottfried refers constantly to the *novelty* of Tristan's music.

20. Gottfried Weber, *Gottfrieds von Strassburg "Tristan" und die Krise des hochmittelalterlichen Weltbildes um 1200*, 2 vols. (Stuttgart: Metzler, 1953), is the most thorough study of the religious elements but it has a definite thesis and cannot be regarded as an objective evaluation. (There is a short version in *ZDA*, LXXXII [1948–50], 335–88.) Bodo Mergell, *Tristan und Isolde: Ursprung und Entwicklung der Tristansage des Mittelalters* (Mainz: Kirchheim, 1949), also attempts to show strong Christian influence on the structure of the various versions. The arguments are hard to accept. See also the works by Schwietering and Ranke cited below.

21. The influence of Bernard of Clairvaux and of mysticism is discussed and stressed by Julius Schwietering, *Der Tristan Gottfrieds von Strassburg und die Berhardische Mystik*, Abhandlungen der preussischen Akademie der Wissenschaften, Phil.-hist. Klasse 5 (Berlin, 1943). See also the collection of articles in *Mystik und höfische Dichtung* (Darmstadt: Wissenschaftliche Buchgesellschaft, 1960).

22. Weber and Hoffmann, p. 71.

23. Gertrude Schoepperle, *Tristan and Isolt: A Study of the Sources of the Romance*, 2 vols., 2d ed., with expanded bibliography by R. S. Loomis (New York: Burt Franklin, 1960), pp. 439 f.

24. Helaine Newstead, "The Origin and Growth of the Tristan Legend," and Frederick Whitehead, "The Early Tristan Poems," in Roger S. Loomis, ed., *Arthurian Literature in the Middle Ages* (Oxford: Clarendon Press, 1959).

25. Weber and Hoffmann, p. 36.

26. In the Middle English *Sir Tristrem*, for example, ed. Eugen Kölbing, *Die nordische und die englische Version der Tristan-sage*, 2 vols. (Heilbronn: Henninger, 1878–82).

27. Schoepperle, pp. 326 ff.

28. Schoepperle, pp. 451 f., 457 f.

29. Saul N. Brody, "The Disease of the Soul: A Study in the Moral Associations of Leprosy in Medieval Literature" (Ph.D. dissertation, Columbia University, 1968).

30. Works on the prologue and acrostics are: Carl von Kraus, "Das Akrostichon in Gottfrieds *Tristan*," *ZDA*, L (1908), 220 ff.; Jan Hendrick Scholte, "Gottfrieds von Strassburg Initialenspiel," *BGDSL*, LXV (1942), 280 ff.; "Gottfrieds *Tristan*-Einleitung," *ZDPh*, LVII (1932), 25 ff.; Jean Fouquet, "Sur l'acrostiche du *Tristan*," *Bulletin de la Faculté de Lettres de Strasbourg*, XXXI (1952–53), 197 ff.; "Le Prologue du Tristan de Gottfried," *loc. cit.*, 251 ff.; Albrecht Schöne, "Zu Gottfrieds Tristanprolog," *DVJS*, XXIX (1955), 447 ff.; Helmut de Boor, "Der strophische Prolog zum *Tristan* Gottfrieds von Strassburg," *BGDSL*, LXXXI (Tübingen) (1959), 47 ff.; Klaus Speckenbach, *Studien zum Begriff "edelez herz" im "Tristan" Gottfrieds von Strassburg* (Munich: Eidos, 1965).

31. See Speckenbach, *Studien zum Begriff* (see above) and the literature there cited.

32. See the works of Schwietering and Weber already cited.

33. See W. T. H. Jackson, "Tristan the Artist in Gottfried's Poem," *PMLA*, LXXVII, (1962), 364–72.

34. *Ibid.*

35. His allocation of his fiefdom to Rual's children may be gratitude or calculation that he will succeed Mark and become a king. He shows little to Queen Isolde or Brangaene. The attitude to Mark naturally fluctuates according to events. He was a child when Gurmun conquered Cornwall for Ireland and it is hardly likely that he could have been more than fourteen years old at that time (5927). Three tributes had already been paid, and the language seems to indicate that they were annual ("si sanden in daz erste jar . . . daz ander silber, daz dritte golt"). Yet this is clearly impossible, for Mark is obviously a grown man when Riwalin came to Cornwall more than fifteen years before Tristan's arrival. If we regard Mark as a contemporary of Riwalin, he would be about thirty-five when he first met Tristan, and we must then assume that the tributes to Ireland were paid once every eight or ten years. Whether we should expect such mathematical consistency from Gottfried is another matter.

36. For an indication of Mark's age, see note 35.

37. Rosemary N. Combridge, *Das Recht im "Tristan" Gottfrieds von Strassburg*, 2d ed., Philologische Studien und Quellen, 15 (Berlin: Erich Schmidt, 1964).

38. Geoffrey of Monmouth, *Historia regum Britanniae*, I, 12.

39. Friedrich Ranke, *Die Allegorie der Minnegrotte in Gottfrieds Tristan*, Schriften der Königsberger gelehrten Gesellschaft, Geisteswissenschaftliche Klasse, 2 (Berlin: Deutsche Verlagsgesellschaft für Politik und Geschichte, 1925).

40. There are good grounds for thinking that Chrétien de Troyes, far from incorporating a unified "courtly love" in his romances, used the different works to illustrate different ideas of love in the courtly milieu.

41. For a summary of research see Eduard Neumann, "Der Streit um das ritterliche Tugendsystem," *Festschrift für Karl Helm* (Tübingen: Niemeyer, 1951), pp. 137 ff.

42. The subject is studied in: Gertrud Hermans, *List: Studien zur Bedeutung und Problemgeschichte*, Dissertation Freiburg im Breisgau, 1953; Gisela Hollandt, *Die Hauptgestalten in Gottfrieds Tristan—Wesenszüge, Handlungsfunktion, Motiv der List*, Philologische Studien und Quellen 30 (Berlin: Erich Schmidt, 1966). The footnote on p. 13 has a useful list of works dealing with *list* and other words of varying meaning.

43. Gottfried could have read the story in Hyginus, *Fabulae*, No. 194 (ed. H. I. Rose [Leiden: Sijthoff, 1933]).

44. Josef Raith, ed., *Die alt- und mittelenglischen Apollonius-Bruchstücke mit dem Text der Historia Apollonii nach der englischen Handschriftengruppe* (Munich: Max Hueber, 1956). Although there are many versions of the romance, the essentials of the plot remain.

45. For a more detailed study of the function of the "literary excursus," see W. T. H. Jackson, "The Literary Views of Gottfried von Strassburg," *PMLA*, LXXXV (1970), 992–1001.

46. The formal rhetorical aspects are discussed by: Stanislaw Sawicki, *Gottfried von Strassburg und die Poetik des Mittelalters* (Berlin: Ebering, 1932); Aaltje Dijksterhuis, *Thomas und Gottfried: Ihre konstruktiven Sprachformen* (Groningen: Noordhoff n.v., 1935); Heinz Scharschuch, *Gottfried von Strassburg: Stilmittel—Stilästhetik* (Berlin: Ebering, 1938). The best studies on the ideal landscape are: Rainer Gruenter, "Daz wunnecliche Tal," *Euphorion*, LV (1961–62), 341 ff; Ingrid Hahn, *Raum und Landschaft in Gottfrieds "Tristan"* (Munich: Eidos, 1963).

47. Kolb, *Der Begriff der Minne*; André Moret, "Qu'est-ce que la Minne? Contribution à l'étude de la terminologie et de la mentalité courtoises," *Etudes germaniques*, IV (1949), 1–12; P. Schmid, "Die Entwicklung der Begriffe 'Minne' und 'liebe' im deutschen Minnesang bis Walther," *ZDPh*, LXVI (1941), 137–63.

48. For a more detailed exposition of the relation between "in-line" and "column" pairs, see W. T. H. Jackson, "The Stylistic Use of Word Pairs and Word Repetitions in Gottfried's *Tristan*," *Euphorion*, LIX (1965), 229–51.

# BIBLIOGRAPHICAL NOTE

I have not provided a bibliography for this book, since the necessary material is readily available and any attempt to reproduce it here would result either in an incomplete list or one of quite inordinate length.

The following works will provide more than adequate bibliographical information:

Hans–Hugo Steinhoff, *Bibliographie zu Gottfried von Strassburg* (Berlin: Erich Schmidt, 1971).

Heinz Küpper, *Bibliographie zur Tristansage*, Deutsche Arbeiten der Universität Köln, No. 17 (Jena, 1941).

Gottfried Weber and Werner Hoffmann, *Gottfrieds Tristan*, Sammlung Metzler, No. M.15, 3d ed. (Stuttgart: Metzler, 1968).

Gertrude Schoepperle, *Tristan and Isolt: A Study of the Sources of the Romance*, 2 vols., 2d ed., with expanded bibliography by R. S. Loomis (New York: Burt Franklin, 1960).

Hans Fromm, "Zum gegenwärtigen Stand der Tristanforschung," *DVJS*, XXVIII (1954), 115–38.

Gisela Hollandt, *Die Hauptgestalten in Gottfrieds Tristan*, Philologische Studien und Quellen, No. 30 (Berlin: Erich Schmidt, 1966).

J. J. Parry, "A Bibliography of Critical Arthurian Literature," *MLQ*, 1940–

*Bulletin bibliographique de la Société Internationale Arthurienne*, 1949–

I have used the text of Friedrich Ranke as given in Gottfried Weber, ed., *Gottfried von Strassburg, Tristan* (Darmstadt: Wissenschaftliche Buchgesellschaft, 1967), except for a few cases where I feel that another manuscript reading makes better sense of a particular passage, e.g., p. 145.

# INDEX

NOTE: No attempt has been made to list proper names. They appear only when they have importance to the purpose of the index, which is to allow the reader to trace the main themes treated in the book.

Acrostic, 194, 195

Adultery: in Chrétien de Troyes, 25–30, 34–36, 40–46; in courtly society, 93; medieval views, 10; in *Tristan*, 87, 162

Allegory: allegory of an allegory, 237; of church building, 126–27, 235–37; Gottfried's use of, 32–33, 86–87, 122–31; 234–37; in *Roman de la Rose*, 11, 237

Arthur, 22–30, 43, 99, 144, 163, 164, 182

Artist, 71–73, 103, 141, 165–70, 188–93; allegorical, in *Minnegrotte*, 125, 183–88; Gandin as lower form of, 103–7; skills of, 98, 105, 166, 171, 172

Audience: for Gottfried's poem, 49–63; for Isolde's music, 179–80, 187; in medieval courts, 14; none in *Minnegrotte*, 180; for Tristan's music, 72–76, 168, 170

Author: creator of Tristan and Isolde, 189–91, 237; inferior to Tristan and Isolde as lover, 237; in *Minnegrotte*, 125–31; narration by, preferred, 215–21; personal intervention by, 92, 96, 132, 218–20, 236–45; use of allegorical technique by, 236–37; views on women, 242–45

Awakening of love: in courtly audience, 74–75; in Eilhart, 39, 40; in Isolde, 75, 78–90; in romance, 19, 20, 23–26, 83; in Tristan, 78–79, 81, 85, 86, 89, 90

Battle: with Morolt, 38, 151, 168, 201–2; in romance, 15, 16, 21, 143, 145–55; style in describing, 249–52

Ceremonial: importance in courtly world, 146–47, 156

Chrétien de Troyes, 12, 23–30, 37, 43, 53, 64, 67, 100

Church: allegory of, 126–27, 235–37; formal attitude to love, 2–6, 9; in ordeal, 112–17

Comic: in seneschal, 100–3, 154

Courtliness: adventure, 24, 26–30, 142–47, 164; Arthurian model, 22–30, 99; behavior standards, 14–16, 23, 45–46, 60, 112, 121, 124, 128, 143–50; children not part of, 12; in Christ, 114–15; description of, 28, 50, 144–51; education for, 14–16; erotic images, 65–67, 84; graphic nature of, 65–67, 69, 70, 84, 98, 115, 117; inadequacy of, 1, 103–7, 146–50, 161, 163–64, 168; influence of

Courtliness (*Continued*)
   women on, 13–14, 16–18; intrigue part
   of, 78–80, 88, 113, 156–60, 220–21;
   ironical treatment of, 23–30; love conventions of, in lyric, 6, 17–19; love conventions of, in romance, 9, 11–14, 17,
   19–20, 23–30, 45–46, 60, 136–41; love
   service in, 6, 9, 17–18, 23–30, 64, 67;
   Mark as example of, 98–99, 104, 155 *et
   passim*; medieval life and, 13, 15–16, 30;
   standards as game rules, 192
Cure of wound: by Morolt, 38, 83

Deceit, 37, 41–46, 79, 85; by artist, 167–
   70; connected with dialogue, 206–10; at
   court, 107–13, 117, 119, 121, 156, 159,
   163, 218, 240–45; of God, 111–14; in
   love, 93, 95–96, 109, 126
Description: through eyes of beholder,
   146, 226–32; landscape, 65, 122–31,
   182–85, 232–36, visual, of courtly
   matters, 229–30, 232, 235
Destructive love: common belief, 6–8,
   179; conflict with society, 9; in Tristan
   stories, 34, 36, 142; in Vergil, 8
Dialogue: Brangaene, 210–11; element in
   role-playing, 205; Mark, 211–12; not
   much used in narrative parts, 204; rare
   between Tristan and Isolde, 206; in
   romance, 90; in structure of *Tristan*,
   204–12
Dragon, 39, 79, 86, 100–3, 153–55

*Edele herzen*: attempts at definition, 53,
   126; audience, 53–54, 59–63, 140, 189–
   90, 239; audience for Tristan and Isolde,
   75, 77, 90–91; contrasted with Mark,
   95–96; in *Minnegrotte*, 181
Education: for courtliness, 14–16; of
   Isolde by Tristan, 71–78, 87, 172, 175–
   76, 180; of Tristan, 37, 173–75, 192,
   203; for Tristan-love, 71, 172
Eilhart von Oberge, 35–48, 90
Envy: in courtiers, 157–61, 164; in Mark,
   97–99, 106–7, 109, 113, 121, 222–24,
   241–42

Harmony, 75–76, 88, 90, 99, 118–31, 174,
   180–88, 202–3, 237; classical, 173–74,

expressed by in-line pairs, 259–69; lack
   of, with Isolde White Hands, 259–69
Honor: in Isolde, 96, 110, 116, 132; and
   law, 112; in lyrics, 17–18, 26; in Mark,
   104, 108; in Tristan, 35, 43, 60–62, 68,
   83, 88–89, 110; in women, 243–45
Hunt, 37, 123, 146, 156

Imagery: of contrast, 262–69; erotic, 65–
   67, 130; erotic, in *Roman d'Enéas*, 19–
   20; flower, 50; love as ruler, 94; in
   lyrics, 18, 67; in *Minnegrotte*, 122–31;
   not characteristic of Tristan, 71; of
   sowing, 93, 240; visual, 65–67, 71, 84,
   98, 115, 117–18, 156, 180, 229–35
Intrigue: at court, 99, 107, 156–60, 162–
   64; against God, 111–17
Irony: in Chrétien de Troyes, 24–25; in
   *Tristan*, 68, 71, 91, 101, 109, 112, 114,
   116, 135–36, 218
Irrational elements in love, 71–75, 83, 87

Landscape, 65, 122–31, 182–88, 232–36;
   connected with courtliness, 233–35; out
   of time and space, 233–34
Law, 111–17, 148–50, 202
Literary excursus, 33, 50, 168, 238, 245
Love: in counterfeit, 94; opposition to
   society, 92, 95, 99, 121–31, 240–45; as
   physician, 91, 239; as pleasure, 99, 108;
   as possession, 106, 223–25; potion, 34–
   35, 39–47, 86–90, 162
Loyalty: Brangaene, 96, 163; in love, 94,
   160, 240; to Mark, 88–89; in Rual, 161
Lyric poetry: importance for Tristan-love,
   19, 73–74, 126, 190; love conventions of,
   13–14, 17–18, 101, 239

Marriage: Christian view of, 9–10, 12–13;
   at court, 100–3, 107, 132, 135; in
   medieval society, 10, 12–15, 79–80,
   85–86; as reward, 105; in romance,
   23–30, 79–80, 96
Metaphor: of feudal relation, 88–90; of
   growth of suspicion, 221; of limed twig,
   66–69, 89, 239; of Sirens, 179
*Minnegrotte*, 40–43, 55, 76, 86, 91–92, 96,
   99, 141, 180–91, 201–4, 225, 233–37,
   240, 243, 245

Minstrel: Gandin, 103–7; as hero in romance, 165–66, 192; Tantris, 39, 71, 80–82, 84, 90, 167, 172, 189; Tristan in Eilhart, 41

Monologue: in *Roman d'Enéas*, 19–20; in *Tristan*, 83, 88, 212–15

*Moraliteit*, 76–77, 81, 96, 176, 181

Music: characteristic of Tristan, 71–73, 173, 176; connection with *moraliteit*, 76–77; difference in performance of, 103–7, 139, 170; effect on court, 104; Gottfried trained in, 32; irrational effects of, 73–75, 169, 179, 226; lack of understanding by Isolde White Hands, 137–40; link between Tristan and Isolde, 75, 77, 88, 118, 173; in *Minnegrotte*, 128–29

Mutuality in love, 55–58, 65, 72–73, 76, 95, 127–36, 182–88, 191; lack of, in Isolde White Hands, 136–40

Parody: of courtly behavior, 103, 134, 154–55, 163, 193; of martyrs, 124; of romance, 79

Persona of poet, 58–59, 124–31, 190

Politics and love: in historical epics, 8, 15, 16; in romances, 15–16, 19–22, 27, 68–69, 100, 105

Prologue to *Tristan*, 49–63

Quatrains: content of, 194–96, 239; structural use of, 49–58, 91–92

Religion: allegory in, 29, 33, 61–63, 126–27; attitude to love, 2–6, 9, 131–32; Catharists, 12–13; in Chrétien de Troyes, 29–30; at court, 158–59; Eucharist parallel to *Tristan*, 62, 96, 127; God and love, 3; in Gottfried's training, 32–33; mystics and love, 3–4, 55, 236; terminology, 5, 32, 55–56, 62; in "Tristan-love," 55–63, 114, 116, 126, 235–36

Rhetoric: absent in descriptions of Isolde by Tristan, 78; in Gottfried's work, 31–32, 225, 247; used by Tristan, 149–50

Role-playing: dialogue as element in, 206–12; by Gandin, 106; by Tristan, 106, 138–40, 164–76, 185, 188–93

*Roman de la Rose*, 1, 11, 33, 237

*Roman d'Enéas*, 8, 19–21, 244

Seneschal: Kay typical of, 100; as symbol of courtly intrigue, 79–84, 100–1, 105, 108–9, 115, 117, 153–57, 161–63

Sensuality: in Mark, 43, 79, 86, 90, 97, 130, 222–24; part of woman's nature, 243–45; in Tristan and Isolde, 79, 86–90, 96

Separation: from court, 122–24, 128–30, 234–35; love in separation, 119–20, 243; of Mark from Isolde, 130; of Tristan and Isolde, 109–10, 117, 132, 134–40

Service-reward motif, 101–2, 107, 144, 152, 165, 182, 190

Sexual love: absent in separation, 119; destructive, 6–8; hostility of church to, 2, 243–45; in Isolde without love, 134; in Mark, 223–25; for procreation, 9–13, 244; sense of guilt, 2, 6–7, 9–10, 13, 24

Structure: description, 225–36; dialogue: 204–12; differences in narrative style, 216–25; expression of author's views, 238–45; intervention of author, 236–45; landscape descriptions, 232–36; monologue, 212–15; narrative blocks, 194–204; point of view in description, 226–32; third-person narrative, 215; use of allegory, 236–37; verbal-nominal contrast, 220–24

Style, 247–69; descriptive-analytic, 203; Gottfried's personal, 247; images of contrast, 262–69; narrative style, 248–49; *see also* Word pairs

Surveillance, 92, 99, 107, 110, 131–32; Gottfried's views on, 239–45

Suspicion: in Mark, 97–99, 111–21, 164, 242–43

Time: suspended in *Minnegrotte*, 123–31

Tristan-love: in absence, 119–20; conflict with society, 89–90; 163; connection with *moraliteit*, 140; death as factor in, 54, 61–62, 68–69, 90; mutuality characteristic of, 65, 71–73, 76, 95, 127–36; not total joy, 53–54, 57, 60, 87; religious aspects, 55–57, 61–62, 68–69, 90; visual not characteristic of, 70–71

Tristan stories, 33–47; Béroul, 33, 35, 42, 48; Brother Robert, 35, 49; Heinrich von Freyberg, 36; *Sir Tristrem*, 36; *Tavola Ritonda*, 36; Thomas of Britain, 33, 35–46, 48–63; Ulrich von Türheim, 36

Uncle-nephew relation, 34–47, 89, 95–96, 98

Word pairs, 253–69; column pairs as disharmony, 259–69; effects of contrasting pairs, 261–63
——, in-line pairs, 257–69; characteristic of court, 254–55; characteristic of Mark, 255–56; conventional, 253–56; show harmony, 259–69
Wounds: by Morolt, 38, 151–53, 171; of Riwalin, 68, 83